Cannabis in Medical Practice

This book is dedicated to all the patients, their families and friends who have suffered needlessly because of prohibitions against the medical use of cannabis. Some have simply never known of the plant's therapeutic potential and thus were denied a possible low-risk therapy option. Some have been criticized and abandoned by health care professionals after confiding how this medicine has helped them. Some have been arrested and incarcerated for years because they used a natural substance that eased their suffering. The cost of this unjust prohibition cannot be measured.

Cannabis in Medical Practice

A Legal, Historical and
Pharmacological Overview of
the Therapeutic Use of Marijuana

Edited by
MARY LYNN MATHRE

McFarland & Company, Inc., Publishers
Jefferson, North Carolina, and London

"To sin by silence when we should protest makes cowards out of man."
—Ella Wheeler Wilcox

"If people let government decide what foods they eat and medicines they take, their bodies will soon be in as sorry a state as are the souls of those who live under tyranny."
—Thomas Jefferson

Front cover illustration by Robert C. Clarke. Used by permission.

British Library Cataloguing-in-Publication data are available

Library of Congress Cataloguing-in-Publication Data

Cannabis in medical practice : a legal, historical and
    pharmacological overview of the therapeutic use of marijuana /
    edited by Mary Lynn Mathre.
        p. cm.
    Includes bibliographical references and index.
    ISBN 0-7864-0361-6 (sewn softcover : 50# alkaline paper) ∞
    1. Marijuana—Therapeutic use.   I. Mathre, Mary Lynn.
    [DNLM: 1. Cannabis.   2. Drug Therapy.
    3. Cannabinoids—therapeutic use.   4. Legislation,
    Drug—United States.   QV77.7 C2248   1997]
    RM666.C266C37   1997
    615'.7827—dc21
    DNLM/DLC
    for Library of Congress   97-10944
                                                                   CIP

Manufactured in the United States of America

McFarland & Company, Inc., Publishers
  Box 611, Jefferson, North Carolina 28640

Contents

Acknowledgments

In addition to the 17 authors who contributed to this book, there are others who have assisted in some way to bring this collaborative work to completion.

Roger Grant and Elizabeth Schupp, our cohorts in a video project, "Marijuana as Medicine," provided encouragement and ideas that got ths project started. Lynn and Judy Osburn helped us understand the dangers of margarine and most polyunsaturated oils in contrast to the healthy alternative of hemp oil, which helped us decide to include therapeutic aspects of the whole plant. Dennis Peron's support and his introduction to Walter Krampf are greatly appreciated. Sandee Burbank and Mark Miller created the Drug Consumer Safety Guidelines, which provide a framework to reduce harm from the use of medicines. Jon Gettman coined the phrase "less is more" to describe safe, long-term use of marijuana. Also, thanks to Dr. David Busch and Jeanne Lang for taking the lead on a related issue.

David Hall and Patty Schweickert, R.N., M.S.N., our neighbors and friends, reviewed the early drafts and offered suggestions to make this book user-friendly for the general public. David Pate, in addition to being a chapter contributor, reviewed the manuscript and offered suggestions. Neil Jacobs; Tod Mikuryia, M.D.; Tom Saint, R.N. P.A.-C.; and Dave Watson have my gratitude for their learned guidance, as does Michael Farmer for helping "the way he did." Alice O'Leary was a wonderful sounding board.

Jiki Pierson and Debbie Mazonne provided their expertise to package the manuscript with a professional appearance. Kelly Hale reviewed the manuscript to provide editorial advice and catch the ever-present grammatical errors prior to sending it off to the publisher.

Lisa Bayne, an Eli Lilly & Co. historian, provided us some beautiful slides of old *Tincture of Cannabis* labels from their archives. David Busch, M.D., Ph.D., provided us with a historic World War II poster noting the importance of hemp in American history. Serelda Bedsole deserves much thanks for the design of the I-CARE logo. Thanks, Eric E. Skidmore, for the quote from Thomas Jefferson.

My sincere gratitude goes to eight of the federally approved medical marijuana patients who have shared their experiences with me: Robert

Randall, Irvin Rosenfeld, Elvy Musikka, Corinne Millet, George McMahon, Kenny and Barbra Jenks, and Barbara Douglass. Their efforts to speak out on behalf of the benefits of therapeutic cannabis so that others may have legal access to this valuable medicine are heroic. Kenny and Barbra both died from AIDS but before their deaths they put forth great effort in educating the HIV-infected population about how to apply for government access to marijuana, despite threats of having their prescriptions canceled.

I am also indebted to the hundreds of patients with whom I have communicated over the years who have shared their stories of their efforts to gain relief from suffering through their medical use of cannabis. To all of you, thank you for providing me the strength and determination to talk and write about a subject that has been condemned to silence over the years.

I also want to thank my family, friends, professional colleagues, and mentors for cheering us along as we sought to create a collaborative reference on therapeutic cannabis that can be used by patients, families and health care professionals. I am especially grateful for the understanding of my nursing colleagues at the University of Virginia, who have stood by me and, in effect, protected my reputation as a professional nurse while I continued to advocate for patients' rights to this medicine. Alone each of us is easily silenced; together we create a roar that will be heard.

And finally, I am grateful to my husband, Al Byrne, who always reminds me to "consider the source," and who managed the process that brought this work from an idea to publication.

MARY LYNN MATHRE, R.N.

Introduction

MARY LYNN MATHRE

Corinne Millet, a physician's widow and glaucoma patient from Nebraska, grew up hearing many stories regarding the dangers of marijuana. It was a lucky coincidence that she learned of marijuana's therapeutic potential because her ophthalmologist was certain that she would be blind within three years. None of the accepted medical therapies nor two surgical procedures were effective in decreasing her intraocular pressure. In 1989 she gained legal access to medicinal marijuana with the support of her physician through the Investigational New Drug Program administered by the FDA. Not only does she still have her sight as a result of the therapeutic use of marijuana, but she also has gained an uncomfortable insight regarding the government she had believed for many years. Ms. Millet has the following to say:

> It's very frustrating for me to know that there are all these people out there that have no idea what they should do. They're going blind, they're losing their sight—they know they are. They don't know what to do. They don't know who to write to. They don't know who to call. They don't know what they have to have. This is very upsetting to me, because these people are desperate as I was desperate. I don't want to be blind. I don't want to be any more handicapped than I already am. And I don't feel that this is justifiably honest for this country to deny these people this information. And who is doing it? Who? Why? I don't know.

Why write a book about an illegal plant that contains a legitimate medicine? Because the cannabis plant (marijuana) does have therapeutic benefits and could ease the suffering of millions of persons with various illnesses such as AIDS, cancer, glaucoma, multiple sclerosis, spinal cord injuries, seizure disorders, chronic pain, and other maladies.

Mary Lynn Mathre, R.N., M.S.N., C.A.R.N., is an addictions consultant at the University of Virginia Medical Center in Charlottesville.

Marijuana is the most commonly used illicit drug in the United States. Estimates regarding its use in the United States range from 20 million to 80 million regular users, and although many cannabis users do consume this drug for enjoyment and relaxation, others use it for medicinal purposes. If they were aware of its therapeutic value and had the opportunity and guidance to use it effectively, countless others could benefit from its therapeutic properties.

Marijuana Prohibition

Legal access to therapeutic cannabis is currently unavailable to most people. Marijuana is a Schedule I drug under the Controlled Substances Act and therefore cannot be prescribed. Although difficult to obtain, medicinal marijuana was at one time available through a special federal program (the Investigational New Drug Program). However, access through this program was closed in 1992. Because marijuana is an illegal drug, accurate information about it is difficult to obtain. Mainstream information includes scare tactics, lies, and faulty research findings that have been repeatedly reported as though they were factually correct. The therapeutic benefits of cannabis are no longer mentioned in the formal education of healthcare professionals (i.e., physicians, nurses, pharmacists) nor are they mentioned in the thousands of medical and healthcare textbooks that discuss the various illnesses against which the plant may be helpful. Thus, many healthcare professionals are simply ignorant of the therapeutic uses of cannabis.

Those healthcare professionals who do learn of its therapeutic value are quite often intimidated by its illegal status. Any association with this drug could result in the loss of prescription privileges or professional licenses, and could possibly lead to criminal charges for possession of or intent to distribute an illegal drug. Those charges could further result in forfeiture of property and prison time. Thus, because of intimidation and fear of penalties, most healthcare professionals do not even want to discuss any positive uses of cannabis.

The contributors to this book are aware of the therapeutic benefits of cannabis and believe this information should be readily available. They recognize that people are currently using this medicine without access to a reliable source of information about it. In fact, they believe that the illegal status of cannabis jeopardizes the health of the American people by denying them access to a remarkably safe and effective medicine.

A patient generally learns of the medicinal value of cannabis through personal experience or by word of mouth from another patient, a friend or a healthcare professional, who has learned of its benefits and is willing to share this information. The patient must then commit the illegal acts of procurement and possession to determine if the drug is effective for his or her illness. If cannabis is effective, the patient must then determine how to obtain this illegal substance on a regular basis.

Because of its illegality, there is no quality control on the ingredients of this medicine, and this places the patient in further jeopardy. Patients are not taught by a healthcare professional about the safe administration of the medicine, the recommended dosages or the medicine's associated risks and benefits. Because the patient fears admitting to using the drug or the healthcare professional refuses to care for a patient using this illegal substance, there is no follow-up by healthcare professionals. And there is no current research on humans regarding its therapeutic use, because it supposedly has no therapeutic benefits, and therefore, there is no funding available for such research.

Government-sponsored (funded) research projects have been aimed at determining the dangers of this drug. However, when these studies have shown minimal risks, they have been buried or the data have been manipulated to indicate a greater risk. For example, in 1980 and 1981, a committee of the Institute of Medicine completed a study, *Marijuana and Health*, supported by the National Institutes of Health, which was published in 1982. When the study, chaired by A.S. Relman, concluded that cannabis had therapeutic value and should be further evaluated, and that the dangers of cannabis were not great enough to warrant its prohibition, fewer than 300 copies of the study were printed. There were not even enough copies for every member of Congress.

Another example can be found with research on the effects of cannabis on the immune system. What the reader will find when reviewing most of the research studies is that extremely high doses are necessary to yield negative effects. In fact, when a study funded by the National Institute on Drug Abuse (NIDA) found little evidence that cannabis was hazardous to the immune system, the researchers had to go outside the United States to find a journal willing to publish their findings. It is a simple case of catch-22 that lack of research is often cited as the reason why marijuana cannot be removed from the Schedule I category; however, one cannot research this drug because it is in Schedule I (forbidden use category).

War on Drugs Based on Faulty Premise

Our modern-day "war on drugs" has given rise to emotionally charged attitudes and dangerously unsafe misconceptions about both medicines and drugs. Under this model, medicines are represented and viewed as "good chemicals," which can be taken to provide a quick fix for just about any health problem. There are over-the-counter (OTC) medicines, which are considered

The Comprehensive Drug Abuse Prevention and Control Act of 1970 was signed by President Richard M. Nixon on October 27, 1970, and became effective on May 1, 1971. Commonly known as the Controlled Substances Act of 1970, this law specifically states that all drugs controlled by the act are under the jurisdiction of federal law. Under this law, five Schedules were created to categorize drugs according to their potential for abuse.

Schedule I: These drugs are not safe, have no accepted medical use in the United States, and have a high potential for abuse. These drugs cannot be prescribed and are available only for research after special application to federal agencies. Examples: marijuana, natural THC, heroin, LSD, peyote, psilocybin.

Schedule II: These drugs have a currently accepted medicinal use and have a high potential for abuse and dependence liability. A written prescription is required by a physician who is registered with the Drug Enforcement Administration (DEA). Telephoned prescriptions are not allowed and no refills are allowed. Examples: opium derivatives (e.g., morphine, codeine), meperidine (Demerol), methadone, Fentanyl, cocaine, amphetamines (Dexedrine), short-acting barbiturates (e.g., Nembutal, Seconal), and dronabinol (Marinol) (synthetic THC).

Schedule III: Medicinal drugs with potential for abuse and dependence liability less than Schedule II, but greater than Schedule IV. A telephoned prescription is permitted to be converted to written form by the dispensing pharmacist. Prescriptions must be renewed every six months and refills are limited to five. Examples: paregoric, some appetite suppressants (e.g., Didrex, Tenuate), some hypnotics (e.g., glutethimide, methyprylon).

Schedule IV: Medicinal drugs with less potential for abuse and dependence liability than Schedule III drugs. Prescription requirements are similar to Schedule III drugs. Examples: pentazocin (Talwin), propoxphene (Darvon), benzodiazepines (e.g., Librium, Valium), meprobamate.

Schedule V: Medicinal drugs with the lowest potential for abuse and dependence liability. Drugs requiring a prescription are handled the same way as any nonscheduled prescription drug. The buyer may be required to sign a log of purchase. Examples: codeine and hydrocodone in combination with other active, non-narcotic drugs usually in cough suppressants and antidiarrheal agents.

Schedules of Controlled Substances

safe enough for individuals to consume at their own risk. In addition, there are prescription medicines, which are judged to be stronger and therefore require the permission and guidance of a physician in the form of a prescription.

Information about specific OTC and prescription medicines is readily available to the healthcare professional as well as to consumers—as it should be. This information generally includes the pharmacology of the drug, indications for use, possible side effects and adverse reactions as well as recommended therapeutic dosage and administration instructions. Advertising for these drugs often stresses the strength and effectiveness of the medicine and minimizes the side effects and risks. And the seller, or prescriber, of medications is a "reputable" pharmacist or physician, who is considered a helpful authority.

Drugs, on the other hand, are misrepresented and viewed as "bad chemicals" used only by drug abusers, drug addicts, or criminals. Once a chemical is determined to be an illegal drug (by bureaucrats and law enforcement officials), no one is allowed to consume it. Accurate information about these drugs is more difficult to come by. Information about drugs is skewed to include only the dangers of the drugs, the extreme potential for abuse and addiction, and the negative effects (which are usually based on extremely high doses). The seller of these drugs is a "drug dealer," who is portrayed as a sleazy and dangerous criminal. The seller of drugs is such a menace to society that the death penalty or life imprisonment has been considered as appropriate punishment for this less-than-human scum.

Under our current system of drug control, people learn (incorrectly) that there is a quick-fix medicine for just about any ailment and assume they can take these good chemicals without any negative health effects. They often take little responsibility to learn about the medicine(s) they are taking, based on the naive perception that because it is legal, it is without risk. This perception could not be further from the truth. Roughly 70 percent of drug-related emergency room visits are due to prescription medications. On the other hand, there is no tolerance for anyone using an illegal drug. Healthcare professionals often do not even inquire why a person is using an illegal drug. Instead, the person is often reprimanded in some manner and assumed to have a drug problem.

The paradigm for the "war on drugs" is based on a belief that there are "bad" drugs and that the solution to our drug problems is to prohibit the use of these drugs. This basic premise is faulty and must be challenged. Clearly, irresponsible use of drugs, legal or illegal, can be dangerous and costly to society. Our government maintains that drug prohibition is the best approach to our drug problem. We would argue that drug prohibition is a costly, intolerant, moralistic, simplistic, irrational, and dishonest approach. The "war on drugs" approach addresses drug use as a criminal issue instead of a health-care issue and focuses on punishing people rather than treating addiction.

In Europe drug problems are addressed with a *harm reduction* approach, which is based on the understanding that a drug is neither "good" nor "bad." Instead it is the manner in which drugs are used that may be good or bad, healthy or unhealthy, safe or very risky. According to this approach, drug problems are addressed as a health issue, and the focus is on helping people to reduce unsafe or irresponsible drug use through educational and medical intervention.

Harm Reduction

Individuals must have knowledge in order to make responsible choices. In the context of using the harm reduction approach, the terms *drug* and *medicine* will be used interchangeably throughout this book. Webster's dictionary defines a *drug* as "any substance used as a medicine, or in making medicines, for internal or external use," and it defines a *medicine* as "any substance or preparation used in treating disease." A *druggist* is synonymous with a pharmacist and is defined as "one who deals in drugs." Whether a drug is over-the-counter, prescription, legal, or illegal, it has potential risks. No drug is completely safe, and any drug can be abused. A drug or medicine is neither good nor bad, but rather the manner of use may be good or bad for a particular person.

In order to decrease any potential harm from a drug, people should obtain some basic information regarding the inherent risks and benefits of the drug. In *Teach Your Children Well: A Rational Guide to Family Drug Education* (Mosier OR: Mothers Against Misuse and Abuse, 1995), M. Miller and S. Burbank list the seven basic questions necessary to evaluate a drug for its benefits and risks:

1. What is the name of the drug (medicine, chemical)?
2. Where is it working in my body (desired effect, side effects)?
3. What is the correct dosage (amount, route, and frequency)?
4. What drug interactions may occur?
5. What allergic actions can occur?
6. Will it produce tolerance?
7. Will it produce dependence?

This book will provide the answers to these questions as they relate to the use of cannabis.

Just Say "Know"

This book is not about a miracle drug, a perfect drug, or a completely safe drug. Such a drug exists only in fantasy. No drug can be everything for everyone. What works for one person may not work for another. All drugs come with risks, some known and some unknown. Prior to using a drug, medicinally or otherwise, both the potential risks and the likely benefits should be considered. The goal is to maximize the benefits and minimize the risks.

This book is not about a drug that causes insanity, leads to heroin addiction, or causes one to commit violent crimes while causing at the same time the amotivational syndrome. That drug, too, exists only in fantasy. That is, however, what was said of marijuana, the new name created for preparations from the cannabis plant in the 1930s. The renaming of cannabis allowed the politically motivated media to create such a nationwide emotional hysteria and fear of this "new" and dangerous drug that the Marihuana Tax Act of 1937 was passed, marking the beginning of the marijuana prohibition. During this time, cannabis was listed in the *U.S. Pharmacopoeia* and recognized for its therapeutic value in the treatment of numerous ailments.

This book is about a plant, the cannabis plant. In colonial times, it was commonly known as the hemp plant, while today in the United States it is commonly known as marijuana (found most often in U.S. government literature misspelled: *marihuana*). Around the world, it is known by other names: *ganja* in Jamaica, *bhang* in India, *dagga* in South Africa, and *kif* in Morocco. The leaves and buds of the cannabis plant have natural therapeutic properties, which have been used for centuries in the treatment of numerous life- and sense-threatening illnesses.

Today, this plant is illegal in the United States. It is illegal for physicians to prescribe it, illegal for anyone to sell it, illegal to possess it, illegal to consume it, and illegal to grow it. Think about that. The goal of marijuana prohibition is to eradicate this plant. What is the merit of this goal?

There is a shrinking population of the elderly in this country who may remember that it was once a patriotic duty for an American farmer to grow marijuana (hemp). In 1942 a film called *Hemp for Victory* was produced and distributed by the U.S. Department of Agriculture to encourage American farmers to grow cannabis for much-needed hemp products, particularly rope. This film was somehow lost from our National Archives at the Library of Congress, but it has been replaced by a persistent hemp researcher, Jack Herer, who found it listed in a catalog of the Department of Agriculture's films and donated a copy of the film to the library.

Many Americans have easily accepted the negative propaganda on cannabis. However, for those millions of Americans who have experiential knowledge of cannabis's properties and potential value, prohibitionist fantasies simply do not measure up to reality.

The 80 million users of marijuana in the United States and the 500 million worldwide have the right to obtain honest and unpoliticized information about cannabis. This book was written in an effort to fill the void of accurate information about medicinal cannabis. It is intended for the healthcare professional, the patient, and the general public. This book will provide essential information regarding the historical use of therapeutic cannabis, the pharmacology of the drug, indications for use, dosage and administration, and potential risks and side effects. To fulfill their ethical obligation of using scientific knowledge to provide optimal care to patients, healthcare professionals must have access to this information in order to provide advice based on knowledge, not on the party line. With little or no help from healthcare professionals, thousands of patients have chosen to go outside the law to obtain a medicine that has significantly improved their quality of life. This book is intended to provide patients with the information they will need.

The book begins with Norman Kent's report of patients who have become victims of the marijuana prohibition. He has defended many of these patients in court and describes a small sample of the numerous patients who have had to endure additional suffering as a result of the marijuana prohibition. Next Kevin Zeese presents a clear overview of the legal risks involved with the therapeutic use of cannabis and provides legal counsel to guide patients in their decision of whether or not to use this medicine and what to do if they, their family members, or their healthcare provider face legal charges as a result of their use or procurement of cannabis.

In chapter 3, Michael Aldrich provides a well-documented historical review of the use of cannabis throughout the world. He begins with the earliest records of cannabis use in China and follows its use throughout the centuries, including its therapeutic use in America prior to the marijuana prohibition. He then describes the progression of the marijuana prohibition despite modern research findings and new indications for use. What was known centuries ago about its various therapeutic applications is being rediscovered and validated with modern research capabilities despite the limiting constraints of the prohibition.

Denis Petro reviews the pharmacology of cannabis in chapter 4, relying highly on the more studied synthetic preparation of delta-9-tetrahydrocannabinol (THC), the primary psychoactive cannabinoid in cannabis. He reviews the toxicity of smoked cannabis as well as of the THC and discusses the significance of the newly discovered cannabinoid receptor and how that will influence future research.

Part III provides several close looks at specific therapeutic indications for use. Dan Dansak begins with his research on the use of cannabis and oral

THC for cancer patients experiencing nausea and vomiting from chemotherapy. The study was initiated as a result of a cancer patient who found cannabis very useful but died before he was ever allowed legal access to this medicine. Walter Krampf cares for AIDS patients in San Francisco and has much experience with its value as an appetite stimulant as well as an effective antiemetic for his patients. His clinical experience and review of the literature indicate beneficial effects for AIDS patients and do not confirm claims that the drug damages the immune system when used in therapeutic dosages. For use in the treatment of glaucoma, Robert Randall, the first legal medical marijuana patient through the IND program, reviews his experience with smoked marijuana and the research in which he was a subject. Manley West offers information about an ophthalmic preparation of cannabis, Canasol, and explains how eye drops can deliver medication directly to the area of need, while eliminating the possible risks associated with smoking. Petro reviews the use of cannabis with spasticity disorders, as seen in patients with multiple sclerosis and spinal cord injuries and its use in alleviating chronic pain. In his review, he notes that research indicates that a cannabinoid other than THC, cannabidiol (CBD), may be the more effective substance. Milton Burglass takes a cautious view of cannabis's possible use in psychiatry. Although research has not shown efficacy in this area, numerous anecdotal accounts, both current and in historical records, discuss its usefulness for depression, anxiety, insomnia, and stress management. This appears to be an area in need of more rigorous research especially with the natural form of cannabinoids other than THC, the plant's main psychoactive cannabinoid. To that end, Antonio Zuardi and Francisco Gimarães present their research on the use of cannabidiol (CBD) in the treatment of anxiety and psychotic symptoms.

Madelyn Brazis and Mary Lynn Mathre provide an educational overview regarding the safe dosage and administration of therapeutic cannabis in chapter 13. All medications present risks and patients need to understand the potential risks and how to avoid them if possible. Brazis presents an application of this information as she instructed many patients in the proper use of cannabis during a research study.

Part IV reviews additional considerations with the use of cannabis. Melanie Dreher reviews the potential risks of women using cannabis during pregnancy. In her review Dreher presents her research of use during pregnancy in Jamaica, a culture in which *ganja* is viewed more favorably. Her studies and those of a Canadian researcher do not confirm reports of negative effects on the fetus of cannabis-using mothers. Mathre examines the potential of dependence and addiction problems associated with regular use of cannabis. She first clarifies the terms *abuse, tolerance, dependence,* and *addiction* and then discusses the relative concerns with the therapeutic use of cannabis.

There is more to know about the cannabis plant than its therapeutic value in the treatment of illnesses. In chapter 16 Don Wirtshafter discusses the nutritional value of hemp seed and hemp seed oil, which is important for all people. Cannabis seeds are a nutritious protein source rich in essential fatty acids. He provides an analysis of the contents of the seed and its oil and an explanation of why they are so nourishing.

A full discussion of the cannabis plant and possible hemp products is presented in chapter 17, which looks at the ecological (or world health) value of this plant. Robert Clarke and David Pate review the plant structure and clarify the difference between the plants grown for medicine and those cultivated for hemp products. The stalk of the plant is valuable because of its pulp and fiber, for paper products, building materials, rope, and textiles, and it also has potential as a fuel source. Clarke and Pate discuss how this crop is environmentally friendly, requires low maintenance, and helps prevent soil erosion through its root structure.

We hope that the reader of this book will learn to question the sources of negative reports about the medical use of marijuana. Are those reports based on scientific research and history? Or do they carry a strong sense of politics, scare tactics, even outright lies? We hope we have provided information that will inspire the reader to ask these questions and more—to ask, above all, why the United States government continues its prohibition of this remarkable plant.

Part I

Legal Dilemmas
of Cannabis Prohibition

1

People Behind the Pain

Norman Elliott Kent

In 1993 south Florida faced the wrath of a natural enemy that challenged our resources as never before. It was a hurricane called Andrew. Now, for a moment, I would like you to join me in a role-playing exercise:

Imagine you live in a beautiful home at the eye of the storm, and you are fortunately blessed with all the necessities and luxuries of life, including, but not necessarily limited to, a comfortable job, a paid-to-date mortgage, and dependable transportation. You are also the parent of two 6-month-old twins, a boy and a girl. You have running water, flowing electricity, food in the pantry, and money in the bank. But now, a natural disaster wreaks sudden havoc in your life.

In the sudden swell of a rising tide and crushing wind, everything you own and cherish, at least materially, is lost to this devastating force of nature. You and your children fortunately survive, making your way from the rubble and ruin of your neighborhood to a shopping center and the crumbling ruins of a supermarket that barely survived the storm. Your children are wet and weary, shivering from unsheltered nights and gale-force winds and rains. The market appears abandoned, and there are no neighbors or governmental agencies around to offer assistance. There is only a threatening sign on the supermarket that reads: "Warning—No Trespassing—Looters will be shot."

You read the sign, but you feel for your children, crying and hungry in your arms, and you see food and clothes inside the market that is within your reach, food and garments that will feed and clothe your children. You proceed to appropriate those items for your own use—not with the intent to steal, but out of the need to survive. As you leave the market, a clerk who was hiding in the warehouse stops you with a gun. The National Guardsmen

Norman Elliott Kent, Esq., is an attorney in Fort Lauderdale, Florida, who has defended many persons involved in cases of medicinal use of marijuana.

are called, and the chief officer, following the storekeeper's request, takes you into custody and charges you with theft.

Who among us would find this person guilty under these circumstances? Who among us would not agree that he or she should not be found guilty because he or she acted out of necessity to survive, not out of an intent to deprive?

If you, as I, would declare this person's conduct excusable, you would in effect be saying that there is certain criminal conduct that becomes excusable and justifiable under certain limited circumstances. You would be making a declaration that the children's biological needs far outweighed some corporation's material and financial interests. Now I ask you—is that so wrong?

You do not need to be a lawyer to understand the nature of this defense. You just need to grasp that there may be circumstances where the value of the law and traditional public policy is superseded by the value of human life and individual liberty. In a case like this we are saying that personal survival weighs in more heavily than the laws and customs of our land.

The following story is not unlike the dilemma many victims of hurricane Andrew faced. It is also the point of connection that enables us to talk about the courageous cases of citizens like Robert Randall, Elvy Musikka, or Brownie Mary. In August of 1988 Elvy Musikka was living a quiet and comfortable life in her suburban home in Hollywood, Florida. One major factor, however, made her life a bit different than that of her neighbors. While most of her friends baked cookies and tended their tulips, Elvy grew cannabis.

A glaucoma patient for decades, Elvy had endured all the tried and traditional treatments for this disease, which would periodically and all too often, steadily, cause the intraocular pressure in her eyes to increase, leading to unbearable pain and inevitable blindness. Doctors had tried to help her. Elvy had experimented with every possible treatment, including 23 surgeries, cataract operations, and even frightening injections into the retina of her eye. But her sight continued to deteriorate, and ultimately she lost sight in one eye.

Elvy had heard through others that smoking marijuana had mild benefits, but a middle-aged woman does not have easy access to marijuana. So Elvy grew a few plants of her own. Harvesting them, she enjoyed the benefits of a particularly rehabilitative drug. However, an angry ex-roommate bent on revenge told the police about her venture, and one afternoon the police paid her a visit. She was asked about her marijuana and openly stated, "Yes, I have a little. I grow it for my survival; for my sight." According to the law, however, she was committing a felony, and she was taken into custody.

Over the next few hours, days, and weeks, Elvy's world turned upside down. She was booked, stripped, searched, and bonded. She was arrested, jailed, prosecuted, and named as a defendant in a criminal system that could have sentenced her to jail for five years. And the prosecutors gave her only one alternative: forgo the further growing of marijuana and its consumption, submit to random drug tests, and we'll give you probation. If you don't like this plea, go to trial and risk the possibility of conviction and a jail sentence.

Elvy stood up for her rights. She demanded a trial and rejected all prosecutorial plea bargains. She hired me as her lawyer, and we went into court together, asserting that this was a woman who grew and smoked marijuana today so that she could preserve her eyesight for tomorrow. We told a startled community that marijuana for Elvy had a medicinal value—that it relieved the pressure, alleviated the pain, and reduced the number of headaches she endured from glaucoma. Remarkably, the community of public opinion, like the court of law, acquitted Elvy Musikka. When we took the case to the public, we found enormous support, and we also discovered that Elvy was not alone.

We received calls from and encountered many cancer patients, one of them a police officer who used marijuana regularly to reduce the pain of chemotherapy, an agonizing hurt that racked his body and sapped his strength. We found multiple sclerosis victims using marijuana to prevent recurring instances of uncontrollable spasticity. We found individuals, lawyers, and doctors with migraines who smoked marijuana to eliminate headache pain and daily stress.

We also found countless AIDS patients, like my friend Jimmy Messer, who sat in a Vero Beach, Florida, hospital fighting nausea and appetite deprivation and consuming marijuana not to get high, but to restore health and retard the pain of a fatal disease. By coming out of the closet, we tore down a veil of secrecy. We found a myriad of patients across the country who shared Elvy's predicament.

Ultimately we unveiled a whole new world of people who smoked and used marijuana—scores and scores of good, decent, and respectable people, who, like the parent of the twins in our hurricane Andrew example, simply sought to survive. We learned that there were patients like Elvy who had a considerable history of success with marijuana as a therapy. But we also learned that the majority of America's states and municipalities had no real interest in protecting the health and welfare of the Elvy Musikkas of America. We learned that medicinal marijuana was not available by prescription. In fact, even after acquittal, Elvy had to threaten the United States with a suit before four-year-old freeze-dried marijuana from the U.S. government-run farm at the University of Mississippi was made available to her on a trial basis. Now she is still only one of a handful of Americans fortunate enough to receive this medicine. Thousands of other patients continue to suffer both the threat of criminal prosecution for seeking it and the fear of increased illness for not getting it.

There are many like Elvy who seek to acquire marijuana legally but must

Prescription container of government-supplied marijuana for legal medical marijuana patient Elvy Musikka. Photo supplied by I-CARE.

resort to obtaining it illegally. One young man, 29-year-old James Messer, an AIDS patient in Stuart, Florida, was arrested in November of 1993 with four grams of marijuana rolled into a couple of cigarettes. James had been taking Marinol (the synthetic THC) by prescription to act as an appetite stimulant. Marinol is the legally prescribed THC pill that stimulates appetite. However, Marinol has a slower onset of action and costs more than smoking. And amazingly, the only pharmacy in the entire county that made Marinol available to James had been out of stock for four weeks prior to his encounter with the law. So James turned to the illegal alternative—not because he wanted to break the law, but because the law gave him no choice. Marijuana was simply the best available medicinal alternative open to James Messer.

James would have been an excellent candidate to receive marijuana legally had our government not turned its head and heart from the Compassionate Use Protocol Program (IND)—a governmental initiative that enabled patients to seek marijuana medicinally, as Elvy did. In chapter 3, Michael Aldrich will review the Bush administration's termination of this program and the Clinton administration's refusal to review or reenact it.

Kenneth Jenks of Pensacola, Florida, was a hemophiliac who contracted AIDS from infected blood during a transfusion. Unknowingly he infected his wife Barbra. Utilizing marijuana to minimize the devastating effects of nausea and vomiting that reduced them to incapacitated human beings, the Jenkses also found themselves the victims of an unwelcome prosecution by district attorneys. In a moving and emotional trial, they were each convicted of felonies. The judge and the jury did not accept the defense of medical necessity. They refused to apply it.

Now the Jenkses not only had a disease to worry about but also the possibility of incarceration. They were saved by a compassionate judge who recognized the true nature of their deeds. His sentence for Barbra and Ken Jenks was simply that they be placed on probation, with the special conditions that "they each take care of the other for the rest of their natural lives." Barbra died in 1992, and Ken died in 1993, but he was alive to hear that the court, in citing the Musikka case, asserted that the defense of medical necessity was indeed available in the state of Florida, and that the facts in the Jenks's case were such that it should have been applied instantly. The convictions were reversed and important case law had gained a strong foothold in the sunshine state, but only because desperate people acted courageously in the face of unjust governmental prosecution.

Mary Rathbun ("Brownie Mary") of San Francisco did not have AIDS. She did, however, bake marijuana brownies and cookies she delivered to AIDS patients. Arrested and prosecuted, she was acquitted of the felony of distribution of marijuana by correctly using a variation of the medical necessity defense. She was able to testify that her deliveries were made to assist others in need, not to advance individual greed, that the nobility of her actions outweighed the reprehensibleness of her offense according to the law.

This legal defense was originated in 1976 by Robert Randall, who eventually became the founder of the Alliance for Cannabis Therapeutics (ACT). In Elvy's case we used him as an expert witness to establish marijuana's medicinal value. Elvy was victorious in 1988. In 1993 and 1994 San Diego and San Francisco jurors again acquitted persons who successfully employed a medicinal marijuana defense. But the Jenkses lost their trial and so did other worthy patients in Minnesota and Massachusetts.

Barbara Sweeny, an AIDS patient of Fairfax, California, was arrested twice in Marin County for growing cannabis. She suffers from a chronic infection, and the drugs she has to take have terrible side effects that marijuana helps alleviate. After her first arrest, she was instructed to try Marinol, the synthetic marijuana substitute, which costs $300 per bottle. Marinol did not work very well and cost nearly $600 per week, paid by MediCal, to replace the medicine she had been growing at home for free.

Valerie Corral of Santa Cruz, California, was also arrested twice for growing cannabis to control seizures due to an accident. After charges were dropped in her first arrest on grounds of medical necessity, the sheriff re-arrested her and destroyed her plants even though he had been told by the local district attorney that he could not prosecute her.

Samuel Skipper, another AIDS patient, was arrested in San Diego for growing his own cannabis. He started growing cannabis when his partner contracted AIDS. When he also contracted AIDS, he started using the medicine to treat himself. After his second arrest, he was acquitted of cultivation by a jury on grounds of medical necessity but was sent to prison for having violated probation from his first arrest!

Scott Hager, a 34-year-old para–Olympic athlete, was raided by Santa Cruz police for growing four marijuana plants. He uses marijuana rather than addictive and debilitating drugs to control violent muscle spasms caused by his quadriplegia. At the time of the raid, Scott was recovering from major surgery, and the loss of his medicine caused serious complications.

 Bryon Stamate, a 74-year-old retiree, was arrested in El Dorado County, California, for growing cannabis to treat his girlfriend's chronic back pain. Not wanting to testify against him in court, his girlfriend committed suicide. As punishment, his home and life savings were seized by the sheriff's department, and he had to go to court to get them back. He also spent more than three months in jail.

Alex D., a 25-year-old hemophiliac, was arrested in Fort Lauderdale, Florida. An AIDS patient, he needed marijuana to combat the effects of chemotherapy. He sat in jail without bond while swelling in his brain nearly proved fatal. A wise judge released him and dismissed the charges for possession of marijuana. Another client of mine faced a jail term of six months in Stuart, Florida, for using marijuana when the only pharmacy in town that carried his Marinol had run out. Fortunately, the state attorney dismissed the charges based on the defense of medical necessity. While each of these last two cases ended favorably, the fear each defendant felt when initially arrested was staggering. As patients in the advanced stages of AIDS, both men had more to worry about than jail. Each was taking marijuana medicinally, but had it not been for the intervention of legal counsel on their behalf, they both would have ended up in jail. I am not trying to congratulate myself, but I am saying that neither patient, given the extent to which he was already suffering, should have been placed in that position.

My last admonition for anyone who may need to use this defense is to be sure to retain a competent and thoroughly professional attorney who will be able to meet the high standards outlined by Kevin Zeese in the following pages. These are not cases for amateurs. Medical necessity is a stringent, demanding defense. To preserve health in a rational, compassionate manner, the practice of medicine, however, cannot be predicated upon the legal requirements of the medical necessity defense.

When the Drug Enforcement Administration (DEA) and the Public Health Service joined hands and rescinded the Compassionate Use Program, Investigational New Drug program, the DEA administrator heartlessly wrote, "Beyond any doubt, the claims that marijuana is medicine are false, dangerous and cruel.... It is a cruel hoax to offer false hope to desperately ill people. It is not a safe or effective drug for any illness." I wish he had met some of these patients, endured some of their pain, or imagined some of their dreams. They aren't criminals. Only the unjust laws have made them so.

As Judge Mark Polen wrote in his legal decision acquitting Elvy Musikka:

> We cannot become blind to the legitimate medical needs of those who are afflicted by incurable diseases and require appropriate medical care. To ignore the plight of such people renders the law callous to the most basic of all human rights: the right of self-preservation.

2

Legal Issues Related to the Medical Use of Marijuana

KEVIN B. ZEESE

Seriously ill Americans are faced with a difficult choice if they need cannabis as a medicine—they can either obey the law and suffer the consequences of their illness and perhaps die, or they can break the law and face criminal prosecution. Similarly, healthcare professionals caring for patients who could benefit from cannabis also face a difficult choice. They can either hide information from their patients on the medical benefits of cannabis or they can tell their patients about its medical utility and advise them to break the law.

Most patients decide it makes more sense to preserve their health than to obey the marijuana laws. Occasionally such patients are prosecuted. Many doctors also conclude that they must tell their patients about marijuana's medical value. Indeed, nearly half the oncologists in a recent survey admitted they recommended that their patients get illegal marijuana to treat the side effects of their cancer treatment (Doblin and Kleinman 1991). So far, no doctor has faced ethics charges or criminal prosecution for giving such advice.

One of the more absurd by-products of the prohibition of marijuana has been the denial of a useful medicine to seriously ill people. As patients have discovered the medical uses of cannabis, they have come into conflict with the criminal law. Some of those patients who have chosen to protect their health rather than obey the marijuana law have sometimes been arrested and prosecuted for marijuana possession or cultivation.

Kevin B. Zeese, Esq., is the president of Common Sense for Drug Policy in Washington, D.C.

Advice to Patients and Doctors

Before discussing legal defenses for patients using marijuana as medicine, I will briefly focus on the advice to give such patients regarding the legal aspects of the matter. Answers to medical questions can be found in the other parts of this book.

Patients who decide to break the law and take this medicine must be advised of their real risk: they could face prosecution, which could result in fine, imprisonment and or forfeiture of property. The patient should be advised that there is currently no legal method of getting medicinal marijuana in the United States. In 1992 the federal government closed the only route available to such patients, the compassionate Investigational New Drug (IND) program.

The IND program was intended to be used for drugs that have not yet been approved for marketing but appear to have therapeutic potential. From 1976 to 1991 the Food and Drug Administration (FDA) allowed limited access to medical marijuana through the IND program. To gain access to this medicine from the government, the patient's physician was required to submit a lengthy, "red-taped" IND application to the FDA that included a specific research protocol for the patient. Once the FDA approved the IND application, the DEA then approved the security of the medicine and the National Institute on Drug Abuse (NIDA) supplied the marijuana to the patient. Over the years, thousands of patients obtained marijuana in this way through either individual or group IND applications. (The group applications came from states seeking marijuana after their legislature approved its use.)

While there is currently no legal source for marijuana, patients can get access to a synthetic THC pill (tetrahydrocannabinol, the primary psychoactive cannabinoid) through a doctor's prescription. Though many patients do not get satisfactory results from the pill, it should be tried before resorting to illegal marijuana. (As a lawyer, I have to give this legal advice.) When patients try the synthetic THC, they should document whether it worked and how it affected them. They should inform their doctor of the results and make sure that their doctor includes these comments in their medical records. In case of arrest, this documentation may be useful in defending against marijuana charges in the future.

The patient, through his or her doctor, should apply to the FDA for an IND before using marijuana illegally even though the IND program is closed at the time of this writing.[1] Similarly, if there is a state agency, the patient should contact it. If a negative response is received, political leaders should

---

[1]*The Alliance for Cannabis Therapeutics in Washington, D.C., can help doctors with the paperwork involved in filing an IND. Its number is 202-483-8595.*

be asked to contact the state or federal bureaucracy on the patient's behalf. It is important for the patient to try all legal means to acquire marijuana before resorting to illegal activity and to keep records of these efforts. Some patients have even called their local police chief to ask for advice or to ask if seized samples can be provided. Previous attempts at legal procurement can be very persuasive if the patient is later arrested for a marijuana violation.

If a patient decides to use marijuana, he or she should avoid letting people know about it, never share his or her medicine with anyone, never sell marijuana to anyone under any circumstances, and only grow or obtain as much as is needed for medical purposes. The patient should let his or her doctor know about the use of marijuana and ask the doctor to keep records of how it affects the course of the patient's illness. In particular, records should be kept on any reductions in other prescription medicines after beginning marijuana use.

If the police come to the patient's residence and ask about marijuana cultivation or possession, the patient should be honest. Right from the outset the patient should explain that it is being used for medical purposes and has not been shared with anyone.

The Medical Necessity Defense

The defense of necessity is one long recognized in common law. The defense has been noted in numerous treatises on criminal law (Kenny 1907; Clark and Marshall 1940; Burdick 1946). The defense has been described as:

> An act which would otherwise be a crime may be excused if the person accused can show that it was done only in order to avoid consequences which could not otherwise be avoided, and which, if they had followed, would have inflicted upon him, or upon others whom he was bound to protect, inevitable and irreparable harm [Clark and Marshall 1940, p. 104].

However, it has been said that the common law defense has been "more discussed than litigated."[2] This has changed somewhat in the use of the defense in marijuana cases (George Washington Law Review 1978). The medical necessity defense has now been successfully used to defend patients suffering from glaucoma,[3] multiple sclerosis[4] and AIDS[5] against marijuana charges.

[2]United States v. Moore, *486 F2d 1139 (D.C. Cir 1973).*
[3]United States v. Randall, *104 Wash Daily L Rep 2249 (D.C. Super Ct 1976);* State v. Musikka, *Case No. 88-4395 CFA (17th Judicial Circuit Broward County, Dec 28, 1988), reported in 14 FLW 2 (Jan 27, 1989).*
[4]State v. Diana, *604 P 2d 1312.*
[5]Jenks v. State, *no. 90-2462 (Ct App 1st Dist, Fl, April 16, 1991).*

The medical necessity defense is highly specific to the individual charged. In order to effectively utilize the defense, the defendant must have a medical condition that can be treated with marijuana and is beyond the reach of legally available medicines. Some states have statutes that authorize the necessity defense and require specified elements of proof needed for the defense to succeed. And while the defense has been successful in some cases, it has failed in an equal number of cases. Thus, it is a difficult defense that requires skilled lawyering in order to succeed.

The first case in which medical necessity was successful was *United States v. Randall* (1976). In that case Robert Randall was charged with possession of marijuana when marijuana plants were seen growing on his porch in Washington, D.C. Randall admitted that he was growing marijuana and defended it by arguing that marijuana was necessary to preserve his eyesight from glaucoma. Conventional drugs, which had initially controlled his eye pressure, had become ineffective, and by the time of his arrest, he had suffered loss of sight in his right eye and considerable impairment in his left. Mr. Randall had begun using marijuana in college and discovered by accident that it provided relief from his eye problems.

The court reviewed the common law history of medical necessity and found the defense available if breaking the law was caused by "the press of events" and "arises from a determination by the individual that any reasonable man in his situation would find the personal consequences of violating the law less severe than the consequences of compliance." The court found three situations in which the defense was *not* applicable.

1. If the circumstances compelling the violation of law were brought about by the accused: The court cited *United States v. Moore*,[6] where a defendant appealed a conviction for heroin possession arguing that because of his addiction, he lacked the capacity to choose to obey the law. The court refused to vacate his conviction because it reasoned that he had freely brought the addiction upon himself.

2. If a less offensive alternative was available: The court cited the case of *Bice v. State*[7] where an individual was convicted of transporting liquor to a church. The defendant appealed, arguing the liquor had been prescribed for medical purposes and that it was kept in his carriage in the vicinity of the church in case it was needed. The court recognized the legal use of liquor in treating certain illnesses but sustained the conviction stating that the defendant should "either stay at home or … take with him other medicine."

3. If the harm avoided is more serious than that performed to escape it: The court illustrated this exception by reference to a case in which prisoners

---

[6]*Infra. note 5.*
[7]*34 S E 202 (Ga 1899).*

overtook a prison to protest its inhumane conditions. The court ruled that prison control was more important than the prisoners' grievances.[8]

With regard to Mr. Randall's glaucoma, the court found only the third exception could possibly apply. With regard to that exception, the court said "the evil he sought to avert, blindness, is greater than that performed to accomplish it, growing marijuana in his residence." Any ill effects from the marijuana would be suffered only by the defendant, and as he was growing marijuana for his own consumption he was not contributing to the illegal market in marijuana.

The second successful case involved a multiple sclerosis (MS) patient, Samuel Diana.[9] In that case the appellate court found that the defense was applicable after the trial court had found Mr. Diana guilty of marijuana possession. The court noted that "the common law has long recognized the existence of a defense of necessity" and said the defense is available "when the physical forces of nature or the pressure of circumstances cause the accused to take unlawful action to avoid a harm which a social policy deems greater than the harm resulting from a violation of law." The appellate court remanded the case to the trial court to determine whether medical necessity existed in Diana's case.

The trial court heard testimony from several sufferers of MS, Mr. Diana, and physicians. Diana and the MS sufferers testified that marijuana relieved their symptoms. Specifically, Diana testified that within thirty seconds of using marijuana, he noticed his double vision leaving, tremors disappearing, the unsteadiness of his walk improving, nausea being alleviated and stiffness in his joints improving.

The court ruled that Mr. Diana had established his defense by a preponderance of the evidence and found him not guilty, setting aside the conviction. The court found that marijuana minimized the crippling effects of multiple sclerosis. The benefits to the defendant outweighed society's interest, and there was no other drug as effective in minimizing his disease. The court emphasized that this ruling applied only to Mr. Diana and the particular facts and circumstances of this case.

The third successful case involved a glaucoma patient Elvy Musikka.[10] Arrested for growing four plants in her home, Ms. Musikka had an extensive medical history, including forty years of trying all available medications and operations for her glaucoma. Indeed, she underwent more than twenty risky surgical procedures in an effort to retain her sight, including experimental procedures. The last of these left her blind in her right eye. Ms. Musikka

[8]People v. Brown, *70 Misc 2d 224, 333 NYS 2d 342 (1972)*.
[9]State v. Diana, *infra.* note 8.
[10]State v. Musikka, *infra.* note 7.

never denied her marijuana use. Her doctor, Paul Palmberg of the Bascom Palmer Eye Institute, testified that he was initially skeptical of the medical value of marijuana, but after monitoring her eye pressure for several years after she started using it, he became convinced that it worked. In fact, its use resulted in significantly lowered eye pressures for Ms. Musikka.

The court compared the defense of necessity to that of self-defense, i.e., an act that would constitute a crime can be justified by the need to protect oneself or another person from harm. In essence, the person is "compelled by circumstances beyond his control to breach the law in order to prevent injury." Thus, with medical necessity, the law forbids a medicine the individual needs. The court found that the defense of medical necessity would apply in Ms. Musikka's case if the trier of fact found by a preponderance of the evidence that:

a. a genuine medical disorder does, in fact, exist;

b. the defendant did not bring about the circumstances causing her to break the law, that is, Ms. Musikka was not responsible for causing her medical disorder, glaucoma;

c. weighed under the totality of the circumstances, Ms. Musikka's decision to do the illegal act, that is, to grow and use marijuana, was genuine and reasonable, tailored to minimize the effects of the medical disorder; and,

d. the benefits derived from the use of the illegal substance are greater than the harm sought to be prevented by the controlled substances law, that is, whether Ms. Musikka's alleged "right to sight" outweighs the social harm that her use of marijuana might cause.

While the above would make a good model for jury instructions, in this case the judge was the trier of fact. The court found that all four tests were met and acquitted Ms. Musikka. In making these findings the court relied heavily on the findings and recommendations of DEA administrative law judge Francis L. Young. Judge Young had been considering a petition filed to have marijuana rescheduled under federal law. In September 1988, after over two years of hearings, Judge Young ruled that marijuana should be rescheduled. He issued a 63-page ruling that included very strong findings of fact (DEA 1988). Even though the DEA administrator refused to follow Judge Young's recommendation, this decision should be relied on by counsel litigating medical necessity defenses.

In acquitting Ms. Musikka, Judge Mark E. Polen was careful to limit the ruling to Ms. Musikka. He did not want his ruling to be perceived as a green light for others to use marijuana. However, he went on to urge the state and federal legislatures to resolve what he described as an "intolerable, untenable legal situation." He expressed concern about a law that "forces law-abiding citizens into the streets—and criminality—to meet their legitimate medical needs."

Another successful medical necessity defense involved two AIDS patients, Barbra and Kenneth Jenks.[11] The trial court refused to accept the defense of medical necessity and convicted the couple for cultivation of marijuana and possession of drug paraphernalia. Mr. Jenks became infected with AIDS when getting a blood transfusion due to his hemophilia. He unknowingly passed it on to his wife. Mrs. Jenks rapidly lost weight, dropping from 150 to 112 pounds during a three week period due to constant vomiting and lack of appetite. Shots for nausea left her unable to function and in a stupor. Mr. Jenks started treatment with AZT. This left him nauseous and unable to eat resulting in significant weight loss. Through an AIDS support group they discovered that marijuana was being used by other patients to control nausea and increase appetite. They asked their doctor if he could get them marijuana legally, but he stated he was unable to do so. The Jenks decided to grow two plants and were arrested.

The court described the defense as follows:

> The pressure of natural physical forces sometimes confronts a person in an emergency with a choice of two evils: either he may violate the criminal law and thus produce a harmful result, or he may comply with those terms and thus produce a greater or equal or lesser amount of harm. For reasons of social policy, if the harm which will result from compliance with the law is greater than that which will result from violation of it, he is by virtue of the defense of necessity justified in violating it.[12]

The court noted that while there was no legislative declaration of necessity, it was recognized at common law[13] and never rejected by the legislature. The court rejected the argument that the legislature, by passing a controlled substances act prohibiting marijuana, and finding it had no accepted medical use, had made the necessity defense unavailable. The court concluded that unless a statute speaks unequivocally, it should not be interpreted to displace common law more than is necessary.[14] The court concluded the Jenkses met

[11]Jenks v. State, *infra. note 9.*

[12]Jenks v. State, *infra., quoting W.R. LaFave and A.W. Scott, Jr., 1 Substantive Criminal Law, § 5.4 at 627; see also Arnolds and Garland, "The Defense of Necessity in Criminal Law: The Right to Choose the Lesser Evil,"J. Crim. L. and Criminology 289 (1974):65; note, "Necessity: The Right to Present a Recognized Defense" 21 N. Eng. L. Rev. 779 (1985–86):21; Brown v. United States, 256 U.S. 335 (1921) (Where Justice Holmes stated: "Detached reflection cannot be expected in the presence of an uplifted knife.")*

[13]*The court cited* Reninger v. Fagossa *1 Plowd 1, 19, Eng Rep. 1, 29-30 (1551):75; ("[W]here the words of [the law] are broken to avoid greater inconvenience or through necessity, or by compulsion," the law has not been broken).*

[14]*The court cited* Carlile v. Game and Fresh Water Fish Comm'n, *354 So2d 362, 364 (Fla 1977);* State v. Egan, *287 So2d 1, 6–7 (Fla 1973);* Sullivan v. Leatherman, *48 So2d 836, 838 (Fla 1950)(en banc).*

the requirements of the defense. It adopted the standards of *United States v. Randall* and *State v. Musikka* in reaching this conclusion.

The final example of a positive case involving medical necessity in marijuana cases was a decision by the Supreme Court of Idaho.[15] This decision merely found that the medical necessity defense existed. It did not rule on the specific claims of the appellant. When the case was remanded for trial, the prosecutor dropped the charges.

The Idaho court did not create a special defense of medical necessity; it merely stated that the common law defense of necessity may apply. The court found the defense had four elements: (1) a specific threat of immediate harm; (2) the circumstances were not brought about by the defendant; (3) the same objective could not have been accomplished by a less offensive alternative; and (4) the harm caused was not disproportionate to the harm avoided.

In addition, to these positive cases there have also been some negative decisions. Usually, the result is brought about by the specific facts of the case. Some cases lost because the defendant did not try all legal channels, particularly the IND program[16] or a state research program.[17] It should be noted that with the closure of the federal IND program, there is no legal source for medical marijuana in the United States. Thus, this is currently not a factor in medical necessity cases.

More troublesome is the view accepted by one court that where a state has passed a law allowing the medical use of marijuana in a research program, there is no medical necessity defense. Thirty-five states have enacted such laws. The theory of the court in these circumstances is that the passage of the law indicates that the legislature considered marijuana's medical use and passed the legislation it thought was appropriate.[18] There are two responses to this position. First, most of these laws were passed in the late 1970s and early 1980s and since that time new diseases have become known that are helped by marijuana, and the federal government has closed the only source for marijuana for such programs. Thus, a patient can no longer apply to the state research program to obtain marijuana. Second, there are many diseases that affect a small number of people, and therefore the legislature would not be aware of the medical use of marijuana in these circumstances.

Another factor that can weigh heavily against a defendant is a situation in which a large amount of marijuana is being grown or possessed—larger than would be needed for medical purposes.[19] This presents a very real problem for many medical marijuana users. Medical users do not use the drug in

---

[15]State v. Hastings, *No. 18444 (Sup Ct Idaho, Nov. 27, 1990).*
[16]United States v. Burton, *894 F2d 188 (6th Cir 1990).*
[17]State v. Tate, *102 NJ 64, 505 A2d 1000 (1983).*
[18]State v. Hanson, *N.W. 2d, C3-90-1628 (Minn 1991).*
[19]*Burton, infra. note 16 ("large quantity of marijuana produced without government sanction").*

the same way recreational users do. For example, Robert Randall is legally prescribed ten marijuana cigarettes per day. Even a heavy recreational user would not consume more than one or two per day. Thus, the court needs to be educated about how patients use marijuana medically.[20] Also, not all patients have green thumbs and therefore grow more than necessary to offset the potential loss of some of their plants.

Only one court has refused to find that a medical necessity defense exists. In *Commonwealth v. Hutchins* (1991),[21] the Supreme Judicial Court of Massachusetts concluded in a 3–2 decision that the defense simply was not available in marijuana cases. The majority accepted the defendant's proffer of evidence concerning his disease, scleroderma, and marijuana's positive impact on it but harshly concluded:

> In our view, the alleviation of the defendant's medical symptoms, the importance to the defendant of which we do not underestimate, would not clearly and significantly outweigh the potential harm to the public were we to declare that the defendant's cultivation of marihuana and its use for his medicinal purposes may not be punishable. We cannot dismiss the reasonably possible negative impact of such a judicial declaration on the enforcement of our drug laws, including but not limited to those dealing with marihuana, nor can we ignore the government's overriding interest in the regulation of such substances.

The dissenters argued that this balancing test should have been made by the jury, not by judges. It went on to criticize the majority for not understanding the "humanitarian and compassionate value in allowing an individual to seek relief from agonizing symptoms." The stinging dissent led to the passage of a marijuana research law in Massachusetts and the defendant was pardoned by Governor William Weld.

Practical Issues in Defending Medical Necessity Cases

There are a series of practical and tactical issues an attorney faces in presenting the medical necessity defense. First, the attorney must recognize that this is a difficult defense, which has succeeded only a handful of times. Therefore, in addition to thinking about presenting a defense, counsel should be thinking about preparing for sentencing. Unlike other defenses, medical necessity defense is helpful in regard to sentencing. The defendant's illness will be graphically described, and the judge will hear in detail about his

[20]*Expert witnesses, including five legal medical marijuana patients, are available through Patients Out of Time (804) 263-4484.*
[21]Commonwealth v. Hutchins, E-5414 (Sup Jud Ct July 24, 1991).

symptoms and medical history. The only potential downside in the defense is the judge perceiving the defendant as deceiving the court about why the defendant used marijuana. Thus, if the defendant has a history of marijuana sales or was in possession of a large amount of marijuana, the defense is not likely to be effective.

One of the most difficult things in presenting the defense is finding good witnesses. While there are expert medical doctors and researchers throughout the United States who will testify that marijuana is medically useful,[22] it is often difficult to get the patient's treating physician to testify because local doctors do not want to be known as the "pot doc" or be harassed by police officials or government regulators. These are very real fears.

The testimony of the treating physician could be the most important of the case. If the doctor is unwilling to testify about marijuana use, it is useful to have the doctor testify about the defendant's illness, medical history, and symptoms. From this the attorney can get testimony about the reduction of the symptoms and the reduction of prescription drug use over particular time periods when the patient was using marijuana. This testimony can be built on by an expert witness. The expert can also submit for the record a great deal of written materials on the issue.[23]

Other helpful testimony can come from other users of marijuana for medicinal purposes. Their testimony is helpful in demonstrating that any reasonable person in the same circumstances would make the same choice. The testimony also helps to demonstrate marijuana's usefulness for a particular illness or symptom. It can be difficult to find illegal users who are willing to come forward and testify. In *State v. Diana*, the court allowed the identities of other patients to be hidden from the public and labeled them John and Jane Does. Another alternative is to have patients who are legally using marijuana testify. Robert Randall of the Alliance for Cannabis Therapeutics (ACT) in Washington, D.C., has successfully testified in many such situations.

Finally, the defendant generally must testify when presenting a medical necessity defense. The finder of fact needs to understand the choice the defendant was faced with, the pain or other symptoms the defendant was suffering from, and the defendant's view of his or her medical history. The defendant needs to impress the trier of facts as an honest and law-abiding citizen who has been forced to make this difficult decision based on circumstances beyond the defendant's control.

---

[22]*Four organizations that have helped find such witnesses are the Alliance for Cannabis Therapeutics (202-483-8595), Patients Out of Time (804-263-4484), Drug Policy Foundation (202-895-1634), and the International Cannabis Alliance of Researchers and Educators (804-263-4484).*

[23]*The same organizations can supply a variety of written materials on this issue. Bob Randall of the Alliance for Cannabis Therapeutics, through Galen Press, has published several books that can be useful in this regard.*

Aside from determining the witnesses, a critical question is whether a jury trial or bench trial (before the judge) is more appropriate. None of the successful medical necessity defenses involved a jury trial, all were bench trials. Perhaps it is more likely for a judge to be able to weigh the violation of the marijuana laws than it is for a jury. While this track record is hard to ignore, if the judge assigned to the case is one who will be unable to understand that marijuana has positive uses because of his or her personal biases then a jury trial will be preferable. If there is to be a jury trial, it could be helpful for the jurors to understand that they have the right to dismiss the defendant if they believe the law is unjust or applied unjustly. More information on this is available from the Fully Informed Jury Association (FIJA).[24]

A final practical question I will consider is how to deal with the prosecutor. There are advantages to a surprise defense of medical necessity given its rare use. However, it is also possible to educate a prosecutor prior to trial and work out an acceptable plea agreement. If the latter path is chosen, any agreement on probation should avoid drug testing so that the patient can continue to use marijuana as medicine.

If a court refuses to allow a defense of necessity, counsel should be prepared to make a thorough proffer of the evidence that would have been presented if the defense had been allowed to proceed. Such a proffer is critical for appellate purposes.

Concluding Thoughts

As a concluding thought it is useful to quote Judge Mark Polen in *State v. Musikka* (1988):

> Finally, the Court is deeply disturbed by the broader implications of the testimony presented in this case. Medical necessity is a stringent, demanding legal defense. The practice of medicine, however, cannot be predicated upon the legal requirements of the medical necessity defense if it is to preserve health in a rational, compassionate manner. As this decision, and the earlier decisions cited herein illustrate, marijuana has "an accepted medical use in treatment." Indeed, the evidence indicates marijuana is now being employed, albeit illegally, by patients throughout the United States. In the vast majority of such cases, these desperately ill people are being forced underground and away from urgently needed medical supervision to acquire marijuana.

Until medicinal marijuana is made legally available, patients, healthcare

---

[24]*For more information contact FIJA: P.O. Box 59 Helmville, MT 59843. (406) 793-5550 or 1-800-TEL-JURY.*

professionals, and lawyers will be in a quandary. The highest concern in such situations should be the health and well-being of the patient, not compliance with the law. Healthcare professionals and lawyers should come to the aid of such patients, not shun them. It is not their fault they are in this position; it is due to circumstances beyond their control. As professionals, we can help to ameliorate this situation, or we can make it worse for someone who is already seriously ill. The choice is obvious.

References

Arnolds and Garland. 1974. The defense of necessity in criminal law: The right to choose the lesser evil. *Journal of Criminal Law and Criminology* 65: 289–301.

Burdick, W. 1946. *The Law of Crime*. Albany, NY: Mathew Bender, p. 260.

Clark, W., and W. Marshall. 1940. *Treatise on the Law of Crimes*. 4th ed. Chicago: Callaghan.

Doblin, R., and M.A.R. Kleinman. 1991. Marijuana as as antiemetic medicine: A survey of oncologists' experiences and attitudes. *Journal of Clinical Oncology* 9 (7): 1314–1319.

Kenny, C. 1907. *Outlines of Criminal Law*. New York: MacMillan, pp. 68–70.

George Washington Law Review. 1978. Medical necessity as a defense to criminal liability. 46: 273–298.

Necessity: The right to present a recognized defense. 1985–86. *New England Law Review* 21: 779–815.

Washington, D.C. U.S. Department of Justice, Drug Enforcement Administration. September 6, 1988. In the matter of marijuana rescheduling petition, Dkt. No. 86-22, opinion, recommended ruling, findings of fact, conclusions of law, and decision of administrative law judge.

Part II

Medicinal Characteristics of Cannabis

3

History of
Therapeutic Cannabis

MICHAEL ALDRICH

On a February morning in 1994, the U.S. District Court of Appeals in Washington, D.C., with a panel of three law judges, issued a finding indicating that in their opinion cannabis has no medicinal value—none.

China: The World's Oldest Pharmacopoeia

Cannabis, called *ta ma* ("great hemp"), was one of the staple crops of ancient China, valued not only for food, fiber, oil, and paper but also as a medicine. According to legend, the ancient Emperor Shen Nung, patron deity of agriculture (c. 2700 B.C.), had a transparent abdomen, which allowed him to see the effects of medicines passing through his body (Wallnofer and von Rottauscher 1965). After experimenting with more than one hundred herbs, he is credited with the discovery of ephedra, ginseng, and cannabis as therapeutic agents.

The world's oldest pharmacopoeia, the *Shen-nung pen-ts'ao ching* (compiled in the first or second century A.D. but based on oral traditions passed down from the time of Shen Nung), gives cannabis the name *ma*, an ideogram that shows two plants (male and female) under a drying shed with the sun beating down on top (Dewey 1913). The text shows that the Chinese understood its psychoactive properties: "*ma-fen* [the fruits of hemp] ... if taken in excess will produce hallucinations [literally, "seeing devils"] ... over a long term, it makes one communicate with spirits and lightens one's body" (Li 1974, 1975). Hua T'o, the founder of Chinese surgery (A.D. 110–207), used a

Michael Aldrich, Ph.D., is a historian of cannabis in San Francisco, California.

Chinese ideogram for cannabis shows two plants (male and female) under a drying shed.

"hemp boiling compound," taken with wine, to anesthetize patients during surgical operations (ibid.).

Later editions of Shen Nung's pharmacopoeia list more than 100 ailments treated with cannabis, including "female weakness, gout, rheumatism, malaria, beri-beri, boils, constipation, and absent-mindedness" (Camp 1936, 113). By the tenth century A.D., the *Cheng-lei pen-ts'ao* summarized the therapeutic value of cannabis: "*Ma-fen* has a spicy taste; it is toxic; it is used for waste diseases and injuries; it clears blood and cools temperature; it relieves fluxes [diarrhea]; it undoes rheumatism; it discharges pus." (Li 1975, 56)

Other therapeutic uses of cannabis were preserved in the classic *Pen ts'ao kang mu* of Li Shih-Chen (A.D. 1578). Many of these uses—as an antiemetic, antibiotic, anthelmintic (treatment of parasites), to treat leprosy, and to stop hemorrhages—deserve modern investigation (Mechoulam 1986).

The historical use of cannabis for wasting diseases is one of its most common medical uses today in the age of AIDS. This is also emphasized in folk medicine throughout modern Asia. For example, in Thailand, "cannabis is frequently used to stimulate the appetite of sick people and make them sleep.... Its use to counteract diarrhea and dysentery is equally common" (Martin 1975, 72).

Ancient texts also refer to cannabis seed eaten as food. Even the Buddha himself, according to Chinese legend, existed for six years under the Bo Tree while awaiting enlightenment, eating only one cannabis seed each day (Abel 1980, 20). The nutritional and medical value of hemp seed and all the ancient economic uses of hemp are currently being reinvestigated (Rubin 1976; Herer 1990; Conrad 1993; Rosenthal 1994); see also chapters 16 and 17 of this book.

India

In India, the *Atharva Veda* (c. 1400 B.C.) mentions cannabis (*bhang*) as one of five sacred plants used for "freedom from distress" (11.6.15), and it also (8.8.3) ordains the practice of throwing hemp boughs into a fire during a magical rite "to overcome enemies" or evil forces (Aldrich 1977). As in China, where hemp stalks were used to strike the beds of sick people to drive out disease demons (Abel 1980), cannabis has been intimately associated with magical, medical, religious, and social customs in India for thousands of years

(Hasan 1975; Aldrich 1977; Touw 1981; Morningstar 1985). Sushruta, the most renowned physician of ancient India, recommended it as an antiphlegmatic (drying mucous membranes and relieving congestion, or more broadly regulating the bodily humors). Sushruta also mentions *vijaya* (cannabis, or perhaps yellow myrobalan) as a remedy for catarrh accompanied by diarrhea and as an ingredient in a cure for fevers (Grierson 1894; Chopra and Chopra 1957). It has thousands of uses in traditional Ayurvedic medicine, is noted in medieval texts as a soporific (sleep medication) and an excitant, appetite stimulant and digestive aid, remedy for many ailments and conditions, analgesic, aphrodisiac, intoxicant and *elixir vitae*.

One of the most famous jokes in the literature of medical cannabis occurs in the *Dhurtasamagama* or "Rogues' Congress," an amusing if coarsely written farce from circa A.D. 1500 (Grierson 1894):

> In the second act, two Shivaite mendicants come before an unjust judge, and demand a decision on a quarrel which they have about a nymph of the bazaar [prostitute]. The judge demands payment of a deposit before he will give any opinion. Not having any money, one of the holy men says, "Here is my ganja bag; let it be accepted as payment." The judge, taking it pompously, and then smelling it greedily, says, "Let me try what it is like" (takes a pinch). "Ah! I have just now got by the merest chance some ganja which is soporific and corrects derangements of the humours, which produces a healthy appetite, sharpens the wits, and acts like an aphrodisiac."

The *Rajavallabha*, a seventeenth century Ayurvedic text, says cannabis:

> is acid, produces infatuation, and destroys leprosy. It creates vital energy, the mental powers, and internal heat; corrects irregularities of the phlegmatic humour; and is an elixir vitae. It was originally produced, like nectar, from the ocean by the churning with Mt. Mandara, and inasmuch as it gives victory in the three worlds, it, the delight of the king of the gods, is called vijaya, the victorious. This desire-fulfilling drug was obtained by men on earth, through desire for the welfare of all people. To those who regularly use it, it begets joy and destroys every anxiety [Grierson 1894].

The Indian Hemp Drugs Commission of 1893–1894 heard testimony from hundreds of native and Western doctors about its therapeutic uses in treatment of cramps, spasms, convulsions, headache, hysteria, neuralgia, sciatica, tetanus, hydrophobia, ague, cholera, dysentery, leprosy, brain fever, gonorrhea, hay fever, asthma, bronchitis, catarrh, tuberculosis, piles, flatulence, dyspepsia, diabetes, delirium tremens, and impotence; as a sedative and febrifuge (substance that reduces fever); as an analgesic for toothache, tooth extraction and many other acute or chronic pains; as an anesthetic for minor surgery including circumcision; as a diuretic, tonic, digestive, disinfectant, aphrodisiac, anaphrodisiac (substance used to decrease sexual desire), food supplement, appetite stimulant, energy-creator, cool refreshing drink to prevent malaria, cure insomnia, alleviate hunger, and ... for freedom from distress (Kaplan 1969; Mikuriya 1968). In sum, the commission concluded:

> It is interesting to note that while the [hemp] drugs appear now to be frequently used for precisely the same purposes and in the same manner as was recommended centuries ago, many uses of these drugs by native doctors are in accord with their application in modern European therapeutics. *Cannabis indica* must be looked upon as one of the most important drugs of Indian materia medica [Kaplan 1969, 175].

For this reason, and because of its importance in religious and social life, the commission "unhesitatingly" gave "their verdict against such a violent measure as total prohibition in respect of any of the hemp drugs" (p. 287).

Ancient Middle East

Mechoulam (1986) provides the best summary of the literary evidence for medical use of cannabis in ancient Assyria, Egypt, and Judea. If the names of plants (*azallu, qunnabu,* and *gan-zi-gun-nu*) in Assyrian tablets of the seventh century B.C. are correctly translated as cannabis, the drug was used externally as a bandage and in salves for swellings and bruises, and internally for depression of spirits, impotence, "poison of all limbs" (arthritis?), kidney stones, for a "female ailment," and for the annulment of witchcraft. Similarly, if the hieroglyph "*smsm.t.*" in the ancient medical papyri of Egypt indicates cannabis, it was used as incense, as an oral medication for "mothers and children" (in childbirth?), in enemas, in eye medications, and as an ointment in bandages. This may be its first mention in world literature as an eye medication.

Although Benet (1975) interpreted the Hebrew term *kaneh-bosm* in the Bible as cannabis, there was until recently no direct evidence of medicinal use of cannabis in ancient Judea. However, in 1992 the skeletal remains of a 14-year-old girl who apparently died while giving birth were discovered in a tomb near Jerusalem dating from the fourth century A.D. (Zias et al. 1993). Ashes in the skeleton's abdominal area were analyzed and were found to contain a cannabinoid, delta-6-tetrahydrocannabinol. The researchers concluded that cannabis was burned in a bowl and administered to the girl as an inhalant to facilitate the birth process. Another possibility is that a mixture of cannabis ashes and honey was used for labor pains, as described in the Greek *Geoponica* for ulcers in the lower back (Brunner 1973). Yet another possibility is that cannabis was burned in a purification rite after her death, as Herodotus describes for the Scythians, who had swept down through Palestine 630 B.C. (Mechoulam 1986; Benet 1975).

Central Asia: The Scythians

The earliest Greek mention of *Kannabis* is Herodotus's famous story of the funeral ceremonies of the Scythians in the *Histories* (c. 450 B.C.). After the death of a king, the Scythians made small head tents, crept inside, threw hemp seeds (or blooms) on red-hot stones in an urn, and "howled for joy" at the vapor (Aldrich 1972). This is the first ethnographic description of a cannabis smoking device in world literature that was later confirmed by modern archaeologists who found kettles containing charred hemp seeds in Scythian tombs in the Altai Mountains (Rudenko 1970) and in Germany (Reininger 1966).

In the same book Herodotus (I: 202) also describes the practice of inhabitants of islands in the Araxes river throwing an unidentified fruit on a fire and getting "drunk" by inhaling its fumes (Brunner 1973, 347). This brings to mind the passage in the *Atharva Veda*, noted above, where Vedic worshippers threw hemp into a fire to ward off evil forces. The ritual intoxicant use of cannabis to communicate with spirits (or ward off evil) is thus found in ancient China, India, Central Asia, and Europe before the Christian era, and this magical use seems to have preceded specific medical uses in each region. Indeed, "folk medicine" tends to preserve ancient rituals simply because many generations have found the rituals medically useful. For example, Benet (1975, 46) notes that "in Poland, Russia, and Lithuania, hemp was used to alleviate toothache by inhaling the vapor from hemp seeds thrown on hot stones," right up into the twentieth century.

It is quite possible that Scythian influence may have introduced ritual use of cannabis throughout the Middle East. Scythian cavalry were employed by Philip of Macedon and by Alexander the Great on his campaign across Persia to the Hindu Kush in 326 B.C. (Aldrich 1972). By and large, however, the early references to hemp in Greek and Roman literature are to its fiber and medical uses rather than its ceremonial uses (Brunner 1973).

Ancient Greece and Rome

Dioscorides, a doctor in Nero's army in the first century A.D., wrote that cannabis seeds, "when eaten in excess, diminish sexual potency. The juice of the fresh seed, dropped in the ear, is beneficial for earaches." He also described a wild cannabis (hemp mallow?) whose roots could assuage inflammations and disperse hard matter about the joints. Pliny the Elder (A.D. 23–79), in his *Natural History* (20.259), combined these two descriptions and wrote that cannabis seed makes the genitals impotent, and its juice drives worms and insects out of the ears, but "at the cost of a headache." It makes water coagulate, and the boiled root "eases cramped joints, gout and similar pains, and is applied raw to burns" (Brunner 1973). Pliny may have been the first in the world to note that cannabis is not very miscible in water.

Galen, the second century physician renowned for making compound drug preparations (still called galenicals), said that cannabis seed is hard to digest and causes headaches; but "cooked and consumed with dessert after dinner, it stimulates the appetite for drinking, and in excess sends a warm and toxic vapor to the head." He added that it "eliminates intestinal gas, and dehydrates [the user] to such a degree that if eaten in excess it quenches sexual potency. Some squeeze juice from the green seeds and use it as an analgesic for pains caused by ear-obstruction" (Brunner 1973, 350). Galen is the only classical author to describe the intoxicating properties of cannabis consumed orally, including appetite stimulation (or at least dry mouth).

In these references, medical properties are described for the *sperma* (seed) of the plant; in many cases the term *sperma* may also refer to the blossom, the whole top of the flower where cannabis resin is produced. Such descriptions were the basis of European knowledge of medicinal cannabis all through the Middle Ages and the Renaissance. An illustration in a Byzantine manuscript of Dioscorides (c. A.D. 512) is the first botanical illustration of the plant in Western literature. It depicts both male and female flowers on the same plant—a mistake often repeated in later herbals (Aldrich 1992).

Medieval Middle East

Reviewing the literature from the thirteenth through the sixteenth centuries, Rosenthal (1971) has produced the only modern scholarly work in English on the subject of hashish in medieval Muslim society. Muslim physicians translated Dioscorides and Galen, poets wrote lovely and often satirical poetry contrasting hashish and wine, and theologians debated whether hashish should be forbidden under Muslim law, since, unlike alcohol, it is not expressly forbidden in the Koran. According to the most conservative legalists, the punishment for using hashish as an intoxicant would be 40 to 80 lashes (which would cripple the recipient for life), but the "medical use, even if it leads to mental derangement, remains exempt" from such punishment. Az-Zarkashi, a fourteenth century scholar whose work gives the fullest information on this subject, speaks of "the permissibility of its use for medical purposes if it is established that it is beneficial. ... Thus, it has been stated that it dissolves flatulence and cleans up dandruff." Other medical uses of hashish mentioned in Muslim texts are as a diuretic, to clean the brain, to soothe pains of the ears, and to aid digestion (Rosenthal, 114–115, 126). In this legal distinction between the intoxicant and the medical uses of cannabis, medieval Muslim theologians were far ahead of present-day American law.

One of the earliest "case reports" of the value of cannabis in treatment of epilepsy is a story told by Ibn al–Badri (c. A.D. 1464) about a poet who visited the epileptic son of the caliph's chamberlain and gave him some hashish as a medication. "It cured him completely, but he became an addict who could not for a moment be without the drug" (Rosenthal 1971, 152). Mechoulam et al. (1976) also mention this story in their discussion of the anticonvulsant effect of cannabidiol derivatives, one of the most promising new studies of the medical cannabinoids. More recent reviews of the use of cannabis derivatives in epilepsy, seizures, dystonia, and other convulsive and neurological disorders may be found in Mechoulam et al. (1984), Consroe and Snider (1986), Randall (1991a) and in chapters 9 and 10 of this book. An interesting offshoot of the research is that cannabidiol is also being reinvestigated as an anxiolytic (Musty 1984)—which takes modern medicine back full circle to the *Atharva Veda*'s "freedom from distress."

Muslims also introduced the art of making hemp paper into Europe, with the first paper mill established in Spain in A.D. 1150 and the second in Italy in 1276. Papermaking finally reached England in 1494. Much of the world's paper contained hemp fiber until the mid–nineteenth century, when sulfite tree pulp processing began to replace hemp paper (Conrad 1993), leading to worldwide deforestation and deterioration in the quality and longevity of books ever since.

Africa

Du Toit (1980) finds that cannabis has been smoked in Africa for at least six centuries, probably introduced by Arab traders down the east coast from Egypt and certainly having some connection to India as evidenced by the similarity of African and Hindi terms for the drug. Most accounts of native medical use come from white explorers and colonists of the nineteenth and twentieth centuries. The plant was used as a remedy for snake bite (Hottentots), to facilitate childbirth (Sotho), and among Africans of Rhodesia as a remedy for malaria, blackwater fever, blood poisoning, anthrax, and dysentery (Du Toit 1980, 58).

In addition, South African *dagga* (cannabis) was "famous in relieving the symptoms of asthma. This belief was shared by rural African farm workers and white farmers and many a pipe was shared between persons who suffered from this respiratory congestion" (Du Toit, 59).

Renaissance Europe

Europe during the Middle Ages did not have hashish and did not know much about the medical uses of the drug even though hemp had been cultivated throughout Europe since Roman times (Godwin 1967). Only one reference to hemp in Anglo-Saxon medicine has survived, that being *haenap* as an ingredient of a "holy salve" in the *Lacnunga*, a magico-medical recipe book of about the tenth century (Grattan and Singer 1952, 123). A few crusaders and Marco Polo told the tale of the assassins (eleventh to thirteenth centuries), without stating which drug was used in the potion that gave initiates a glimpse of paradise (Aldrich 1970). The Latin herbal of Rufinis (thirteenth century) mentions it as *canape*, and many subsequent herbals give crude illustrations of the plant along with its names in European languages. Fuchs's *De Historia Stirpium* (1542) describes the morphology and cultivation of Cannabis sativa and quotes Dioscorides, Galen, Pliny, and Simeon Sethi about its medical uses. Fuchs has the finest Renaissance illustration of cannabis, drawn from life but still displaying male and female flowers on the same plant (Aldrich 1992).

Parkinson, the king's herbalist (1640), summarized most of the herbalist uses of cannabis in treating dry cough, jaundice, fluxes (diarrhea), colic, gout, hard tumors, or knots of the joints, the "paines and shrinking of sinewes," burns or scalds, and to stay bleeding, and to kill worms. These are based on the classical sources with occasional local additions. For example, Parkinson says that a hemp decoction "powred into the holes of earthwormes, will draw them forth, and fishermen and anglers have used this feate to get wormes to bait their hookes" (Mechoulam 1986, 5).

Explorers and travelers in Africa, the Middle East, and especially India sent back reports of the use of hemp by natives, reports that were often superficial, always condescending, and usually confused hemp with opium (Aldrich 1970). An outstanding exception is Garcia da Orta's *Colloquies on the Simples and Drugs of India* (1563), in which a Portuguese physician, who grew cannabis in his own garden in Goa, consulted with native herbalists (as well as household servants), and gave a clear, scientific, and amusing account of *bangue*. He noted that it is quite distinct from opium, that unlike European hemp it is not used to make cords, and "the Indians eat either the seeds or the pounded leaves to assist or quiet the women. They also take it for another purpose, to give an appetite." (Da Orta 1563).

Rabelais (c. 1535), physician and author of *Gargantua and Pantagruel*, says that juice of the herb *Pantagruelion* (hemp), kills every kind of vermin ... [and is] a prompt remedy for horses with colic and broken wind. Its root, boiled in water, softens hardened sinews, contracted joints, sclerotic gout, and gouty swellings. If you want to quickly heal a scald or burn, apply some *Pantagruelion* raw [Grinspoon 1971, 397].

Rabelais expands on his main source, Pliny, noting a veterinary use of hemp and specifying its antibiotic ("kills vermin") properties.

The antibiotic use was verified by Czech scientists in the 1950s in a remarkable series of experiments (Kabelik, Krejci, and Santavy 1960; Rubin 1976) that showed "hemp extract proved itself valuable often when all modern antibiotic measures, including Terramycin [and others] failed." The Czech researchers also confirmed the value of cannabis unguent or spray in the treatment of burns, and found, as Dioscorides had said almost 2,000 years earlier, cannabis extracts achieved "rapid success" in the treatment of otitis media—earache (Rubin 1976, 6–7).

Eighteenth Century: Botany and Bounties

European botany lagged behind Chinese knowledge of the two sexes of the plant by several thousand years. In most pre–Linnaean botanical authors, the longer-living bushier plant was called male and the other one female—which is the opposite of the true situation in regard to cannabis, where the bushier pistillate plant is female (Stearn 1974). Hemp cultivation manuals, such as that appended to Barrufaldi's book of hemp poetry (1741), showed pictures of both sexes but reversed. Linnaeus corrected this mistake when he classified the plant as Cannabis sativa in 1753, and a few years later he grew cannabis on his windowsill and showed incontrovertibly that cannabis is dioecious by separating the male (staminate) and female (pistillate) plants at various stages of development (Linnaeus 1760; Stearn 1974). In 1783 the French naturalist Lamarck described Cannabis indica as a separate species based on a specimen collected in India, and botanists are still debating whether there are one, two, or three distinct species of this cultigen (Schultes et al. 1974).

From the sixteenth to the eighteenth centuries, military demand for cannabis (ship rigging and sails) and its widespread use for textiles and rope made all the royal houses of Europe command that their colonies grow hemp (Abel 1980; Conrad 1993). The Ludlow Library in San Francisco has originals of two of the most famous royal hemp edicts. In 1764 King George III offered American colonists a bounty of eight pounds sterling for every bale of raw hemp delivered to London, to which Ben Franklin's reply was, "We have not yet enough for our own consumption" (Abel 1980, 80). In 1788 the viceroy of Mexico ordered the mission at Monterey to plant hemp, thus starting hemp cultivation in California (Aldrich 1992).

So that the United States would not have to depend on England and Russia for hemp, George Washington tried, not very successfully, to grow hemp for seed at Mt. Vernon in the 1790s. And Thomas Jefferson invented a new type of hemp brake to mitigate the hard labor of extracting the bast fibers from hemp stalks (Conrad 1993, 304–305). Although African slaves may have known about cannabis intoxication, there is no evidence that the American plantation owners used it for intoxicating or medical purposes.

Nineteenth Century Europe: Cannabis Therapeutics

During Napoleon's disastrous expedition to Egypt in 1798, many of his troops discovered the pleasures of hashish, and his apothecary Rouyer wrote an article about the Egyptians' use of the drug in 1810 (O'Shaughnessy 1839). Interest in North African hashish and the assassins legend was the context in which the "Club des Haschichins" was founded in Paris in the 1840s, attracting the cream of French literary society (Aldrich 1970; Mickel 1969). One of its founders was Jacques Joseph Moreau de Tours, who began experimenting with the drug as a psychotomimetic (thinking cannabis intoxication might provide some insight into the genesis of mental illness) and as a possible treatment for fixed ideas in depressed patients (Moreau 1845). Although neither approach was successful, Moreau is justly regarded as the father of modern psychopharmacology.

It was not Moreau, however, but William B. O'Shaughnessy, a young Irish doctor serving the British Raj at the Medical College of Calcutta, who in 1839 introduced cannabis into Western medicine. By 1831 O'Shaughnessy had already discovered the modern fluid electrolyte treatment for cholera and would later be knighted by Queen Victoria for establishing the telegraph in India (Moon 1967).

> After studying the literature on cannabis and conferring with contemporary Hindu and Mohammedan scholars, O'Shaughnessy tested the effects of various hemp preparations on animals, before attempting to use them to treat humans. Satisfied that the drug was reasonably safe, he administered preparations of cannabis extract to patients, and discovered that it had analgesic and sedative properties. O'Shaughnessy successfully relieved the pain of rheumatism and stilled the convulsions of an infant with this strange new drug. His most spectacular success came, however, when he quelled the wrenching muscle spasms of tetanus and rabies with the fragrant resin [Mikuriya, 1973].

He also gave cannabis tinctures to cholera victims during an epidemic and found that ten drops every half hour would usually stop the vomiting and diarrhea that make the disease fatal (O'Shaughnessy 1839). This seems to be the first mention in European clinical literature of cannabis as an antiemetic.

Any drug that demonstrated success in the treatment of the most wretched diseases of the nineteenth century—rabies, tetanus, cholera—would be hailed as a wonder drug; and that's what happened when O'Shaughnessy brought his research back to London along with specimens for the Royal Botanical Gardens. Between 1840 and 1900 more than 100 articles about the therapeutic value of cannabis were published in Europe and North America (Grinspoon 1971).

Mikuriya (1973) collected the key nineteenth and twentieth century documents and summarized them in *Marijuana: Medical Papers, 1839–1972*. Other detailed accounts of cannabis therapy in the nineteenth century may be found in Mikuriya (1969), Grinspoon (1971), Snyder (1971), Carlson (1974), Cole (1976), Cohen and Stillman (1976), Abel (1980), and Mechoulam (1986). Mikuriya (1973) lists the following therapeutic applications of cannabis based on the literature:

1. Analgesic-hypnotic
2. Appetite stimulant
3. Antiepileptic and antispasmodic
4. Prophylactic and treatment of the neuralgias, including migraine
5. Antidepressant and tranquilizer
6. Antiasthmatic
7. Oxytocic (stimulates uterine contractions in childbirth)
8. Childbirth analgesic
9. Antitussive
10. Topical anesthetic
11. Withdrawal agent for opiate and alcohol addiction
12. Antibiotic

Queen Victoria's physician, Sir J. Russell Reynolds (1890), summed up 30 years of clinical experience with the drug finding it useful as a nocturnal sedative in senile insomnia and valuable in treating dysmenorrhea, neuralgias including tic douloureux and tabetic symptoms, migraine headache, and certain epileptoid or choreoid muscle spasms. He thought it less beneficial in asthma, alcoholic delirium and depressions, joint pains, or true epilepsy. He also advised doctors to start with very small doses of cannabis extracts and tinctures, gradually increasing the dose until relief is obtained; "with these precautions I have never met with any toxic effects" (Mikuriya, 1973, p. xviii).

Nineteenth–Twentieth Century America: Cannabis Therapeutics

Fitz Hugh Ludlow made a perceptive prediction in America's first drug book, *The Hasheesh Eater* (1857, 368): "Except as an antispasmodic in a very limited number of diseases, the cannabis is known and prized very little among our practitioners, and I am persuaded that its uses are far wider and more important than has yet been imagined." Ludlow also appended an article by an American physician, J.W. Palmer, which summarized O'Shaughnessy's work and recommended it to American doctors especially in hydrophobia and tetanus.

The first American clinical conference on medical marijuana was a meeting of the Ohio State Medical Society in 1860, which reported successful treatments of stomach pain, childbirth psychosis, chronic cough, gonorrhea, and marijuana's general usefulness as an analgesic for inflammatory or neuralgic pains (McMeens 1860). The Civil War edition of the *U.S. Dispensatory* (Wood and Bache 1868) devoted four pages to the medical properties of *Extractum Cannabis,* including its action as "a decided aphrodisiac, to increase the appetite, and occasionally to induce the cataleptic state ... to cause sleep, to allay spasm, to compose nervous inquietude, and to relieve pain." It was preferable to opium because it did not cause constipation, and it was recommended specifically for "neuralgia, gout, rheumatism, tetanus, hydrophobia, epidemic cholera, convulsions, chorea, hysteria, mental depression, delirium tremens, insanity, and uterine hemorrhage." The book also mentioned that Dr. Alexander Christison in Edinburgh had "found it to have the property of hastening and increasing the contractions of the uterus in delivery" based on clinical experiments to confirm its ancient use in childbirth.

Laboratories around the world experimented with different tinctures and extracts of cannabis, searching for a standard preparation with an established dose-response curve. Problems with the variable potency of such preparations led to the inclusion of cannabis itself—"the flowering tops of the female plant of *C. sativa*"—in medical practice. The *U.S. Dispensatory* of 1899 finally noticed that when ganja is cultivated in India, "The utmost care is taken to prevent fertilization, it being affirmed that a single male plant will spoil a whole field" (Wood, Remington, and Sadtler 1899). This forced American pharmaceutical companies to learn what is now called sinsemilla cultivation, removing male from female plants before seeds are set, and by 1918 it was shown that American-grown cannabis and its extracts were as fully reliable as those from India. By the 1930s both Eli Lilly and Parke-Davis were marketing cannabis extracts and tinctures that were uniformly effective at dose levels of 10 mg (Mikuriya and Aldrich 1988).

Amazingly little clinical work was done to investigate the smoking of cannabis for medical purposes. Walton (1938, 49) reports that in 1899 a researcher named Dixon experimented with powdered ganja and noted the ease with which patients titrated their own dose, with "little danger of taking an excess." He considered that smoking cannabis was "a satisfactory expedient in combating fatigue, headache and exhaustion, whereas the oral ingestion of cannabis results chiefly in a narcotic effect which may cause serious alarm."

This is very similar to the reports of present-day AIDS patients who much prefer smoking cannabis to taking Marinol

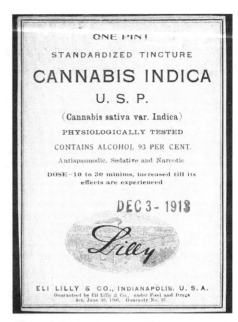

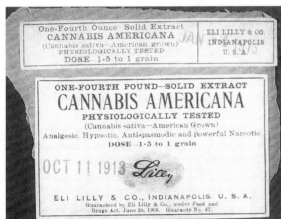

Top and bottom: *Labels from cannabis medicinal products developed and sold by Eli Lilly & Co. before the prohibition began with the Marihuana Tax Act of 1937. Photos supplied by Lisa Bayne from the Eli Lilly archives.*

pills (Randall 1991b, 99–112). So far the United States government has rejected a well-designed research project proposed by Dr. Donald Abrams and his colleagues at the University of California, San Francisco to compare the value of smoked marijuana to that of oral THC pills as a treatment for the wasting syndrome accompanying AIDS (Klinger 1995).

Straub (1931) also emphasized the self-regulation of dosage with smoking due to the rapid absorption of the smoke, leading to milder and shorter-acting effects. Walton (1938, 49) remarked that despite these recommendations, "the smoking of cannabis as a medicinal has been very limited," mainly to the anti-asthma cigarettes of Grimault & Company. Today the value of aerosol cannabis as a bronchodilator for asthma attacks is being investigated (Graham 1986).

Robinson (1912) stated,

> In medicinal doses cannabis is used as an aphrodisiac, for neuralgia, to quiet maniacs, for the cure of chronic alcoholism and morphine and chloral habits, for mental depression, hysteria, softening of the brain, nervous vomiting, for distressing cough, for St. Vitus' Dance, and for ... epileptic fits of the most appalling kind. It is used in spasm of the bladder, in migraine, and when the dreaded *Bacillus tetanus* makes the muscles rigid. It is a uterine tonic, and a remedy in the headaches and hemorrhages occurring at the final cessation of the menses. It has been pressed into the service of the diseases that mankind has named in honor of Venus [sexually transmitted diseases] ... [It] is sometimes useful in locomotor ataxia ... the intense itching of eczema ... as a hypnotic ... as a specific in hydrophobia ... Hemp enters into four galenicals; in chloral and bromine compound which is used as a sedative and hypnotic, in chloroform anodyne which is used in diarrhoea and cholera, in Brown Sequard's antineuralgic pills, and in corn collodions. Hemp is a constituent in the majority of corn remedies. Not many drugs are used for both the brain and the feet, but with cannabis we have this anomaly: a man may see visions by swallowing his corn-cure [30–32].

Robinson's little joke obscures an important point in the history of drug delivery systems, namely that cannabis corn plasters were among the first transdermal patches employed in medicine for timed release of water-insoluble drugs through the skin.

Sajous's Analytic Cyclopedia of Practical Medicine (1924) succinctly summarized early twentieth century cannabis therapy in three areas:

1. As a sedative or hypnotic in insomnia, senile insomnia, melancholia, mania, delirium tremens, chorea, tetanus, rabies, hay fever, bronchitis, pulmonary tuberculosis, coughs, paralysis agitans, exophthalmic goiter, spasm of the bladder, and gonorrhea.

2. As an analgesic in headaches, migraine, eye-strain, menopause, and brain tumors; tic douloureux, neuralgia, gastric ulcer, gastralgia (indigestion), tabes, multiple neuritis, and pain not due to lesions; in uterine disturbances, dysmenorrhea, subinvolution and chronic inflammatory states, menorrhagia and impending abortion, postpartum hemorrhage, acute rheumatism, eczema, senile pruritus, tingling, formication and numbness of gout, and for relief of dental pain.

3. Other uses to improve appetite and digestion, for the "pronounced anorexia following exhausting diseases," also in gastric neuroses, dyspepsia, diarrhea, dysentery, cholera, nephritis, hematuria, diabetes mellitus, cardiac palpitation, vertigo, sexual atony in the female, and impotence in the male.

Marihuana Tax Act, 1937–1969

While police waged campaigns against the "marihuana menace," medical use of cannabis preparations began to decline in the 1930s as they were gradually replaced by synthetic drugs. When the United States House of Representatives held hearings on the Marihuana Tax Act of 1937, Dr. W.C. Woodward of the American Medical Association (AMA) was the only witness who opposed the bill. The legislative activities committee of the AMA wrote to protest the impending legislation (Grinspoon 1971):

> There is positively no evidence to indicate the abuse of cannabis as a medicinal agent or to show that its medicinal use is leading to the development of cannabis addiction. Cannabis at the present time is slightly used for medicinal purposes, but it would seem worthwhile to maintain its status as a medicinal agent.... There is a possibility that a restudy of the drug by modern means may show other advantages to be derived from its medicinal use [p. 226].

Against all medical advice, the Marihuana Tax Act was passed in 1937 and cannabis preparations were removed from the United States pharmacopoeia in 1941 (Bonnie and Whitebread 1974). As Walton (1938, 162) noted, "Sasman in 1937 listed 28 pharmaceuticals which contained Cannabis indica. Most of the manufacturers are now removing cannabis from such combinations since the 1937 federal restrictions make it inconvenient to use such formulae."

Only a few years later, the LaGuardia Committee took a clear-headed look at the marijuana "problem" in New York and found most of the police claims that it caused crime, violence, insanity and death were completely unsubstantiated. In regard to medical use, the LaGuardia Report said,

> Marihuana possesses two qualities which suggest that it might have useful actions in man. The first is the typical euphoria-producing action which might be applicable in the treatment of various types of mental depression; the second is the rather unique property which results in stimulation of the appetite [1944, 147].

It is interesting that the committee did not shrink from commending euphoria itself as having therapeutic potential, and that it noted more than 50 years ago the greatest contemporary (1990s) use of cannabis as an appetite stimulant for patients with cancer or AIDS.

1970s–1990s: Rediscovering Medical Marijuana

In 1969, the United States Supreme Court ruled in the case of Timothy Leary that the Marihuana Tax Act could no longer be enforced because, had Dr. Leary tried to pay the tax on cannabis required by federal law, he would have broken Texas state law prohibiting possession of marijuana. This meant President Richard M. Nixon had to rewrite the federal drug laws in 1970, when marijuana was associated with war protesters and hippies, rather than with medical patients. The Controlled Substances Act of 1970 placed illicit drugs in one of five schedules, and the final decision about *which* schedule a drug was put in was made not by medical experts but by the Justice Department—the attorney general (John Mitchell) and the Bureau of Narcotics and Dangerous Drugs, later named the Drug Enforcement Administration (DEA). Cannabis and its derivatives were placed in Schedule I, for drugs with a high potential for abuse and no medical use (Baum 1996).

Ironically, two new medical uses were discovered shortly after the law was passed. The first was the ability of cannabis to reduce intraocular pressure (Hepler and Frank 1971; Hepler, Frank, and Petrus 1976; Roffman 1982; Colasanti 1986; Adler and Geller 1986), which suggested its use as a treatment for glaucoma. Robert Randall, a schoolteacher suffering from glaucoma who was arrested for using cannabis to keep from going blind, fought his case through the courts and finally in 1976 forced the federal government to provide him with cannabis for this purpose—the first legal marijuana smoker in the United States since 1937 (see the articles by Randall and West, in chapters 7 and 8 of this book).

The second discovery can be considered new because of a new context, the horrors of more than 40 kinds of chemotherapy used by contemporary doctors as treatment for cancer (Roffman 1982). The most frequent toxic side effect of chemotherapy is violent, uncontrollable nausea and vomiting that lasts for hours, and conventional antiemetics often do not help. Patients who smoked cannabis before chemotherapy, however, reported to their doctors that the illegal drug helped them enormously, stopping the vomiting and even making them hungry (Grinspoon and Bakalar 1995). This led to many clinical reports on the antiemetic effect of cannabis and the cannabinoids, starting with Sallan, Zinberg, and Frei (1975). Most of the research in this field has been summarized by Regelson et al. (1976), Roffman (1982), Levitt (1986), and Randall (1990) (see Dansak's review in chapter 5 of this book). The successful use of cannabis in cancer chemotherapy led to the marketing of an expensive synthetic tetrahydrocannabinol under the name Marinol and the rescheduling of this synthetic drug into Schedule II, though the plant and THC extracted from the natural source, remain in Schedule I.

The proven antiemetic value of cannabis also led to its use by many AIDS patients in the 1980s, both as an appetite stimulant against the AIDS wasting syndrome and as a remedy against the intense nausea often caused by the HIV's gradual takeover of the immune system and by the toxicity of AZT therapy. There are AIDS and cancer patients all over the country using cannabis for these purposes, regardless of the laws. Ironically, so many people with AIDS applied for admission to the federal "Compassionate Access" program for marijuana that in 1992 the United States Department of Health and Human Services shut down the only way for people to get this medicine legally (Randall 1991b). The use of Marinol in Schedule II is allowed in AIDS wasting syndrome, but the plant itself is not (see Krampf's review in chapter 6 of this book).

In San Francisco, a major AIDS epicenter, voters in 1991 approved a local ballot proposition recommending that cannabis be restored to the list of approved medicines by nearly 80 percent, the largest popular vote for marijuana in world history. As a result, the San Francisco board of supervisors approved a resolution in 1992 recognizing the therapeutic value of cannabis in AIDS, glaucoma, cancer, spastic and convulsive diseases, for the control of chronic pain and any other healing purposes. The resolution stated that arresting patients for medical use of marijuana would be the lowest of police enforcement priorities as long as patients obtained a letter of diagnosis from their physician. As a result, Dennis Peron was able to establish the Cannabis Buyer's Club, along the lines of AIDS drug buyer's clubs, which allows more than 10,000 registered patients, mostly people with AIDS, cancer, and painful paraplegic or spastic conditions (see Petro's review in chapter 9), to use the drug therapeutically without fear of arrest (Rathbun and Peron 1993). Cannabis clubs have also sprung up in several other cities. Bills approving the medical use of marijuana have passed the California legislature three times and have been vetoed by Governor Pete Wilson. A statewide initiative (Proposition 215) allowing doctors to prescribe, and patients to use, cannabis without fear of arrest was passed (by 56 percent) on November 5, 1996, as did a similar initiative in Arizona, Proposition 200 (by 65 percent). They cannot be vetoed by the governor; whether they can supersede the federal Schedule I classification will be for the courts to decide.

The improper classification of cannabis in Schedule I was challenged in 1972 by the National Organization for Reform of Marijuana Laws (NORML). For decades NORML, the Alliance for Cannabis Therapeutics (ACT), and other groups have petitioned the courts for hearings on rescheduling medicinal marijuana. Finally hearings were held in 1986, with dozens of doctors, patients, and health experts testifying that marijuana should at least be placed in Schedule II, for drugs with medical use and some potential for abuse (Grinspoon and Bakalar 1995). Testimony from the hearings has been published in a series of five books written and compiled by Randall (1988–1991).

On September 6, 1988, the DEA's own administrative law judge, Francis L. Young, ruled that,

> The evidence in this record clearly shows that marijuana has been accepted as capable of relieving the distress of great numbers of very ill people, and doing so with safety under medical supervision. It would be unreasonable,

arbitrary and capricious for DEA to continue to stand between those sufferers and the benefits of this substance in this record.

The administrative-law judge recommends that the (DEA) Administrator conclude that the marijuana plant considered as a whole has a currently accepted medical use in treatment in the United States, that there is no lack of accepted safety for use of it under medical supervision and that it may lawfully be transferred from Schedule I to Schedule II. The judge recommends that the Administrator transfer marijuana from Schedule I to Schedule II [Young 1988].

That should have been the end of it. Medical experts had shown conclusively that there is an accepted medical use for cannabis in the United States, and the DEA's own judge had agreed that it should be placed in Schedule II, where it belongs according to the definitions in the law itself. Nonetheless, on December 29, 1989, DEA Administrator John Lawn ignored the recommendations and findings of fact and stated that the DEA would not allow the rescheduling.

And on a February morning in 1994, the U.S. District Court of Appeals in Washington, D.C., with a panel of three judges, issued a finding indicating that in its opinion cannabis has no medicinal value—none.

References

Abel, E.L. 1980. *Marihuana: The First Twelve Thousand Years*. New York: Plenum.

Adler, M.W., and E.B. Geller. 1986. Ocular effects of cannabinoids. In *Cannabinoids as Therapeutic Agents*, ed. R. Mechoulam, 51–70. Boca Raton, FL: CRC Press.

Aldrich, M.R. 1970. *Cannabis Myths and Folklore*. Ph.D. diss., State University of New York at Buffalo (available from University Microfilms, Ann Arbor, Michigan).

Aldrich, M.R. 1972. A brief legal history of marihuana. In *Marihuana: Debate and Data*, ed. P.H. Blachly, 15–33. Corvallis, OR: Oregon State University, Continuing Education Book.

Aldrich, M.R. 1977. Tantric cannabis use in India. *Journal of Psychedelic Drugs* 9 (3): 227–233.

Aldrich, M.R. (Speaker). September 1992. *The History of Medical Marijuana*. Slide presentation at NORML's 22nd Anniversary Conference, San Francisco. (Videotape #3834 by Jim Turney, available from NORML, 1001 Connecticut Ave NW, Washington, DC 20036.)

Baruffaldi, G. 1741. *Il Canapajo...* Book 8. Bologna: Lelio dalle Volpe. Appended is GA Berti's *Coltivazione della canape*, with illustrations showing the male and the female hemp plant (reversed).

Baum, D. 1996. *Smoke and Mirrors: The War on Drugs and the Politics of Failure*. Boston: Little, Brown.

Benet, S. 1975. Early diffusion and folk uses of hemp. In *Cannabis and Culture*, ed. V. Rubin, 39–49. The Hague: Mouton.

Bonnie, R.J. and C.H. Whitebread, 1974. *The Marihuana Conviction: A History of Marihuana Prohibition in the United States*. Charlottesville: University Press of Virginia.

Brunner, T.F. 1973. Marijuana in ancient Greece and Rome?: The literary evidence. *Bulletin of the History of Medicine* 47 (4): 344–355.

Camp, W.H. 1936. The antiquity of hemp as an economic plant. *Journal of the New York Botanical Garden* 37 (437): 110–114.

Carlson, E.T. 1974. *Cannabis indica* in nineteenth century psychiatry. *American Journal of Psychiatry* 131 (9): 1004–1007.

Chopra I.C., and R.N. Chopra, 1957. The use of the cannabis drugs in India. *Bulletin on Narcotics* 9 (1): 4–29.

Cohen, S., and R.C. Stillman, eds. 1976. *The Therapeutic Potential of Marihuana*. New York and London: Plenum.

Colasanti, B.K. 1986. Review: Ocular hypotensive effect of marihuana cannabinoids: Correlate of central action or separate phenomenon. *Journal of Ocular Pharmacology* 2 (3): 295–304.

Cole, C. 1976. Stash notes: Marijuana as medicine, a historical perspective. *STASH Capsules* 8 (3): 1–5. (Madison, Wisconsin, Student Association for the Study of Hallucinogens, Inc.)

Conrad, C. 1993. *Hemp: Lifeline to the Future*. Los Angeles: Creative Xpressions.

Consroe, P. and S.R. Snider. 1986. Therapeutic potential of cannabinoids in neurological disorders. In *Cannabinoids as Therapeutic Agents* ed. R. Mechoulam, 21–49. Boca Raton, FL: CRC Press.

Da Orta, G. 1563. *Colloquies on the Simples & Drugs of India*. (Goa). Trans. Sir Clements Markham. 1913. London: Henry Sotheran.

Dewey, L.E. 1913. Hemp. *Yearbook of the U.S. Department of Agriculture*. Washington, DC: USDA. Reprinted in Rosenthal, 1994, pp. 339–376.

Du Toit, B.M. 1980. *Cannabis in Africa*. Rotterdam: Balkema.

Fuchs, L. 1542. *De Historia Stirpium...* Basle: Michael Isengrin.

Godwin, H. 1967. The ancient cultivation of hemp. *Antiquity* 41: 42–50.

Graham, J.D.P. 1986. The bronchodilator action of cannabinoids. In *Cannabinoids as Therapeutic Agents*, ed. R. Mechoulam, 147–157. Boca Raton, FL: CRC Press.

Grattan, J.H.G., and C. Singer, 1952. *Anglo-Saxon Magic and Medicine*. London: Oxford University Press.

Grierson, G.A., 1894. Note on references to the hemp plant occurring in Sanskrit and Hindi literature: Appendix to *Report of the Indian Hemp Drugs Commission, 1893–94*. 3: 247–249. (Summarized in Kaplan edition, pp. 174–175.)

Grinspoon, L. 1971. *Marihuana Reconsidered*. Cambridge, MA: Harvard University Press.

Grinspoon, L. and J.B. Bakalar. 1995. *Marihuana: The Forbidden Medicine*. New Haven and London: Yale University Press.

Hasan, K.A. 1975. Social aspects of the use of cannabis in India. In *Cannabis and Culture*, ed. V. Rubin, 235–246. The Hague: Mouton.

Hepler, R.S. and I.M. Frank. 1971. Marihuana smoking and intraocular pressure. *Journal of the American Medical Association* 217: 1392.

Hepler, R.S., I.M. Frank, and R. Petrus. 1976. Ocular effects of marihuana smoking. In *The Pharmacology of Marihuana*, ed. M.C. Braude and S. Szara, 815–824. New York: Raven Press.

Herer, J. 1990. *Hemp and the Marijuana Conspiracy: The Emperor Wears No Clothes*. Van Nuys, CA: HEMP Publishing.

Kabelik, J., Z. Krejci, and F. Santavy. 1960. Hemp as a medicament. *Bulletin on Narcotics* 12 (3): 5–22.

Kaplan, J., ed. 1969. *Marijuana: Report of the Indian Hemp Drugs Commission, 1893–1894*. Silver Spring, MD: Thos. Jefferson.

Klinger, K. September 14, 1995. Government blocks UCSF marijuana study. *Bay Area Reporter*, 25.

LaGuardia Committee (Mayor LaGuardia's Committee on Marihuana). 1973. *The Marihuana Problem in the City of New York 1944*. Metuchen, NJ: Scarecrow Reprint Corporation.

Levitt, M. 1986. Cannabinoids as antiemetics in cancer chemotherapy. In *Cannabinoids as Therapeutic Agents*, ed. R. Mechoulam, 71–83. Boca Raton, FL: CRC Press.

Li, H.L. 1974. An archaeological and historical account of cannabis in China. *Economic Botany* 28: 437–448.

Li, H.L. 1975. The origin and use of cannabis in Eastern Asia: Their linguistic-cultural implications. In *Cannabis and Culture*, ed. V. Rubin, 51–62. The Hague and Paris: Mouton.

Linnaeus, C. 1786. *A Dissertation on the Sexes of Plants, 1760*. Trans. James Edward Smith, F.R.S. London: George Nicol.

Ludlow, F.H. 1857. *The Hasheesh Eater: Being Passages from the Life of a Pythagorean*. New York: Harper.

McMeens, R.R. 1860. Report of the committee on Cannabis indica. In *Transactions of the 15th Annual Meeting of the Ohio State Medical Society*. Columbus, Ohio: Follett, Foster & Co. Reprinted in T.H. Mikuriya. 1973. *Marijuana: Medical Papers, 1839–1972*, pp. 117–140. Oakland: Medi-Comp Press.

Martin, M.A. 1975. Ethnobotanical aspects of cannabis in Southeast Asia. In *Cannabis and Culture*, ed. V. Rubin, 63–75. The Hague and Paris: Mouton.

Mechoulam, R. 1986. The pharmacohistory of Cannabis sativa. In *Cannabinoids as Therapeutic Agents*, ed. R. Mechoulam, 1–19. Boca Raton, FL: CRC Press.

Mechoulam R., N. Lander, S. Dikstein, E.A. Carlini, and M. Blumenthal. 1976. On the therapeutic possibilities of some cannabinoids. In *The Therapeutic Potential of Marihuana*, ed. S. Cohen and R.C. Stillman, 35–45. New York and London: Plenum.

Mechoulam, R., N. Lander, M. Srebnik, I. Zamir, A. Breuer, B. Shalita, S. Dikstein, E.A. Carlini, J. Roberto Leite, H. Edery, G. Porath. 1984. Recent advances in the use of cannabinoids as therapeutic agents. In *The Cannabinoids: Chemical, Pharmacologic, and Therapeutic Aspects*, ed. S. Agurell, 777–793. Orlando, FL: Academic Press.

Mickel, E.J., Jr. 1969. *The artificial paradises in French literature*. Chapel Hill: University of North Carolina.

Mikuriya, T.H. 1968. Physical, mental, and moral effects of marijuana: The Indian Hemp Drugs Commission Report. *International Journal of the Addictions* 3 (2): 253–270.

Mikuriya, T.H. 1969. Marihuana in medicine: Past, present, and future. *California Medicine* 110: 34–40.

Mikuriya, T.H. 1973. *Marijuana: Medical Papers 1839–1972*. Oakland: Medi-Comp Press.

Mikuriya, T.H. and M.R. Aldrich. 1988. Cannabis 1988: Old drug, new dangers, the potency question. *Journal of Psychoactive Drugs* 20 (1): 47–55.

Moon, J.B. 1967. Sir William Brooke O'Shaughnessy: The foundations of fluid therapy and the Indian telegraph service. *New England Journal of Medicine* 276: 283–284.

Moreau, J.J. 1845. *Du Hachisch et de l'alienation mental: Etudes psychologiques*. Trans. G.J. Barnett. In *Hashish and Mental Illness*, ed. H. Peters and G. Nahas. New York: Raven.

Morningstar, P.J. 1985. *Thandai* and *Chilam*: Traditional Hindu beliefs about the proper uses of cannabis. *Journal of Psychoactive Drugs* 17 (3): 141–165.

Musty, R.E. 1984. Possible anxiolytic effects of cannabidiol. In *The Cannabinoids: Chemical, Pharmacologic, and Therapeutic Aspects*, ed. S. Agurell, 795–813. Orlando, FL: Academic Press.

O'Shaughnessy, W.B. 1838–1840 and 1842. On the preparations of the Indian hemp, or gunjah. Transactions of the Medical and Physical Society of Bengal, 71–102, 421–461. Reprinted in T.H. Mikuriya. 1973. Marijuana: Medical Papers 1839–1972, 3–30. Oakland: Medi-Comp Press.

Randall, R.C. 1988. *Marijuana, Medicine and the Law*. Vol. I: *The Direct Testimony*. Washington, DC: Galen Press.

Randall, R.C. 1989. *Marijuana, Medicine and the Law*. Vol. II: *The Legal Argument*. Washington, DC: Galen Press.

Randall, R.C. 1990. *Cancer Treatment and Marijuana Therapy*. Washington, DC: Galen Press.

Randall, R.C. 1991a. *Muscle Spasm, Pain, and Marijuana Therapy*. Washington, DC: Galen Press.

Randall, R.C. 1991b. *Marijuana and AIDS: Pot, Politics, and PWAs in America*. Washington, DC: Galen Press.

Rathbun, M. and D. Peron, 1993. *Brownie Mary's Marijuana Cookbook and Dennis Peron's Recipe for Social Change*. San Francisco: Craig Lombardi.

Regelson W., J.R. Butler, J. Schulz, T. Kirk, L. Peek, M.L. Green, and M.O. Zalis, 1976. Delta-9-tetrahydrocannabinol as an effective antidepressant and appetite-stimulating agent in advanced cancer patients. In *The Pharmacology of Marihuana*, ed. M.C. Braude and S. Szara, 2: 763–776. New York: Raven Press.

Reininger, W., 1966. Historical notes. In *The Marihuana Papers*, ed. D. Solomon. Indianapolis, Kansas and New York: Bobbs-Merrill, 100–101.

Reynolds, J.R. March 22, 1890. Therapeutical uses and toxic effects of Cannabis indica. *Lancet*. 1: 637–638. Reprinted in *Marijuana: Medical Papers, 1839–1972*, ed. T.H. Mikuriya, 145–149.

Robinson, V. 1912. *An Essay on Hasheesh*. New York: Medical Review of Reviews, E.H. Ringer.

Roffman, R.A. 1982. *Marijuana as Medicine*. Seattle: Madrona Publishers.

Rosenthal, E., ed. 1994. *Hemp Today*. Oakland: Quick American Archives.

Rosenthal, F. 1971. *The Herb: Hashish Versus Medieval Muslim Society*. Leiden: Brill.

Rubin, V. 1976. Cross-cultural perspectives on therapeutic uses of cannabis. In *The Therapeutic Potential of Marihuana*, ed. S. Cohen and R.C. Stillman, 1–17. New York and London: Plenum.

Rudenko, S.I. 1970. *Frozen Tombs of Siberia: The Pazyryk Burials of Iron-Age Horsemen*. Berkeley and Los Angeles: University of California.

Sajous C., and M. Sajous. 1924. Cannabis indica (Indian hemp: hashish). *Sajous's Analytic Cyclopedia of Practical Medicine*. 9th ed. 3: 1–9. Philadelphia: Davis.

Sallan, S.E., N.E. Zinberg, and E. Frei. 1975. Antiemetic effect of delta-9-tetrahydrocannabinol in patients receiving cancer chemotherapy. *New England Journal of Medicine* 293 (16): 795–797.

Schultes, R.E., W.M. Klein, T. Plowman, and T.E. Lockwood. 1974. Cannabis: An example of taxonomic neglect. *Botanical Museum Leaflets, Harvard University* 23 (9): 337–367. Reprinted in V. Rubin, ed., *Cannabis and Culture*, 21–38. The Hague and Paris: Mouton, 1975.

Stearn, W.T. 1974. Typification of Cannabis sativa L. *Botanical Museum Leaflets, Harvard University*. 23 (9): 325–336. Reprinted in V. Rubin, ed. *Cannabis and Culture*, 13–20. The Hague and Paris: Mouton.

Snyder, S.H. 1971. *Uses of Marijuana*. New York, London, Toronto: Oxford University Press.

Touw, M. 1981. The religious and medicinal uses of cannabis in China, India, and Tibet. *Journal of Psychoactive Drugs* 13 (1): 23–34.

Wallnofer, H., and A. von Rottauscher. 1965. *Chinese Folk Medicine and Acupuncture*. New York: Bell.

Walton, R.P. 1938. *Marihuana: America's New Drug Problem*, Philadelphia: Lippincott.

Wood, G.B., and F. Bache. 1868. *The Dispensatory of the United States of America*. 12th ed. Pp. 379–382. Philadelphia: Lippincott.

Wood, H.C., J.P. Remington, and S.P. Sadtler. 1899. *The Dispensatory of the United States of America*. 18th ed. Pp. 313–316. Philadelphia: Lippincott.

Young, F.L. September 6, 1988. In the Matter of Marijuana Rescheduling Petition, Docket #86-22, Opinion and Recommended Ruling, Findings of Fact, Conclusions of Law and Decision of Administrative Law Judge. Washington DC: U.S. Department of Justice, Drug Enforcement Administration.

Zias, J., H. Stark, J. Seligman, R. Levy, E. Werker, A. Breuer, and R. Mechoulam. May 20, 1993. Early medical use of cannabis. *Nature* 263: 215.

4

Pharmacology and Toxicity of Cannabis

DENIS J. PETRO

While the history of the medical uses of cannabis extends over 5,000 years, an understanding of the pharmacological properties of this most interesting plant remains a subject of intense interest. In the past ten years, new and exciting developments have emerged in cannabinoid research. *Marijuana* is the popular term for the group of substances derived from the herbaceous plant, Cannabis sativa. When the flowering tops and leaves of the plant are dried and rolled into cigarettes, marijuana can be smoked to deliver volatilized substances to the lungs. In addition to the psychoactive compounds unique to the cannabis plant, the smoke can contain particulate matter and tars as found in tobacco. Pathogens, such as aspergillus and salmonella can be delivered in the inhaled smoke. Transmission of contaminants can be limited with the use of a water pipe or alternative delivery system, such as use of the leaves in food for oral ingestion. The pharmacological properties of cannabis depend on the route of administration and will be discussed in relation to either the smoked form or the synthetic oral preparation, Marinol (delta-9-THC), a more recent form. Much of the clinical data obtained in the Marinol research program can be generalized to include cannabis, except for the route of administration.

Chemistry

Among the more than 400 chemical entities in the cannabis plant, the cannabinoids have been the group of compounds studied the most. At least

Denis J. Petro, M.D., is a practicing neurologist and clinical drug researcher in Arlington, Virginia.

60 cannabinoids have been identified and studied. It should be noted that a particular plant has only trace amounts of most of the cannabinoids, not enough to have any clinical effect. The most thoroughly studied cannabinoids include delta-9-tetrahydrocannabinol (delta-9-THC), delta-8-tetrahydrocannabinol (delta-8-THC), cannabidiol (CBD), and cannabinol (CBN). After two decades of clinical research, a synthetic oral preparation, Marinol, has been approved by regulatory authorities for therapeutic use in the United States. The approved indications for the use of Marinol are for treatment of: (1) anorexia associated with weight loss in patients with AIDS; and (2) nausea and vomiting associated with cancer chemotherapy in patients who have failed to respond adequately to conventional treatments.

Cannabinoids have only limited solubility in water and are usually prepared in a vehicle such as alcohol or sesame oil. The pharmacological actions of any cannabinoid may depend on the nature of the vehicle used to administer it. For example, if serum albumin is the vehicle, the cannabinoid will bind to the albumin and subsequently limit the availability of the drug to the target tissue. Thus, studies comparing the relative potency of specific cannabinoids may not represent the true effect of cannabis when administered as a smoked cigarette. Since the clinical pharmacology of orally administered delta-9-THC (Marinol) has been extensively studied, most of the data relevant to cannabis has been obtained in studies of oral Marinol. Marinol is formulated in soft gelatin capsules containing either 2.5 mg, 5 mg or 10 mg delta-9-THC.

Pharmacokinetics

No significant differences have been found between the sexes in the metabolism, disposition, and kinetics of delta-9-THC in humans (Wall et al. 1983). The absorption, distribution, metabolism, and secretion of cannabis depends on the method of administration and potency of the individual plant in use. In addition, the amount of cannabinoid delivered to the circulation depends on the inhalation technique of the subject. When inhaled, a standard 1-gram cigarette containing 2 percent delta-9-THC could deliver 0.4 to 10 mg of the drug to the circulation. Because of the high lipid solubility and first pass hepatic metabolism, only 10 percent to 20 percent of the dose reaches the circulation when administered orally. Plasma protein binding of delta-9-THC and its metabolites is approximately 97 percent. Plasma concentrations reach their peak within seven to ten minutes after smoking and within one to two hours after oral ingestion. The subjective and physiological effects are maximal within a half-hour after smoking and at two hours after oral ingestion.

The distribution of cannabis metabolites throughout the body is extremely rapid with uptake in liver, lung, spleen, and fat. Less than 1 percent of the administered dose reaches the brain. The elimination half-life is about 30 hours with 80 percent excreted via the intestine and liver and 20 percent excreted in the urine. At least 80 cannabinoid metabolites have been identified in man. Detectable levels of cannabinoid metabolites can be found in the blood and urine for up to one month after exposure to marijuana. Secondary exposure to cannabis smoke can result in inhalation of sufficient cannabinoids to produce positive urine test results.

The biotransformation pathways of cannabis in humans have been studied extensively. The metabolic profile includes hydroxylation, oxidation to carboxylic acids, ß-oxidation, conjugation, and epoxidation. Together with the observation of wide variations in cannabinoid metabolism among species, these data may explain the differential effects of cannabis on experimental animals and man and on different human subjects.

Analytic techniques have been developed to detect the presence of cannabis metabolites in the urine. The metabolite of cannabis usually detected in the highest concentration is 11-nor-delta-THC-9-carboxylic acid (THC-COOH). This metabolite is found in urine in the free or conjugated state as a glucuronide. Most analytic techniques use THC-COOH as an indicator of cannabis use. The analysis is conducted in two steps beginning with a screening immunoassay for THC metabolites. Confirmation of a positive test is achieved using the more sensitive gas chromatography with mass spectrophotometry (GC-MS). A positive THC-COOH test is a level of 15 to 20 ng/dl using the GC-MS test.

The test can be positive for three days after a single use of cannabis. In a chronic cannabis user, the urine test can detect residual positive levels for up to four to six weeks after last use, thus a positive urine test for a chronic user does not necessarily indicate recent or continued use (Ellis et al. 1985). Metabolite concentrations in the urine have been found to be higher following oral ingestion than after smoking cannabis (Cone 1990). Lower but still detectable concentrations in the urine have been found with ingestion by passive inhalation.

Studies by Perez-Reyes et al. (1972, 1973) demonstrated that THC metabolites are not excreted by the salivary glands. However, THC has been detected in saliva and is the result of direct absorption into the buccal mucosa as the cannabis is smoked. Amounts are highest within an hour of inhalation and drop thereafter. Although the amount of absorption is relatively small, it seems reasonable that additional small amounts are probably absorbed in the mucous membranes of the upper respiratory tract as well (Perez-Reyes 1990).

Pharmacological Effects in Humans

The two effects of cannabis that have been demonstrated to be of therapeutic value, to the extent that Marinol is marketed for treatment, are as an antiemetic and as an appetite stimulant in AIDS patients manifesting anorexia. The approval of Marinol for these indications represents de facto recognition that the risk-benefit ratio of delta-9-THC is favorable. Adequate and well-controlled studies are required for approval, and Marinol has met all standards set by the Food and Drug Administration (FDA). This fact is often forgotten by those critics who claim that cannabinoids have no therapeutic effects. In spite of lack of evidence to support any diversion of Marinol in these patients, the drug remains in Schedule II under the Controlled Substances Act.

While therapeutic effects have been demonstrated, most pharmacological studies have emphasized central nervous system (CNS) effects and other system actions that might be considered toxic. Behavioral responses in healthy subjects, at varying doses and under different conditions, have been reported. In addition, clinical experience with 474 patients exposed to Marinol has been published. In healthy subjects, CNS effects on mood, memory, motor coordination, cognition, sensorium, time sense, and self-perception are noted. The most prominent cardiovascular effect in healthy subjects is tachycardia at rest. The increase in heart rate is dose-related, and its duration correlates with concentrations of delta-9-THC in blood. Other cardiovascular effects include increased supine blood pressure, decreased blood pressure on standing and conjunctival reddening (bloodshot eyes). The respiratory effect of a single dose of inhaled cannabis is significant to induce bronchodilatation. Bronchitis and asthma have been reported in chronic cannabis smokers. This observation is not unexpected due to the presence of tars in marijuana smoke and the tendency of recreational smokers to inhale deeply.

Immunosuppression is reported in animals and in vitro. Clinical experience has not indicated an increased susceptibility to infections. Ironically, Marinol is indicated to treat the anorexia associated with AIDS with no reports of increased immunosuppression. Among the endocrine effects reported are decreased testosterone and inhibition of spermatogenesis in men and anovulatory cycles in women.

Mechanism of Action

An understanding of the mechanism of action of cannabinoids remains an exciting challenge to the neurosciences. In the past decade researchers have made discoveries that promise answers to fundamental questions about cannabis. If the active ingredients in cannabis trigger specific receptors in the brain, what is their normal role in brain function? For the receptor theory of cannabis action to be proven, two questions must be answered: what is the nature of the THC receptor and what is the natural brain chemical (the endogenous ligand)?

Before 1988 many neuroscientists thought that since THC is a fat-soluble molecule, the logical explanation was for THC to insert itself in cell membranes. Researchers in the United States and Israel were able to extract membrane receptors from the brain cortex, hippocampus, and basal ganglia that demonstrated binding with cannabinoid compounds in a dose-dependent and pharmacologically specific manner. Isolation of the cannabinoid receptor in 1988 was a signal event in neuroscientific research. The receptor is involved in the regulation of the cellular cyclic AMP (cAMP) second messenger system and the inhibition of adenylate cyclase. The cannabinoid receptor has been cloned and binding sites have been identified (Matsuda et al. 1990; Munroe et al. 1993; Pertwee 1993).

The search for a brain chemical that binds the receptor has focused on a molecule derived from arachidonic acid, christened "anandamide," from a Sanskrit word meaning "bliss." Other candidate molecules have been proposed that, unlike anandamide, are water-soluble. The discovery of the cannabinoid receptor and the endogenous ligand has infused new energy in the field of cannabinoid pharmacology (Devane et al. 1992).

Toxicity

No drug is free of toxic effects. One of the most important roles of the clinician is to balance the risks of a potential medical treatment against the benefits to be gained from its use. After 5,000 years of use, cannabis remains a remarkably safe drug. To date, there exists no reported case of a fatal overdose. Considering that hundreds of people die each year from aspirin overdoses, one can only be impressed by the safety of cannabis. In the hearings concerning the rescheduling of marijuana in 1988, the Drug Enforcement Administration's (DEA) own administrative law judge declared that marijuana in its natural form was "one of the safest, therapeutically active substances known to man." It is often said that if aspirin were a new drug submitted to the FDA for review, regulatory approval would not be a certainty. Yet, the most psychoactive cannabinoid, delta-9-THC, is marked for two indications that are, by definition, untreatable by any other drug available to the physician.

With the marketing of Marinol in the United States, well-controlled clinical trials have been conducted that provide some indication of the safety of Marinol. Adverse reactions to Marinol were identified in clinical trials in the United States and its territories involving 474 patients (157 patients with AIDS-related weight loss and 317 patients with nausea and vomiting associated with cancer chemotherapy). A cannabinoid dose-related "high" (easy laughing, elation, and heightened awareness) has been reported by patients receiving Marinol in both the antiemetic (24 percent) and appetite stimulant clinical trials (8 percent). Adverse reactions from these trials have been classified by frequency and body system. For those reactions that occurred while the subjects were being treated with Marinol and that were felt to be probably causally related to Marinol, the results are presented by incidence:

Incidence of events: 3 percent to 10 percent:
    Digestive: Abdominal pain, nausea, vomiting.
    Nervous system: Dizziness, euphoria, paranoid reaction, somnolence, thinking abnormally.

Incidents of events: 1 percent to 3 percent:
    Body as a whole: Asthenia.
    Nervous system: Amnesia, anxiety/nervousness, ataxia, confusion, depersonalization, hallucination.

Incidence of events: less than 1 percent:
    Cardiovascular: Conjunctivitis, hypotension.
    Digestive: Diarrhea, fecal incontinence.
    Musculoskeletal: Myalgias.
    Nervous system: Depression, nightmares, speech difficulties, tinnitus.
    Skin and appendages: Flushing.
    Special senses: Vision difficulties.

In addition, other events that occurred with a frequency of less than 1 percent and had an unknown relationship to the use of Marinol include:

    Body as a whole: Chills, headache, malaise.
    Digestive: Anorexia, hepatic enzyme elevation.
    Respiratory: Cough, rhinitis, sinusitis.
    Skin and appendages: Sweating.

Reviewing the adverse reactions to Marinol reveals no unusual or unexpected effects of this drug, which is given to patients with the difficult medical problems of cancer and AIDS. In keeping with the restrictions placed on Marinol (Schedule II), the product labeling includes a strong warning regarding possible addiction or diversion. No evidence to support such a warning has been found in the studies of Marinol. In studies, on patients with AIDS who received Marinol for up to five months, no abuse, diversion, or systematic change in personality or social functioning were observed, despite the inclusion of a substantial number of patients with a past history of drug abuse.

While abuse of Marinol has not occurred, the drug can cause signs of an abstinence syndrome on abrupt withdrawal. Electroencephalographic changes consistent with the effects of drug withdrawal (hyperexcitation) were recorded in patients after abrupt discontinuation. Patients also complained of disturbed sleep for several weeks after discontinuing therapy with high dosages of Marinol. Volunteers receiving dosages of 210 mg/day for 12 to 16 consecutive days reported symptoms such as irritability, insomnia, and restlessness within 12 hours after discontinuation. By approximately 24 hours after discontinuation, withdrawal symptoms intensified and included "hot flashes," sweating, rhinorrhea, loose stools, hiccups, and anorexia. These withdrawal symptoms gradually dissipated over the next 48 hours.

Accidental or intentional overdose with Marinol has not occurred. Side effects are usually dose-related and improve with reduction in the daily dose. In antiemetic studies, drowsiness and other nonpsychotropic symptoms were equal in incidence in the higher and lower doses. The incidence of dysphoric effects was only 12 percent in the low-dose group as compared to 28 percent in the high-dose group. Interestingly, in the antiemetic studies the efficacy of Marinol was not reduced in the low-dose group. Thus, the use of a low dose of Marinol can minimize side effects while maintaining therapeutic benefit. The signs and symptoms of a mild Marinol overdose include drowsiness, euphoria, heightened sensory awareness, altered time perception, reddened conjunctiva, dry mouth, and tachycardia. A moderate overdose causes memory impairment, depersonalization, mood alteration, urinary retention, and reduced bowel motility. Severe intoxication includes decreased motor coordination, lethargy, slurred speech, and postural hypotension.

The estimated lethal human dose of intravenous Marinol is 30 mg/kg (2100 mg/70 kg). Using this estimation of the lethal dose, the equivalent inhaled THC would represent the smoking of 240 cannabis cigarettes with total systemic absorption of the average 8.8 mg of THC in each cigarette. Since absorption is much less than 100 percent, the amount of smoked marijuana required to reach lethality is on the order of one to two thousand cigarettes. The physical impossibility of a fatal overdose using smoked cannabis is obvious.

The safety data obtained in clinical trials of Marinol provide some insight into the potential toxicity of cannabis. Clearly, inhaled cannabis presents hazards related to this method of administration. The presence of contaminating herbicides and infectious agents is avoidable with organic cultivation techniques and sanitary cigarette production. The presence of tars and other particulate matter can be minimized using water pipes. Water pipes also can limit direct oral exposure to tars and other potential carcinogens.

A consistent response to the acute administration of cannabis is an increase in heart rate; however, tolerance to this effect develops after approximately one week of regular use. Also seen are blood pressure changes including increased supine pressure and orthostatic hypotension. In the clinical trials of Marinol less than 3 percent of patients experienced cardiovascular adverse reactions (palpitations or tachycardia). Since Marinol has not been studied in the elderly or in patients with preexisting cardiovascular disease, caution should be exercised with these patients. In the Marinol antiemetic studies, no difference was found in efficacy or tolerance in patients over 55 years old. As always, the clinical judgment of the clinician has to balance the possible risks against the potential benefits in any population, such as the elderly or those with heart disease.

While a large body of preclinical data exists regarding the effects of cannabinoids on endocrine gland activity, studies on humans have been the subject of controversy. There are reports of cannabis-induced decreases in testosterone and hormone levels to the lower end of the normal range, but the interpretation of these results is uncertain. Likewise, the increase in anovulatory menstrual cycles in females is consistent with the suppression of LH secretion as seen in rats, but the clinical correlation in terms of fertility is unknown.

The potential for a drug to induce cancer is always studied when a new drug is considered. Animal studies are only an indirect measure of the potential carcinogenicity of a drug. Mutagenicity testing of Marinol was negative in the Ames test. Inhaled cannabis contains many of the same toxic substances found in tobacco cigarettes. Exposure to these substances can be limited or even eliminated with the use of alternative delivery systems for cannabinoids.

A potential connection between marijuana and leukemia was reported in a controlled study of 204 pairs of children. Two hundred and four children with acute non-lymphoblastic leukemia (ANLL) were matched with an equal number by age, race, and residence (area code and exchange). Marijuana use was reported by ten mothers (during or within three months prior to pregnancy) of the children with ANLL and in one control case. This observation represents a tenfold risk (P = 0.005). Marijuana use by fathers, in the year prior to conception, did not demonstrate a significant association with increased risk. This unexpected result may have been influenced by limitations in the study design. The observed rate of cannabis use of 5 percent in study cases is lower than the rate of 10 percent seen in a group of new mothers. The 0.5 percent rate found in the control group may be due to underreporting by subjects who were contacted by telephone and were perhaps unwilling to admit to an activity that is still illegal. In addition, in any study with a large number of outcome variables, the possibility of a random, but incorrect finding, is increased.

Over the years, in vitro studies of human and animal cells have suggested that cell-mediated immunity may be adversely affected by cannabis. If these in vitro results have any merit, one would expect to see increased opportunistic infections in AIDS patients who use Marinol to treat the cachexia (wasting syndrome) associated with AIDS. However, no increase in infections has been found. Likewise, patients undergoing cancer chemotherapy might be expected to show more problems with infections. Again, no relationship between the use of Marinol and opportunistic infection was seen.

A working definition of *neurotoxicity* is any adverse effect on the structure or function of the central or peripheral nervous system by a biological, chemical, or physical agent that may result from direct or indirect actions or reflect permanent or reversible changes in the nervous system. This definition includes temporary and reversible effects on the nervous system as neurotoxic. Neuroscientists have attempted to create animal models to test for neurotoxicity with cannabinoids. As with human studies, route of administration, duration, and age at exposure are variables influencing the results of the studies. In summary, prepubescent rats developed hippocampal lesions after chronic cannabis exposure. A therapeutic window for the production of an effect was seen when 40-day-old rats were more severely affected than 70-day-old rats. Periods of exposure to cannabis, shorter than three months have not demonstrated neurotoxic effects in rats. Studies on prepubescent rhesus monkeys, using up to one-year exposure to cannabis smoke, did not produce neurotoxicity as seen in rats.

The range of psychopathological effects said to be related to cannabis use is wide. However, the fact that cannabis users have experienced virtually every psychiatric illness may be an indication that cannabis is the cause of psychiatric illness, but it is no proof of causality. In many cases, reports of amotivational syndrome, marijuana-induced cerebral atrophy, or acute paranoid reactions have been published with only a minimal concern for scientific objectivity. Widespread media attention to anecdotal reports of brain damage obscure the search for scientific truth. In subjects using marijuana as a recreational drug, one can expect the usual range of mental effects coincident with their search for a "high." If the subject is paranoid or depressed, one would not expect a pleasant experience in all cases.

The effects of cannabis on driving have been extensively studied. It takes no stretch of the imagination to assume that an individual experiencing a "high" should not be on the road. The degree of impairment after cannabis use has been studied in comparison with that caused by alcohol, and both drugs produced impairment of driving performance, with the combination leading to worse results than either drug alone. The Marinol patient instruction is the standard warning seen with many drugs, i.e., not to drive, operate machinery, or engage in any hazardous activity until it is established that patients are able to tolerate the drug and to perform such tasks safely.

Conclusion

This chapter reviewed the chemistry and pharmacology of cannabis. The past decade has seen exciting developments in cannabinoid research. Isolation of specific cannabinoid receptors and the search for the endogenous ligand active at these receptors is ongoing. The decade has seen the regulatory approval of Marinol for the treatment of anorexia in AIDS and in patients with nausea and vomiting associated with cancer chemotherapy. Future developments of other cannabinoids and more acceptable administration of cannabis to avoid the adverse pulmonary effects of smoking are exciting new areas for research. These research developments have to be balanced against the restrictive public policy decisions of governmental agencies, such as the DEA. It is hoped that a rational discussion of the issues will occur as progress in this most interesting therapeutic approach continues.

References

Cone, E.J. 1990. Marijuana effects and urinalysis after passive inhalation and oral ingestion. *NIDA Research Monograph* 99: 88–96.

Devane, W.A., L. Hanus, A. Breuer, R.G. Pertwee, L.A. Stevenson, G. Griffin, D. Gibson, A. Mandelbaum, A. Epinger, and R. Mechoulam. 1992. Isolation and structure of a brain constituent that binds to the cannabinoid receptor. *Science* 258: 1946–1949.

Dewey, W.L. 1986. Cannabinoid pharmacology. *Pharmacological Reviews* 38: 151–178.

Ellis, G.M., M.A. Mann, B.A. Judson, N.T. Schramm, and A. Tashchian. 1985. Excretion patterns of cannabinoid metabolites after last use in a group of chronic users. *Clinical Pharmacology and Therapeutics* 38 (5): 572–578.

Grinspoon, L. and J.B. Bakalar. 1992. Marihuana. In *Substance Abuse: A Comprehensive Textbook*, ed. J.H. Lowinson, P. Ruiz, R.M. Millman, and J.G. Langrod, 236–246. 2d ed. Baltimore: Williams and Wilkins.

Grinspoon, L. and J.B. Bakalar. 1995. Marihuana as medicine. *Journal of the American Medical Association* 273: 1875–1876.

Hollister, L.E. 1986. Health aspects of cannabis. *Pharmacological Reviews* 38: 1–20.

Matsuda, L.A., S.J. Lolait, M.J. Brownstein, A.C. Young, and T.I. Bonner. August 9, 1990. Structure of a cannabinoid receptor and functional expression of the cloned cDNA. *Nature* 346: 561–564.

Munro, S., K.L. Thomas, M. Abu-Shaar. September 2, 1993. Molecular characterization of a peripheral receptor for cannabinoids. *Nature* 365: 61–65.

Musty, R.E., P. Consroe, and A. Makriyannis. 1991. Pharmacological, chemical, biochemical, and behavioral research on cannabis and the cannabinoids. *Pharmacology, Biochemistry, and Behavior* 40: 457–708.

Perez-Reyez, M. 1990. Marijuana smoking: factors that influence the bioavailability of tetrahydrocannabinol. *NIDA Research Monograph* 99: 42–62.

Perez-Reyes, M., M.A. Lipton, M.C. Timmons, M.E. Wall, D.R. Brine, and K.H. Davis. 1973. Pharmacology of orally administered 9-tetrahydrocannabinol. *Clinical Pharmacology and Therapeutics* 14: 48–55.

Perez-Reyes, M., M.C. Timmons, M.A. Lipton, K.H. Davis, and M.E. Wall. 1972. Intravenous infection in man of 9-tetrahydocannabinol and 11-OH-9-tetrahydrocannabinol. *Science* 177: 633–635.

Pertwee, R. 1993. The evidence for the existence of cannabinoid receptors. *General Pharmacology* 24 (4): 811–824.

Thomas, B.F., D.R. Compton, B.R. Martin, and S.F. Semus. 1991. Modeling the cannabinoid receptor: A three-dimensional quantitative structure-activity analysis. *Molecular Pharmacology* 20: 656–665.

Wall, M.E, B.M. Sadler, D. Brine, H. Taylor, and M. Perez-Reyes. 1983. Metabolism, disposition, and kinetics of delta-9-tetrahydrocannabinol in men and women. *Clinical Pharmacology and Therapeutics* 34 (3): 352–363.

Part III

Indications for
Therapeutic Use
of Cannabis

5

As an Antiemetic and Appetite Stimulant for Cancer Patients

DANIEL A. DANSAK

In 1977, a 26-year-old male cancer patient from New Mexico approached the state's legislature with an astounding proposal: legalize marijuana for cancer patients. His reason: smoking marijuana reduced the nausea and vomiting side effects of the therapeutic drugs given by doctors to combat his metastatic cancer. Many other cancer patients could have the same benefit, he argued, except for the fact that marijuana was illegal to purchase or possess. Apparently legal antiemetic drugs were not very effective for the severe symptoms of nausea and vomiting that cancer patients suffered. Some patients even chose to stop anticancer chemotherapy because of the discomfort. And worse, because they stopped treatment, some patients died. This young cancer patient named Lynn Pierson also knew of other cancer patients around the United States who had used or were using marijuana to control the nausea and vomiting side effects of anti-cancer drugs.

One sympathetic New Mexican legislator, Tom Rutherford, sent Lynn Pierson's request on for further research. The Legislative Counsel Office then approached the University of New Mexico's Cancer Research and Treatment Center for assistance. A review of the scientific literature produced a number of reports by reputable investigators in high-quality journals attesting to the effectiveness of cannabis in reducing the nausea and vomiting side effects of anticancer medications. The most notable report was that of Dr. Steven Sallan and his group at Massachusetts General Hospital in Boston, a teaching hospital associated with Harvard University's Medical School (Sallan et al. 1975).

Daniel A. Dansak, M.D., is a practicing psychiatrist at the University of Southern Alabama in Mobile.

Based on the available evidence, the state legislature of New Mexico subsequently passed a law allowing cancer patients to use cannabis to control the nausea and emetic side effects caused by their treatment. However, because federal laws under the Food and Drug Administration (FDA) and Drug Enforcement Administration (DEA) also applied, the legislature required that marijuana or its psychoactive chemical (delta-9-THC) be given to cancer patients *only* under the auspices of a research program that would meet the scientific and legal requirements of the above two federal agencies and any others with similar authority. The National Institute of Drug Abuse (NIDA) and the National Cancer Institute (NCI) were two such additional agencies. The intent of the state legislature was to get marijuana or delta-9-THC to cancer patients in New Mexico who wanted and needed it. Federal agencies, however, wanted reasonable, scientific information to help in making decisions about the drug. Both intentions were equally important.

Many scientists in New Mexico and elsewhere were initially interested in conducting research on the effects of marijuana and delta-9-THC on nausea and vomiting in cancer patients. Their interest gradually disappeared as it became clear that neither the state of New Mexico nor the federal government would provide funds to start or run any program. However, a few concerned individuals at the New Mexico Cancer Control Program, a federally funded community cancer education and training program, found that such a research and service program would mesh extremely well with the program's other missions. A research protocol was prepared and submitted through the University of New Mexico to the FDA, DEA, NCI, and NIDA. After many months of review and refinement, and with much encouragement and assistance from federal and state scientists and administrators, the protocol was approved. Nearly one year after New Mexico passed the law allowing marijuana for cancer patients, medication supplies arrived and were dispensed under this protocol to those who wanted and needed them. Regrettably, Lynn Pierson, who had started the entire process, was not one of the recipients. He had died of cancer several months before the program began. Once begun, the research program attracted a steady flow of patients from all over the state of New Mexico. Eventually, the state of New Mexico funded the project and renamed it the Lynn Pierson Therapeutic Research Program. Five other states (Georgia, Michigan, New York, Tennessee and California) conducted similar studies in the late 1970s to mid–1980s, all concluding marijuana was an effective antiemetic (Randall 1989, 36–54).

Background: Adverse Effects of Chemotherapy

Many of the chemotherapeutic drugs used to treat cancer are highly lethal agents with intense and potentially overwhelming side effects. The goal of chemotherapy is to kill cancer cells. However, the chemotherapeutic agent cannot differentiate between cancer cells and healthy cells and destroys the latter as well. In addition, devastating side effects can also result depending on the type of chemotherapy administered. Some commonly used chemotherapy drugs are so strong that some individuals vomit for hours or days, followed by days or weeks of nausea. This nausea prevents eating, and many chemotherapy patients cannot tolerate the sight or smell of cooked foods. In addition, a metallic taste often develops after treatment. The inability to eat, or to retain food once it is eaten, can obviously result in drastic weight loss. And as weight is lost, strength is lost as well, and the individual becomes less and less able to cope with the disease and treatment. In some individuals, anticipatory nausea and vomiting begins. One patient reported feeling nauseated from merely driving past the doctor's office. Upon seeing the chemotherapy nurse at the grocery store, another patient reported being so nauseated that he had to leave the store. These episodes of nausea are conditioned responses due to associations with past treatment experiences. In fact, anything that reminds the patient of a negative chemotherapy experience may trigger nausea and vomiting (Redd 1984).

The response to repeated episodes of chemotherapy compromises the already stressed system with further weight loss, nutritional deficit, and dehydration. Resultant psychological problems can include dread of the next treatment and later depression. The individual's sense of control over his or her life is lost. Consequently, not only does the individual have to deal with cancer, he or she also has to deal with the side effects of treatment. Given this, the individual may ultimately give up. For a person with cancer undergoing chemotherapy or radiation therapy there is probably nothing worse (except uncontrollable pain) than the added stress of loss of control related to nausea and vomiting.

Study Description

The Lynn Pierson Therapeutic Research Program allowed selected cancer patients to smoke natural cannabis, in standard-dose cigarette form, or take pills containing the psychoactive ingredient of cannabis, delta-9-THC. To participate in the cannabis program, individuals had to meet several criteria. First, the cancer patient was required to initially try at least one conventional antiemetic drug, such as Reglan, Torecan, or Compazine. If one of these drugs was effective and there were no side effects, the individual was not accepted for participation in the marijuana study. Second, it was required that the treating physician be fully informed of the individual's desire to participate and agree to allow him to do so. All oncologists in New Mexico were informed about the program, and a majority of them referred patients. And finally, patients could not be so physically ill that the drug, smoked or swallowed, would cause significant side effects or worsen the patient's condition. Cannabis, like many legal drugs and all illegal drugs, has psychological effects. Therefore, patients also had to be screened for mental disorders that might be affected by its use. After successfully clearing these medical and psychiatric hurdles (fewer than 10 patients of more than 220 who applied did not participate), patients were arbitrarily assigned to receive either oral or smoked cannabis.

Patients who refused to or could not smoke (about ten people) were given oral medication. All patients received their medication under controlled conditions at the same time they were receiving their anticancer chemotherapy. A cannabis cigarette was smoked immediately before or the capsules were swallowed about 30 minutes prior to anticancer treatment. For the next four hours following ingestion of cannabis or delta-9-THC, the patients were closely watched by a nurse or physician. Blood pressure, pulse rate, psychological condition, and known side effects were monitored periodically. Each patient also rated the intensity of nausea, vomiting, and appetite problems experienced. In addition, a few patients gave blood samples at specified intervals during the four-hour observation period so that levels of delta-9-THC and its metabolite could be measured. If no significant problems occurred, patients could then take the medication home to be used as prescribed for the next two to five days, the usual duration. To assure the safety of the patients and effectiveness of the medication, telephone contact was maintained with patients or family during this period as well.

Patients who decided to continue using either form of medication after this initial dosing were then seen at each subsequent chemotherapy treatment. Their medical and psychiatric status was briefly evaluated to assure continued need for the medication and to assess any changes that may have occurred and could interfere with or be worsened by marijuana. Sometimes chemotherapy was changed to types that did not induce nausea or vomiting. At such times, patients were not given additional cannabis or delta-9-THC. In other situations, the cancer progressed so rapidly that it produced physical changes that would interfere with the use of one form of the drug or both. Patients could then be switched or discontinued as appropriate. Although patients were followed closely after the initial dosing, subsequent dosings did not require the close, four-hour observation and monitoring described above.

It must be emphasized that all patients chose to participate in this study. A standard research-informed consent was read and signed by the patient. If a patient was under the age of 18, special permission from the Human Research Review Committee (HRRC) was obtained. There was no payment or other incentive for them beyond the hope of reducing or alleviating their discomfort. There was also no charge to the patients for the cannabis or THC capsules, and patients could drop out at any time, for any reason, without any penalty. And, as I have described above in some detail, patients were evaluated closely and regularly for their safety and comfort. The patients always knew what drug they were getting, and there was no use of placebos or ineffective agents in this study.

From 1979 to 1986 approximately 256 women and men, ages 18 to 77, from all walks of life, participated in the Lynn Pierson Therapeutic Research and Treatment Program at the University of New Mexico. These individuals, from 46 communities in New Mexico, suffered from 22 different types of cancer and had a combined experience of over 2,000 episodes of chemotherapy-induced nausea and vomiting, lasting one day to several weeks per episode. Not all individuals experienced the same intensity of response to particular types of chemotherapy; however, for some people with cancer, it is easy to understand why treatment sometimes feels worse than the disease itself.

One of the major difficulties in a study like this is to find a reasonably accurate baseline measure of nausea and vomiting to compare against the effectiveness of cannabis or delta-9-THC. This was done by asking patients at the time they were applying for admission to the study to rate the severity of their nausea, vomiting, and appetite problems at their most recent chemotherapy session. All patients also received some form of conventional antiemetic during that session so the effect of cannabis or delta-9-THC as an antiemetic or appetite stimulant could be compared with standard treatments.

The main reason for not using those measures of symptoms taken immediately prior to chemotherapy administration was the problem of anticipatory nausea and vomiting. It was well known then that many patients began experiencing nausea, vomiting and appetite problems hours before ever receiving anticancer drugs, in anticipation or expectation of such side effects. In summary, the comparison points were: chemotherapy plus conventional antiemetics versus chemotherapy plus cannabis or delta-9-THC.

Because patients may not accurately recall what happened at their most recent chemotherapy treatment, patients had to rate their past nausea and vomiting twice. They made an assessment at the time of applying to the program and again just before receiving cannabis and chemotherapy. Data was available for 74 patients at these two times and showed no statistical difference in the mean ratings. The median time between the two ratings was 11 days (range 1 to 150 days).

Knowledgeable or experienced readers may well be aware that physicians change chemotherapy for cancer patients. Sometimes they switch from drugs that produce little or no side effects to ones that produce severe nausea and vomiting, or vice versa. Thus, one additional factor that had to be considered was that patients received the same type of chemotherapy at the two treatment sessions. That is, a patient, who had severe nausea and vomiting from a most recent treatment session, would again receive chemotherapy expected to produce severe nausea and vomiting for the session during which the cannabis would be given.

In this regard the scientific literature was reviewed to classify chemotherapy agents and doses as mild, moderate, and severe, depending on the severity of nausea and vomiting induced. Then, physician oncologists (specialists in cancer treatment) and oncology nurses (specialists in cancer patient care) were asked to rate the same chemotherapy agents and doses as mild, moderate, or severe emetics. They had no idea about the investigating team's rating and thus were only reporting their own knowledge and experience. Using a statistical procedure called correlation, moderate to high correlations were found among the ratings, indicating the earlier classification was reasonably accurate (Table 1).

SEVERE (vomiting every 15–30 minutes for 24–48 hours or longer)	
Cisplatin Nitrogen mustard Dacarbazine	
MODERATE (vomiting every 2–4 hours lasting up to 36 hours)	
Doxorubicin Lomustine Mitomycin	Altretamine Ifosfamide
MILD (vomiting every 4–6 hours lasting up to 24 hours)	
Bleomycin Cytosine arabinoside Cyclophosphamide Daunorubicin Estramustine Fluorouracil	Hydroxyurea Methotrexate Vinblastine Vincristine Asparaginase

Table 1. Nausea and Vomiting Severity by Chemotherapy Agent*

This is a very general classification. There is wide variation among patients in frequency, severity, and duration of nausea and vomiting. Moreover, many patients receive combinations of agents which further complicates any rigid classification.

A number of new antiemetics have come on the market the past few years, agents that were not available during the time of this study with cancer patients. The first of these was ondansetron (Zofran). It is effective in reducing or blocking nausea and vomiting in 80 percent of patients, but it is associated with headaches, constipation, and or abdominal pain in 4 percent to 23 percent of patients. The cost per tablet is quite variable but can be $45.00. At three 8 mg tablets per day for two days, the total cost may be $270.00. Granesetron (Kytril) is a related antiemetic effective in reducing nausea and vomiting in 60 percent to 90 percent of patients. Headache, constipation, and or weakness are the most common side effects, occurring in 14 percent to 21 percent of patients. For two 1 mg tablets given daily for a two-day chemotherapy treatment the total cost can be $380.00.

Dronabinol (Marinol), the synthetic oral form of the active ingredient of marijuana (delta-9-tetrahydrocannabinol) is given four to six times per day to control nausea and vomiting. The common side effects are drowsiness, dizziness, euphoria, and abdominal pain in 3 percent to 10 percent of patients. The cost for two days of chemotherapy is about $90.00 to $138.00.

A combination treatment sometimes used is metachlopromide and depamethasome. This may be effective in 60 percent of patients but has side effects of mood changes, drowsiness, and possibly hallucinations or bizarre thinking. The cost of this treatment is lowest, perhaps $2.00 to $3.00 for a two-day chemotherapy treatment, but it has limited effectiveness and the side effects are considered extreme.

Results: Nausea and Vomiting

Although many more patients participated in the study, data analysis was done for 169 patients. Using the comparison points noted above and having ascertained that 92 percent of the patients received the same or worse chemotherapy in the experimental session, it was found that both nausea and vomiting average scores were reduced by half with the use of cannabis (Table 2). In scientific terms, this was a "statistically significant" result. Mild, moderate, and severe chemotherapy classes were looked at next. Patients on chemotherapy drugs causing mild or moderate nausea and vomiting improved by about 60 percent, while those on severe agents had a 40 percent reduction in symptoms. The latter, though less, was still "statistically significant" (Table 3). Given the evidence already existing in the scientific literature, this result was not unexpected.

	Nausea Mean Score	Vomiting Mean Score
Baseline (most recent chemotherapy)	4.53	4.26
Pre-Marijuana Dosing	2.26	1.67
4 Hours Post-Dosing	2.03	1.73

Table 2. Overall Patient Self-ratings of Nausea and Vomiting Severity

Chemotherapy:	Oral			Inhaled		
	Mild	Moderate	Severe	Mild	Moderate	Severe
Baseline Nausea	4.25	4.56	4.58	4.76	4.33	4.60
Post-Marijuana Nausea	2.38	1.67	2.44	1.42	1.69	2.45
Baseline Vomiting	2.88	4.25	4.43	4.46	4.21	4.38
Post-Marijuana Vomiting	1.50	1.35	2.32	1.06	1.40	2.05

Table 3. Group (oral vs. inhaled marijuana) vs. Chemotherapy Severity

Nausea/vomiting rating scale:
1 = not a problem; 2 = slight; 3 = mild; 4 = moderate; 5 = severe

A central question for this study concerned the effectiveness of oral versus inhaled forms of medication. People who smoked had a greater than 50 percent reduction in nausea and vomiting, while those who took the pills had slightly less than a 50 percent reduction. For both forms, improvement was statistically significant. For nausea alone, the difference in effectiveness between the two forms was quite small. For vomiting, however, the difference was larger, and smokers had somewhat greater improvement. One possible explanation for this was that some patients threw up the capsules shortly after receiving chemotherapy. Administering the pills earlier than 30 minutes before chemotherapy may offset this apparent advantage of smoking.

Prior to this study, some scientists suspected that patients who had previously used cannabis illicitly, perhaps as a mood-altering compound, would be more likely to show an antiemetic response. Forty-one percent of study patients had used it previously; the remainder had not. Contrary to expectation, those who had never used cannabis improved more than those who had. Prior users showed slightly less than 50 percent improvement, while those without prior use showed a change of slightly more than 50 percent. Another interesting result appeared in the nausea and vomiting ratings at baseline, immediately prior to dosing and four hours after dosing. Prior users had lower ratings of severity on both nausea and vomiting at all three times. This suggested that the patients in general were probably not exaggerating their discomfort just to get marijuana.

After the first test dose of cannabis or delta-9-THC, 90 percent of patients elected to continue on the study. We learned that prior users were more likely to continue whether on oral (96 percent) or inhaled form (95 percent). People who said they had not used cannabis before the study were more likely to continue if they were smoking (94 percent) than if they were taking the pills (82 percent). In other words, patients without prior use were three times more likely to drop out after initial dosing if they were taking pills than if they were smoking (18 percent versus 6 percent). Irrespective of dose form, patients with no prior use were three times more likely to drop out after the initial dosing than those with prior use (14 percent versus 4 percent).

The presence or absence of eight side effects of cannabis was tallied before and hourly after dosing for the four-hour observation period. The side effects were: euphoria (being "high"), sleepiness, agitation, depression, fearfulness, anxiety, visual and auditory hallucinations. The most common side effect was sleepiness. In fact, so many patients fell asleep that questions went unanswered. Of the approximately 90 patients who were awake, 50 percent reported sleepiness. About 45 percent reported feeling "high" at one and two hours after dosing. Before dosing, 14 percent had reported feeling agitated, declining to 10 percent at one hour and 13 percent at two hours. Of the patients in the study, 17 percent reported feeling depressed before treatment, but only 6 percent were at two hours. Before medication 15 percent reported being fearful and 45 percent felt anxious. Only 6 percent were fearful at one hour, less afterward. And only 21 percent were anxious at one hour, 18 percent at two hours and less afterward. Three patients reported hallucinations; one only before dosing. Of the two others, one was felt to have a heightened awareness of a piece of medical machinery in the room, and the other experienced a series of pleasant pictures. However, there were three cases of side effects requiring medical attention. Two patients had paranoid/fear responses after the four-hour observation period, and one had a strongly elevated heart rate due to an underlying heart condition. The first two situations were managed by simply talking to the patients and waiting for the medication to leave their system. The third problem was quickly resolved by the patient's physician, who had treated similar episodes in the patient in the past.

At the time of data analysis, 154 patients had finished the program with the remaining 15 still receiving medication. Forty-four patients stopped because they believed the cannabis or delta-9-THC capsules to be ineffective (29 percent). Thirty-four (77 percent) of those who stopped had been on the oral drug, the remainder smoked. Twenty-two patients (14 percent) stopped because of side effects; 17 of those patients (77 percent) were on oral medication. Forty-one patients stopped when chemotherapy was changed or discontinued, and 21 patients died in the course of treatment. The remaining patients failed to report their reason for stopping (Table 4).

	Patient Status
Still using oral or inhaled marijuana	15
Drop-out, ineffective	44
Oral Drug	(34)
Inhaled Drug	(10)
Drop out, side effects	22
Oral Drug	(17)
Inhaled Drug	(5)
Chemotherapy changed or discontinued	41
Died	21
No reason given	26
Total	169

Table 4. Patient Status at Time of Data Analysis

The average patient received about 50 doses of medication (cigarettes or pills) while on the program. Patients on the oral form averaged 35 doses, and those on the inhaled form averaged 60. The latter amount is magnified because of a small group of patients on daily chemotherapy that produced mild to moderate persistent nausea. These values are below expectation, as we found that most patients reduced the number of pills ingested or cigarettes smoked to the minimum needed for comfort. Unused medication was returned to the pharmacy. However, there was one unsubstantiated allegation of a patient diverting the drug illegally.

A final issue has to do with patient "controls." Scientists like to measure the same variables in people not being treated as in those treated. In this study there were two such cancer patient groups: one group requested but was not able to receive the cannabis, and a second group did not request the cannabis even though the patients knew of its experimental availability. These two patient groups were asked to rate their nausea and vomiting at their most recent chemotherapy. There was no difference between the two on these symptoms. The two groups were then combined and compared with patients who received oral or inhaled medication. The experimental group was found to have significantly worse nausea and vomiting than the control group. This is as it should be, considering that the study aimed at working with "worst case" patients. When the type of chemotherapy was assessed (mild, moderate, or severe), there were far more people with severe chemotherapy in the experimental group than in the control group. And that fact probably accounted for why nausea and vomiting were also worse. An additional analysis comparing sex, stage of cancer, and prior use of marijuana showed no difference between the experimental and control groups. The results of this study thus seem to be reasonably honest, reliable, and accurate, given the many difficulties in conducting such an experiment.

Patient Examples

A 67-year-old man requested marijuana after having severe nausea and vomiting with several anticancer chemotherapy treatments with cis-platinum, a severe emetogenic agent. Several different conventional antiemetics failed to provide any relief. Except for his cancer and side effects of treatment, he was in good physical health. He denied ever having used marijuana or any other illegal drug, and he rarely used alcohol. He was a pipe smoker of many years and wanted to smoke the marijuana by pipe, instead of in a cigarette form. During his first dosing, he achieved moderate relief through smoking. He requested and was given a supply to take home. On follow-up he reported excellent control of his nausea and vomiting, indicating that he even ate small meals without nausea or vomiting within hours of receiving chemotherapy. Moreover, he experimented with his doses and found that he could inhale just small amounts and suppress his symptoms for several hours. In this fashion, he used much less marijuana than prescribed and, of course, returned the unused portion for "someone else to use." That, of course, could not be done.

Ms. T. was a 35-year-old cancer patient who initially smoked marijuana at the suggestion of a friend to treat her nausea and vomiting. She was taking chemotherapy considered moderately emetogenic but was having far worse symptoms than expected for the classification of "moderate." She received delta-9-THC in capsule form and slept through her next chemotherapy session. At home, she cut the dosage to the minimum available, one capsule every four to six hours, and achieved excellent results over the next six months of treatment. Her cancer went into remission, chemotherapy was stopped, and she left the program to continue her life.

A young man with severe cancer initially received the pills, but threw up shortly after swallowing them. He is a nonresponder for the purposes of the study, but he was allowed to smoke at a later chemotherapy session. He then attained very good control of his symptoms, but this is not reflected in the data presented. There were other patients who faced similar problems with the capsules and who refused to smoke. Some patients could not tolerate the smoke and were switched to the capsules. Some did well, some did not, but all patients were very appreciative of having the chance to try the medication in either form regardless of whether the treatment was successful.

Appetite

The data on appetite was obtained in the same manner and under the same conditions as described above. The same baseline of most recent chemotherapy versus four hours after receiving the marijuana dose applied. Overall, there was a statistically significant difference, indicating that appetite was less of a problem after using marijuana or delta-9-THC than after using conventional antiemetics for chemotherapy side effects. The average baseline measure was in the moderate to severe range of difficulty. The typical improvement was about 30 percent to 40 percent. But there were some differences, depending on the severity of chemotherapy-induced nausea and vomiting. Patients on mild and moderate emetogenic chemotherapy showed more improvement than those on chemotherapy rated as severe. This is consistent with the results for nausea and vomiting.

Next, the oral form was compared to the inhaled form, and the improvement was found to be identical, roughly a 20 percent change. This does not seem like much at first, but it must be kept in mind that these patients were predominantly concerned with nausea and vomiting and, to some extent, were experiencing these symptoms despite the use of cannabis. Hence, they may not have been as attentive to their appetite, or their nausea and vomiting made it difficult to have much appetite.

The data were scrutinized closely to see if there was a correlation between chemotherapy severity and the form of medication. It was found that patients receiving mild or moderately severe emetogenic chemotherapy showed the best improvement, about 30 percent to 40 percent, whether they were smoking or taking pills. Those on severe chemotherapy improved the least, only about 10 percent, and those smoking had less improvement than those taking the pills. There are, however, differences in how the body handles inhaled drugs compared to those taken orally, especially as regards cannabis and delta-9-THC. For example, a breakdown product of delta-9-THC, whether entering the body orally or by inhalation, tends to be higher after oral ingestion. Thus, it may be the metabolite rather than the original drug that accounts for appetite stimulation. It also must be remembered that people who use cannabis recreationally report appetite stimulation some hours after ingesting the drug. Therefore, our four-hour measurement period may not have included the best time to assess this effect. It is quite possible that a different type of study is necessary to demonstrate more effectively the appetite stimulating properties of marijuana, if this has not yet been done.

As mentioned above, there was a control group that could be compared to the experimental group in terms of severity of appetite problems. Briefly, there was no difference. Both groups rated their appetite problems as moderate to severe in intensity. However, it was not possible to measure the control group's appetite during chemotherapy and treatment with conventional antiemetics. Hence, a gap in knowledge does exist here.

Patient Examples

Mr. Z. was a middle-aged man, who had developed a serious stomach cancer and was slowly dying. His appetite was poor, and his weight loss accelerated after nausea and vomiting from chemotherapy. Cure of his cancer was a very remote prospect. He asked for marijuana, so he could have "more time" with his family, thinking that if he could relieve his nausea and vomiting even a little, his weight would stabilize. Decades before, he had smoked marijuana once or twice and so chose that route for his treatment. Not only did he have good control of nausea and vomiting, but he proudly announced that he had "eaten his first steak in months" because his appetite returned. For humanitarian reasons, he was approved to smoke daily at each meal, and his weight stabilized, then increased. On two occasions the delivery of marijuana supplies to him was delayed, and without the appetite stimulation, his weight began to fall each time. It is nice to imagine that he did receive a positive response to his request for "more time" to be with his wife and children.

Ms. K. said the capsules did a very good job of controlling her nausea and vomiting side effects. But she was most pleased that she was finally able to eat, as her appetite returned with the medication. In fact, she was able to reduce the amount needed to control nausea and vomiting so that the extra capsules could then be used to get her appetite and weight up between chemotherapy treatments. Her biggest problem was a close relative, who was shunning her as a "drug addict" because of the capsule. Since it was crucial for her to complete the entire course of chemotherapy, lasting many more months, time was taken to educate the relative about the therapeutic use of the drug versus its recreational use. Ms. K. did complete her prescribed course of cancer treatment with the full support and encouragement of the relative.

Summary

The Lynn Pierson Therapeutic Research Program was a unique opportunity to assess the medical uses of a Schedule I illegal drug with "no known medical use." The results achieved strongly indicate that both the inhaled natural cannabis and the pill form of its active ingredient, delta-9-THC, are effective for control of nausea and vomiting as well as for appetite stimulation. I think that if Lynn Pierson could read this chapter today, he would smile knowingly and approvingly.

References

Abrahamov, A., A. Abrahamov, and R. Mechoulam. 1995. An efficient new cannabinoid antiemetic in pediatric oncology. *Life Sciences* 56 (23/24): 2097–2102.

Anderson, P.O., and C.G. McGuire. 1981. Delta-9-tetrahydrocannabinol as an antiemetic. *American Journal of Hospital Pharmacy* 38: 639–646.

Chang, A.E., D.J. Shiling, R.C. Stillman, N.H. Goldberg, C.A. Seipp, I. Barofsky, R.M. Simon, and S.A. Rosenberg. 1979. Delta-9-tetrahydrocannabinol as an antiemetic in cancer patients receiving high doses of methotrexate: A prospective, randomized evaluation. *Annals of Internal Medicine* 91: 819–824.

Frytak, S., C.G. Moertel, J.R. O'Fallon, J. Rubin, E.T. Creagan, M.J. O'Connell, A.J. Schutt, and N.W. Schwartau. 1979. Delta-9-tetrahydrocannabinol as an antiemetic for patients receiving cancer chemotherapy. *Annals of Internal Medicine* 91: 825–830.

Lucas, V.S., Jr., and J. Laszlo. 1980. Δ-9-tetrahydrocannabinol for refractory vomiting induced by cancer chemotherapy. *Journal of the American Medical Association* 243 (12): 1241–1243.

Mechoulam, R. 1986. *Cannabinoids as Therapeutic Agents.* Boca Raton, FL: CRC Press.

Milne, G.M., M.R. Johnson, E.H. Wiseman, and D.E. Hutcheon, eds. 1981. Therapeutic progress in cannabinoid research: Proceedings of a symposium held at University of Connecticut at Avery Point, Groton, CN, Oct. 20–21, 1980. *Journal of Clinical Pharmacology* 21 Supplement (8&9): 11S–142S.

Nelson, K., D. Walsh, P. Deeter, and F. Sheehan. 1994. A phase II study of delta-9-tetrahydrocannabinol for appetite stimulation in cancer-associated anorexia. *Journal of Palliative Care* 10 (1): 14–18.

Poster, D.S., J.S. Penta, S. Bruno, and J.S. MacDonald. 1981. Delta-9-tetrahydrocannabinol in clinical oncology. *Journal of the American Medical Association* 245: 2047–2051.

Randall, R.C. 1989. *Marijuana, Medicine & the Law, Volume II.* Washington, DC: Galen Press.

Redd, W.H. 1984. Control of nausea and vomiting in chemotherapy patients. *Postgraduate Medicine* 75 (5): 105–113.

Sallan, S.E., C. Cronin, M. Zelen, and N.E. Zinberg. 1980. Antiemetics in patients receiving chemotherapy for cancer: A randomized comparison of delta-9-tetrahydrocannabinol and prochlorperazine. *New England Journal of Medicine* 302 (3): 135–138.

Sallan, S.E., N.E. Zinberg, and E. Frei, III. 1975. Antiemetic effect of delta-9-tetrahydrocannabinol in patients receiving cancer chemotherapy. *New England Journal of Medicine* 293 (16): 795–797.

Ungerleider, J.T., T. Andrysiak, L. Fairbanks, J. Goodnight, G. Sarna, and K. Jamison. 1982. Cannabis and cancer chemotherapy: A comparison of oral delta-9-THC and prochlorperazine. *Cancer* 50: 636–645.

6

AIDS and the
Wasting Syndrome

WALTER KRAMPF

Since July 1981, when the Centers for Disease Control (CDC) first described the disease known as acquired immune deficiency syndrome (AIDS), there have been approximately 513,000 reported cases in the United States and 320,000 deaths (as of March 31, 1996). The World Health Organization stated that as of late 1995 there have been 1,300,000 persons reported with AIDS worldwide and has estimated that there were probably 6 million cases. Furthermore, it estimated that as of 1995 there were probably 17 million people alive with HIV/AIDS. The epidemic is expanding rapidly, and the degree of morbidity associated with it is enormous. There are certain AIDS conditions for which the therapeutic use of cannabis has been found helpful. For the persons affected cannabis should be readily available and healthcare providers should be educated about the benefits of its use.

Definition of the Wasting Syndrome

One of the worst symptoms of AIDS is a condition known in the United States as the *wasting syndrome*. It is characterized by a significant (>10 percent) loss of body weight in a person who is HIV antibody positive and may be associated with fever and diarrhea. The presence of this syndrome alone, without any other conditions of AIDS, is sufficient to justify an AIDS diagnosis (CDC, 1987). In Africa the wasting syndrome is so prevalent it has been named "slim disease." It is the most common clinical manifestation of HIV infection in Africa and has been observed to be a precursor of death.

Walter Krampf, M.D., M.P.H., is a practicing physician and AIDS patient specialist in San Francisco, California.

The wasting syndrome is very common. In one study of AIDS diagnoses, 17.8 percent of all AIDS patients were diagnosed with AIDS on the basis of having the wasting syndrome (Nahlen et al. 1993). Of those 17.8 percent, 7.1 percent had only the wasting syndrome and 10.7 percent had the wasting syndrome and one other AIDS condition. However, the wasting syndrome is even more prevalent than this data indicates. Persons with AIDS are reported to the Department of Public Health when a first diagnosis of AIDS occurs. Subsequent diagnoses are frequently not reported. Thus patients who develop the wasting syndrome after their first AIDS diagnosis will go unreported. Patients with only wasting syndrome as their AIDS diagnosis are more likely to be women, more likely to be black or Hispanic, and less likely to be homosexual men.

In addition to the classic wasting syndrome, where no apparent cause for weight loss is found except HIV itself, there are a number of gastrointestinal infections that can lead to severe diarrhea, vomiting, pain, and fever, all of which can be accompanied by weight loss. These include those caused by bacteria (shigella, salmonella, campylobacter), protozoa (cryptosporidia, microsporidia, amebiasis, giardiasis), mycobacteria (*Mycobacterium avium* complex), and viruses (cytomegalovirus). Weight loss itself is such a debilitating condition that it can quickly predispose the body to further infections, to significant weakness, and can render the patient unable to care for himself or herself. Death in AIDS patients can be predicted by the magnitude of body wasting (Grunfeld and Kotler 1992).

Another cause of wasting in AIDS is the patient's inability to eat due to a loss of appetite. Ironically, many of the medications that persons with HIV take to treat or prevent specific illnesses have a loss of appetite or nausea as a side effect. Nausea is a common side effect of retrovir (AZT), the main antiretroviral drug used to treat HIV infection. Two malignancies are also frequently seen in persons with AIDS: non–Hodgkin's lymphoma and the much more prevalent Kaposi's sarcoma, both of which are often treated with chemotherapy. This treatment frequently causes further significant nausea and vomiting and appetite depression.

Current Treatments of Wasting and Appetite Stimulation

Because the consequences of wasting are so severe, nutritional interventions as well as medications have been tested to try to stop and reverse the loss of weight. Both oral and intravenous food preparations have been used. Among the different drugs studied have been various antinausea and antiemetic preparations, a synthetic progesterone called Megace, growth hormone, and cannabinoids.

Megace, a hormone used to treat inoperable breast cancer, was found to produce weight gain in a significant number of patients. This drug has also been studied in persons with AIDS, and a similar stimulation of appetite and subsequent weight gain has been observed (Tierney, Cuff and Kotler 1991; Von Roenn et al. 1991). Its appetite stimulation effect, however, seems to decrease over time. Megace is now available in a high-concentration, liquid suspension and is relatively easy to take. Cost of the recommended 800 mg daily dose is approximately $10.00 per day.

An old medication that was taken off the market because of severe teratogenic effects in pregnant women but is now being studied again is the sedative thalidomide. Due to its devastating effects on limb development in the fetus, it is no longer prescribable, but it has been shown to selectively inhibit tumor necrosis factor alpha, a factor implicated in the pathogenesis of wasting. Multiple studies are currently evaluating its effectiveness, and it seems promising (Klauser et al. 1994; Reyes-Teran et al. 1994). Side effects include sedation, neuropathy, and rash. Thalidomide is also being studied to treat aphthous ulcers, a common oral manifestation in persons with HIV that also interferes with eating because of pain.

Another drug under investigation to promote weight gain is recombinant human growth hormone (Schambelan et al. 1995). It generally produces an increase in lean body mass rather than just fat. Growth hormone is an already approved drug, but it has not been approved for this specific indication, that is, weight gain in persons with AIDS. Although this may ultimately prove to be an effective and useful medication, it needs to be injected daily, and its current cost to the patient is about $150.00 per day. This price makes it essentially unavailable to the vast majority of HIV-infected people.

Another modality for treating the wasting syndrome has been the use of intravenous nutritional supplements known as total parenteral nutrition (TPN). Large amounts of nutritional supplements (sugars, vitamins, minerals and electrolytes) are administered between 8 and 24 hours a day through an indwelling intravenous catheter. Not only are the nutritional supplements expensive (several hundred dollars per day), but the maintenance of this system is very costly, and requires skilled medical personnel, catheter installation, and blood tests to continually monitor the solutions given. Furthermore, the limitations of TPN in reversing the wasting syndrome are well known. Catheter infections are a constant threat, and the infusions are very disruptive. This intervention is not one that can be embarked upon lightly nor could it ever be suggested for large populations of affected individuals.

Studies of smoked cannabis in healthy volunteers to test its effects on appetite stimulation and weight gain have shown it to be effective (Foltin, Fischman and Byrne 1988). Most of the current research on the effectiveness of cannabinoids, however, is based on the studies with dronabinol (brand name Marinol), a synthetic preparation of delta-9-tetrahydrocannabinol

(THC), the major psychoactive ingredient in cannabis (Gorter 1991; Gorter, Seefried and Volberding 1991; Plasse et al. 1991 and 1992; Struwe et al. 1992). Repeatedly, these studies have shown that dronabinol suppresses nausea, stimulates appetite, and prevents further weight loss or actually leads to weight gain. In addition, there are very few side effects, and if present, they are not life-threatening and reverse quickly when the drug is discontinued. The FDA has approved Marinol as both an antinausea and antivomiting agent for cancer chemotherapy, and more recently it has been approved for stimulating appetite and preventing weight loss in people with AIDS.

Dronabinol at 2.5 mg twice a day has been found useful in combating the wasting syndrome. In studies this dosage correlated with minimal side effects and maximal beneficial effects. Higher doses are generally needed for antinausea and antivomiting action to counteract the effects of chemotherapy. One major drawback to prescribed dronabinol is its cost. A 2.5 mg capsule retails for about $4.00, costing the patient $8.00 per day for this one medication alone if taken twice a day. Five milligram Marinol capsules retail between $7.00 and $8.00 per capsule. If the patient has health insurance that covers prescription medications, this cost is then passed on to the insurance company. Cannabis is a much cheaper alternative, but the current illegal status of the plant keeps the cost unnecessarily high. For persons without health insurance or without a policy covering drugs (such as Medicaid or MediCal), dronabinol becomes yet one more very expensive drug among a host of other very expensive AIDS drugs, and one for which an inexpensive alternative exists.

Adverse Effects

One of the major reasons presented against the use of cannabis in people with HIV infection is its supposed suppression of the immune system. At this time, this conclusion is unsubstantiated. The studies this conclusion is based on have been predominantly in vitro studies of cells exposed to very high concentrations of THC (Hollister 1992). The clinical significance of this data is not clear, but all current clinical and epidemiological studies have shown no difference in immune function between users and nonusers of cannabis (Dax et al. 1989; Dax et al. 1991; Hollister, 1992). Therefore, any immune suppressant effect must be quite small and does not compare to the potential gain from the positive effects of cannabis use in AIDS, particularly in counteracting the wasting syndrome. Epidemiological studies have shown that persons who use cannabis are no more likely than nonusers to progress to AIDS or to become HIV infected. Furthermore, starvation and malnutrition are themselves significantly immunosuppressive, much more so than any suppressive effects ascribed to cannabis. It is hard to overemphasize the severity of the debilitation and malnutrition accompanying the wasting syndrome or the need for good nutrition to maintain a functioning immune system. Methods that encourage a patient's own increased intake of food are to be endorsed and cannabis seems to do just that. That aspect of cannabis use greatly outweighs any clinical immunosuppressive effects ascribed to it that have yet to be demonstrated.

Among the more commonly described side effects of the use of dronabinol and cannabis are drowsiness or anxiety. For many users, these side effects pass with continued use although dose modifications may be required. Acute agitation and paranoia are much less frequently encountered symptoms, but some patients may not be able to tolerate cannabis at all. The description of Marinol that accompanies the drug, written by the manufacturer, lists feeling "high" as an adverse reaction that occurred in 24 percent of the persons enrolled in clinical trials of the drug. However, this adverse reaction could be seen as a beneficial effect, particularly in a patient who is feeling ill, depressed, or dysphoric, symptoms frequently encountered in people with AIDS. Incidentally, depression is a very common symptom in people with AIDS and is very frequently treated with antidepressant medications that often have significant side effects.

Smoking cannabis has concerned some physicians because of an infection called aspergillosis, caused by the fungus aspergillus. The spores of this fungus have been found on marijuana, and it is feared that persons with suppressed immune systems who inhale these fungi might be at risk for a pulmonary or systemic infection caused by it (Levitz and Diamond 1991; Sutton, Lum and Torti 1986). Aspergillosis has been described in persons with AIDS, but it is a very uncommon infection (particularly considering the numbers of persons believed to inhale marijuana). Baking cannabis in the oven prior to smoking will kill these spores as does baking it for eating. If a sterilized commercially prepared cannabis were legally available, this concern would be obviated.

Anecdotal Experience with Marinol and Cannabis

In the past 13 years, I have treated hundreds of people with HIV infection. Many patients had the severe weight loss that characterizes the wasting syndrome as well as the wasting that accompanies other AIDS-related infections and malignancies. I have found the use of dronabinol, and particularly the use of cannabis, to be beneficial.

I first started prescribing dronabinol to treat the nausea and vomiting associated with chemotherapy for AIDS-related malignancies and discovered that it was very well tolerated and effective. Patients often reported that they both smoked and ate cannabis. Many who had tried dronabinol preferred cannabis. They reported that with smoked cannabis they could much better control their dosage than with dronabinol. They could smoke a small amount, wait for the alleviation of symptoms or for appetite to increase, and smoke more if needed. They avoided the experience observed with oral medication: ingesting more than was needed and getting more side effects. Some patients remarked that although they preferred smoking cannabis, Marinol, being an approved drug, was covered on their health insurance plans. For financial reasons, they felt they had to choose the less desirable option.

One of the most positive effects of cannabis is the euphoria that accompanies the drug's other effects. For many patients who are severely debilitated by the disease, this effect was appreciated and should not be minimized or underestimated. Cannabis often has a tendency to make patients more philosophical about mortality and about the course of their illness. When the patient is in that state of mind, it can be beneficial for the healthcare provider and caretakers as well as for the patient.

Cannabis is used during chemotherapy for a short period of time, generally several weeks, during which a cycle of chemotherapy is given. Cannabis is used as needed during this treatment and then is stopped when chemotherapy is completed. In those patients who use cannabis to mitigate the wasting and loss of appetite accompanying advanced disease, cannabis could be used on a more extended or permanent basis. I have never seen any long-term negative effects from the use of either dronabinol or cannabis in treating people with HIV/AIDS, and considering the many and frequently severe side effects from drugs I routinely prescribe to treat AIDS and AIDS complications, this is quite remarkable.

Some patients using cannabis or dronabinol complain of drowsiness and occasionally of anxiety. These effects generally are more common among persons who were new to cannabis at the time when they first used it therapeutically, and it is well known that cannabis use requires a learning process to get the maximum benefit from its psychoactivity. It has been noted that among younger persons there is often less incidence of cannabis-related side effects presumably because this is a population that has had more cannabis experience. The major complaint from patients using dronabinol is drowsiness particularly for those who were still working or otherwise active. There are varieties of cannabis that are more sedating and others that are more stimulating, but most people cannot control the type of cannabis they purchase. If cannabis were legally available or people could grow their own plants, varying strains and potencies could be much more precisely adjusted to the individual patient's needs.

When I agreed to write this chapter for this book, I started to ask my patients during their regular appointments whether or not they had used cannabis in relation to their illness and to describe their experiences with it. Many of my patients reported using cannabis to stimulate appetite or to suppress nausea (frequently caused by other medications I was prescribing!). They reported that it was quite successful in treating these symptoms, and many felt they would have succumbed or sickened sooner if not for cannabis. One patient reported, "That's what's keeping me going." This information is anecdotal but indicates to me that many patients have discovered the use of cannabis is quite helpful and not harmful.

I was surprised at the number of my patients who indicated they had used cannabis to control their symptoms. Whether this reflects a patient population that was not new to cannabis, being urban (San Francisco) and young (mostly aged 25–50), or that information about the effectiveness of cannabis for these symptoms has become widely circulated, I cannot determine. It is true that the use of cannabis for treating chemotherapy-induced nausea and vomiting has received much publicity, particularly in local newspapers and on national television. In San Francisco there has been much coverage of the use of cannabis in AIDS both from a medical point of view as well as the much publicized legal case of Mary Rathbun, a 73-year-old woman who was arrested for baking marijuana brownies for people with AIDS. Due to much popular support, the charges against "Brownie Mary" were dropped. San Franciscans have voted on a city proposition to support the use of medical marijuana, and it was approved by 80 percent of the voters.

Furthermore, San Francisco (as do several other cities in the United States) has a Cannabis Buyers' Club (CBC) that specifically sells marijuana (the dried plant) and marijuana products (e.g., cookies, capsules, and tinctures) to patients. Patients are admitted to the club on the presentation of a letter from their physician indicating that they have HIV disease or another medical condition for which their physician would prescribe marijuana if it were legal. The San Francisco CBC has been in operation since 1993 under the direction of Dennis Peron, an activist who has been trying to get marijuana back into the formulary of the American physician. The CBC operates as a club as well as a supermarket, where patients can sit around and talk, smoke, and meet with other patients like themselves. The city of San Francisco has made the enforcement of anti-marijuana laws one of its lowest priorities. The legislature of the state of California also passed laws to allow the legal prescription of cannabis for medical reasons, but they were vetoed by Governor Wilson. In November of 1996, Proposition 215, an initiative which allows physicians to recommend marijuana for medicinal use, was passed by the people of the State of California by 56 percent. (A similar measure passed in Arizona by 67 percent.) Prior to the passage of Proposition 215 the San Francisco CBC was busted by state law enforcement agencies. Following the passage of the initiative the city's Superior Court judge ruled that the CBC be reopened and it did so in January of 1997 under the new name of the Cannabis Cultivators Club. Thus, there is much positive "lore" about the use of cannabis in AIDS that might account for this population's willingness to try it and find it helpful.

My patients' use of cannabis to treat their symptoms was also instructive in terms of how easily they determined how much and how frequently they needed to ingest it to obtain the desired effects. They did not need a physician to write a prescription and explain how to use it. In my experience, physicians are not needed to prescribe or otherwise control the use of cannabis for patients who are ill, and it would be desirable to minimize the amount of extra paperwork a physician must do to make this treatment available. The major role physicians could have would be to dispel years of misinformation about cannabis spread by the legal and medical professions as well as by prohibition activists. Accurate information from physicians can give patients who have concerns based on earlier misinformation permission to use the drug.

Two problems that my patients reported concerning cannabis were the difficulty of obtaining it and its current high price. Many of the patients who seemed to be most helped by cannabis were sicker, disabled and not working, and in poorer financial situations than others. The unnecessarily high prices for illicit cannabis were difficult for them to manage. In addition, because of their poor health, they themselves could not go out and buy it but had to get others to obtain it. This created much anxiety as they were getting more and more dependent on their family and friends and were now putting them also at legal risk for buying cannabis.

Further Research and Its Problems

Reading the medical and scientific literature and hearing the abundant anecdotal information available, one sees an obvious need for well-planned clinical trials of cannabis in persons with HIV/AIDS. That these studies have not yet been done is shameful and reveals the political nature of this research and that marijuana's controversial status interferes with good science (Grinspoon, Bakalar and Doblin 1995; Voelker 1994). A professor of medicine at the University of California in San Francisco (UCSF), and chair of the Community Consortium of San Francisco (a group of community providers that has been conducting HIV research over the last ten years), Dr. Donald Abrams has been trying for over two years to pilot a study of the effects of various doses of inhaled cannabis versus Marinol in counteracting the symptoms of wasting (Abrams, Child and Mitchell 1995). This sophisticated and privately financed study was designed not only to look at the effects on wasting but also to measure pulmonary function, T-cells, and HIV levels. These are some of the many questions that should be answered but so far have remained unanswered. The study protocol has been approved by the California Research Advisory Panel, the UCSF Review Board, the Executive Board of the Community Consortium, and the FDA. The study has been stopped by the refusal of the DEA to permit the importation of marijuana for the study (cloned standardized cannabis is available in the Netherlands) and by the refusal of the NIDA to provide domestic marijuana. Each agency has taken many long months of inaction before denying the study protocol.

Many physicians feel that the only way to answer questions about cannabis is to do the appropriate controlled studies so they can advise their patients based on the best knowledge available. That these government agencies have chosen to delay and thereby prevent needed and meaningful studies, at no financial cost to them, can only be interpreted as a political decision. Such decisions are inappropriate for agencies that should be concerned with good science, with protecting public health—and that are supported by the taxpayers.

Conclusion

There is an obvious beneficial role for the use of cannabis in the treatment of HIV/AIDS. Marinol has been approved by the FDA to treat the wasting syndrome in people with AIDS. Many studies of cannabis itself have shown it to be well tolerated, to have a very wide therapeutic range, to not have a lethal dose, and it appears to be superior to Marinol. Few drugs are as well tolerated as it is. For many patients, cannabis is the medicine that makes the use of other medicines possible. Concerns about the immunosuppressive effects of cannabis are not supported by clinical data whereas the immunosuppressive effects of starvation and wasting are well documented. Cannabis has been used for centuries. Any further delay in making it widely available now, particularly to the ill, is both irrational and cruel.

References

Abrams, D.I., C.C. Child, and T.F. Mitchell. 1995. Marijuana, the AIDS wasting syndrome, and the U. S. government. [Letter] *New England Journal of Medicine* 333 (100): 671.
Centers for Disease Control. 1987. Revision of the CDC case surveillance definition for acquired immunodeficiency syndrome. *Morbidity and Mortality Weekly Report* 36 (1S Suppl): 3S–14S.
Dax, E.M., N.S. Pilotte, W.H. Adler, J.E. Nagel, W.R. Lange. 1989. The effects of 9-ene-tetrahydrocannabinol on hormone release and immune function. *Journal of Steroid Biochemistry* 34 (1–6): 263–270.
Dax, E.M., N.S. Pilotte, W.H. Adler, J.E. Nagel, W.R. Lange. 1991. Short-term D-9-tetrahydrocannabinol (THC) does not affect neuroendocrine or immune parameters. *NIDA Research Monograph* 105: 567–578.

Foltin, R.W., M.W. Fischman, M.F. Byrne. 1988. Effects of smoked marijuana on food intake and body weight of humans living in a residential laboratory. *Appetite* 11 (1–14).

Gorter, R. 1991. Management of anorexia-cachexia associated with cancer and HIV infection. *Oncology* 5 (9 Suppl): 13–17.

Gorter, R., M. Seefried, and P. Volberding. 1991. Dronabinol effects on weight in patients with HIV infection. [Letter] *AIDS* 6: 127.

Grinspoon, L., J.B. Bakalar, and R. Doblin. 1995. Marijuana, the AIDS wasting syndrome, and the U.S. government. [Letter] *New England Journal of Medicine* 333 (10): 670–671.

Grunfeld, C. and D.P. Kotler. 1992. Pathophysiology of the AIDS wasting syndrome. [Review] *AIDS Clinical Review* 191–224.

Hollister, L.E. 1992. Marijuana and immunity. [Review] *Journal of Psychoactive Drugs* 24 (2): 159–164.

Klausner, J.D., S. Makonkawkeyoon, P. Akarasewi, W. Kasinrerk, K. Nakata, and G. Kaplan. 1994. Treatment with thalidomide in AIDS patients. *International Conference on AIDS* 10 (1) 221 (abstract no PB0312).

Levitz, S.M. and R.D. Diamond. 1991. Aspergillosis and marijuana. [Letter]. *Annals of Internal Medicine* 115 (7): 578–579.

Nahlen, B.L., S.Y. Chu, O.C. Nwanyanwu, R.L. Berkelman, S.A. Martinez, and J.V. Rullan. 1993. HIV wasting syndrome in the United States. *AIDS* 7 (2): 183–188.

Plasse, T., M. Conant, R. Gorter, and K.V. Shepard. 1992. Dronabinol stimulates appetite and causes weight gain in HIV patients. *International Conference on AIDS* 8 (3): 122 (abstract no. PuB 7442).

Plasse, T.F., R.W. Gorter, S.H. Krasnow, M. Lane, K.V. Shepard, and R.G. Wadleigh. 1991. Recent clinical experience with dronabinol. *Pharmacology, Biochemistry, and Behavior* 40 (3): 695–700.

Reyes-Teran, G., J.G. Sierra-Madero, V. Martinez del Cerro, T. Munoz-Trejo, H. Arroyo-Figueroa, A. Pasquetti, J.J. Calva, and G.M. Ruiz-Palacios. 1994. Effects of thalidomide on wasting in patients with AIDS: A randomized, double-blind, placebo controlled clinical trial. *International Conference on AIDS* 10 (2): 65.

Schambelan, M., K. Mulligan, C. Grunfeld, E. Daar, A. Lamarca, and J. Breitmeyer. 1995. Recombinant human growth hormone (rhGH) increases lean body mass and improves functional performance in patients with HIV-associated wasting. American Society for Microbiology. Human Retroviruses and Related Infections; 2nd Annual Conference, Washington, DC January 29 to February 2, 1995.

Struwe, M., S.H. Kaempfer, A.T. Pavia, C.J. Geiger, K.V. Shepard, T.F. Plasse, and T. Evans. 1992. Randomized study of dronabinol in HIV-related weight loss. *International Conference on AIDS* 8 (3): 137 (abstract no. PuB 7531).

Sutton, S., B.L. Lum, and F.M. Torti. 1986. Possible risk of invasive pulmonary aspergillosis with marijuana use during chemotherapy for small cell lung cancer. *Drug Intelligence and Clinical Pharmacy* 20: 289–290.

Tierney, A., P. Cuff, and D.P. Kotler. 1991. The effect of megestrol acetate (Megace) on appetite, nutritional repletion, and quality of life in AIDS cachexia. *International Conference on AIDS* 7 (1): 247 (abstract no. M.B. 2263).

Voelker, R. 1994. Medical marijuana: A trial of science and politics. *Journal of the American Medical Association* 271 (21): 1645, 1947–1948.

Von Roenn, J., E. Roth, R. Murphy, S. Weitzman, and D. Armstrong. 1991. Controlled trial of megestrol acetate for the treatment of AIDS-related anorexia and cachexia. *International Conference on AIDS* 7 (2): 280 (abstract no. W.B. 2392).

7

Glaucoma: A Patient's View

ROBERT C. RANDALL

Marijuana can make the difference between years of functional vision or blindness for people afflicted with glaucoma. I know this firsthand. Marijuana has given me nearly 20 years of vision.

Despite marijuana's therapeutic value in the treatment of glaucoma, only three glaucoma patients in the United States currently receive legal, medically supervised access to marijuana. In each instance, marijuana has dramatically improved medical control over glaucoma and provided safe, effective relief from progressive nerve damage.

If glaucoma were a rare disorder or current therapies were more successful in controlling the disease, marijuana's medical use might seem unnecessary. Glaucoma, however, is commonly cited as the leading cause of blindness in the United States. While conventional medical therapy is successful in dealing with the majority of cases, the failure of existing medical treatments compel significant numbers of Americans into risky surgical treatments.

These problems are not unique to the United States. Outside the post-industrial states of North America, Europe, Australia, and Japan, glaucoma is even less likely to be successfully treated. Data also suggest the incidence of glaucoma is racially disproportionate; the disease may occur eight times more frequently among people of color. This combination of increased incidence and restricted access to modern and expensive synthetic medical treatments suggests marijuana may have a very important role to play in glaucoma therapy.

Briefly stated, glaucoma occurs when elevated fluid pressure inside the eye, commonly called intraocular pressure, damages the optic nerve. While

---

Robert C. Randall is the president of the Alliance for Cannabis Therapeutics and a legal medicinal marijuana patient.

the precise mechanics of glaucoma remain elusive, all treatment for glaucoma, medical or surgical, centers on reducing intraocular pressure.

Marijuana and Reduced Ocular Pressure

Unlike many of the medical uses for cannabis that were identified in earlier times, marijuana's role in the treatment of glaucoma is much more recent. While there are indications that ancient cultures were aware of cannabis' ocular effects, all of the glaucoma-specific data dates from the early 1970s.

Early Studies

In 1970 the University of California in Los Angeles (UCLA) initiated a series of studies on marijuana's effects on various biological systems. One aspect of this study sought to address marijuana's impact on pupil size. At the time, it was commonly believed that marijuana caused pupillary dilation, and law enforcement interests wanted to determine if pupil dilation could be used as an indication of marijuana use.

Dr. Robert S. Hepler of the Jules Stein Eye Institute at UCLA was asked to conduct these studies. Hepler agreed and received a constant flow of research subjects from the umbrella UCLA project. From photographic and other evidence it quickly became clear that the theory of pupillary dilation was wrong. In fact, smoking marijuana actually causes a slight pupillary constriction.

Pupillary constriction is a common consequence of several drugs that lower intraocular pressure and are frequently used in glaucoma therapy. This effect is particularly obvious in short-term and long-term miotics like pilocarpine and phospholine iodide. Hepler made this connection and began to systematically check the intraocular pressure (IOP) of research subjects in the UCLA program. He quickly discovered that marijuana induced a rapid, very significant decline in IOP in both the normal and glaucomatose eye and that the effect was dose-related. Hepler filed the first report of his finding in a letter to *Journal of the American Medical Association* in September 1971 (Hepler and Frank 1971).

For the next five years Hepler and his research technician, Robert Petrus, continued to explore marijuana's IOP-reducing utility. Briefly summarized, they reported marijuana significantly reduced IOP in approximately 80 percent of their subjects. The reduction in ocular pressure was quite significant, usually between 25 percent and 50 percent of baseline pressure. The IOP-lowering effect of marijuana occurs approximately 45 minutes to one hour after smoking and lasts from three to five hours.

The prospect of a plant that is inexpensive to produce and that could significantly improve the medical welfare of people afflicted by glaucoma was not, however, aggressively pursued by the federal government or the ophthalmic establishment. Federal law specifically defines marijuana as a highly dangerous, medically useless substance. Given a choice between upholding this legal fiction or working to meet the real treatment needs of seriously ill Americans, bureaucrats at the FDA, DEA, and the National Eye Institute (NEI) preferred fiction.

Personal Experience

I was oblivious to these events when I was diagnosed in September 1972 as having glaucoma. At the time of diagnosis glaucoma had already destroyed the central vision in my right eye and had greatly eroded peripheral vision in my left eye. My IOP was 42 mm Hg, more than double the highest "normal" pressure of 20 mm Hg. Prognosis at diagnosis was three to five years of remaining vision. I was 24 years old.

My physician, noted ocular pathologist Dr. Ben Fine of Washington, D.C., honestly discussed my various treatment options, and I was immediately placed on conventional glaucoma control drugs, beginning with pilocarpine. The visually distorting effects of pilocarpine were so severe that I became temporarily disabled. Within a year of diagnosis my use of pilocarpine escalated dramatically. Initially I was prescribed 0.5 percent pilocarpine once a day. By September 1973 I was using 4 percent pilocarpine four to six times daily.

Unfortunately, as Fine had predicted, even this rapidly accelerating use of pilocarpine failed to adequately control my elevated IOP. I was continuing to lose my vision. Additional medicines were prescribed, including topical epinephrine and oral diuretics. While each of these new medicines provided short periods of IOP reduction, my ocular pressure quickly escaped medical control.

Then in the fall of 1973 someone provided me with two marijuana cigarettes. I had smoked marijuana frequently while in college. And I had noticed already then that marijuana helped ease visual symptoms my doctors at the time referred to as "eye strain." Upon graduating from college, however, I moved to Washington, D.C., and stopped smoking marijuana.

After having been diagnosed with glaucoma, I learned that these visual symptoms were, in fact, indications of dangerously elevated IOP. These symptoms typically began with a slight blurring of vision. If my IOP continued to increase, this blurring was followed by the appearance of tricolored haloes around sources of light. In extreme but not uncommon circumstances these haloes were followed by an onset of "white blindness," a condition in which IOP is so elevated it causes the light coming into the eye to diffuse. When this occurs IOP is very elevated, and one can become functionally blind, and additional damage to the optic disk often follows. In effect, one is watching oneself go blind.

I was experiencing tricolored haloes that evening in 1973 when I smoked one of the marijuana cigarettes I had been given. I had no great expectations and was certainly not smoking marijuana because of my glaucoma. Forty-five minutes later, however, I noticed that the tricolored haloes were gone. Then I remembered my college experiences with "eye strain." I was suddenly overwhelmed by the fact marijuana was medically helpful.

The next morning I reconsidered. It is, after all, difficult to believe that an illegal weed one associates with pleasure is somehow going to save one's sight when all the modern pharmaceutical drugs have failed to work. It took me six months of careful trial and error evaluation to accept marijuana's important role in my medical care. By the summer of 1974, however, it was very obvious that marijuana was having a profound and beneficial impact on my disease. For the first time my IOP came under stable medical management. And for the first time visual field analysis indicated that I was no longer losing vision.

Illegal Treatment

Against this promising backdrop, I confronted a stark problem that still plagues most patients who need marijuana for medical purposes. It is illegal for physicians to prescribe or for patients to smoke marijuana. So I was forced to purchase unregulated supplies of marijuana at illegal, prohibition-inflated prices. Trying to afford enough marijuana to meet my medical need—about three cigarettes daily—was ruinously expensive. In addition, the criminal market in marijuana means that supplies are not always available.

In an effort to compensate for these difficulties, I decided to grow enough marijuana to meet my medical needs during those times when I could not afford or find marijuana in the street market. In 1974 I lost my first few marijuana plants to spider mites. In 1975, however, I succeeded in growing six beautiful marijuana plants on my sun deck. These were coming along well when I was arrested in August 1975 in the District of Columbia for the crime of marijuana cultivation. I immediately informed my attorneys that I was smoking marijuana for medical purposes, to control my glaucoma. They said I would have to "prove it." So that is what I set out to do.

Building a Case

Within weeks of my arrest I discovered that the United States government also knew of marijuana's important IOP-reducing properties. Then I became aware of Hepler's extensive studies of marijuana's use as a glaucoma control agent. In December 1975 I spent 13 days undergoing controlled medical test at the Jules Stein Eye Institute. The first stage of this controlled medical evaluation assessed the utility of conventional glaucoma control agents. In very quick order Hepler concluded that if left on standard glaucoma control drugs, I would become blind. Even with the use of all available glaucoma control drugs my IOP was consistently elevated for much of the day. In the evening my IOP often spiked above 40 mm Hg, Hepler then tested my IOP-response to oral, synthetic delta-9-THC pills similar to those now marketed under the brand name Marinol. The synthetic THC failed to reduce my IOP.

Finally, Hepler tested my IOP response to prerolled marijuana cigarettes prepared by the National Institute on Drug Abuse (NIDA). Initially, a dose of one cigarette failed to reduce my IOP. Both Hepler and I found this puzzling. In my experience I usually smoked less than a complete cigarette to achieve IOP-reduction. Perplexed, we agreed to increase the dose. I was told to smoke as much marijuana as I cared to. I smoked seven cigarettes in an hour. My IOP decreased dramatically.

Over the next few days Hepler worked to establish a marijuana dose that would effectively reduce my IOP on a consistent basis. By the conclusion of the UCLA study, it was clear that I would need between eight to ten NIDA marijuana cigarettes daily to achieve desired levels of IOP-reduction throughout the course of a day.

After reviewing the UCLA data, my physician, Dr. Fine, recommended a second controlled medical experiment to confirm his and Hepler's conclusion that my IOP was beyond the reach of conventional glaucoma therapies. This second, confirmatory study was conducted over a period of six days at the Wilmer Eye Institute at Johns Hopkins University.

At the end of the six-day, in-hospital evaluation, Wilmer ophthalmologists agreed with the UCLA findings and concluded that even under maximal medical treatment, employing all available glaucoma control drugs in combination and at the highest recommended dosages, my disease could not be adequately controlled. The Wilmer physicians concluded that if I were left on these therapies, I would quickly lose my remaining vision. They recommended immediate surgical intervention to save my sight.

Nearly all credible ophthalmologists would agree that surgery for glaucoma entails very real risks. In many instances, such surgery fails to reduce IOP. Glaucoma surgery can also trigger the development of cataracts or result in sight-destroying infections. One study suggests that nearly one-third of patients suffering from "end-stage" glaucoma are blinded as a result of surgery.

Fine agreed with Hepler that surgical intervention would probably destroy the small island of healthy optic nerve that gave me functional vision. After carefully reviewing my medical history and the results of the controlled medical studies conducted at the Jules Stein Eye Institute and the Wilmer Eye Institute, Dr. Fine concluded it would be medically unethical to deprive me of therapeutic access to marijuana.

Medical Necessity

In July 1976 I went on trial in the District of Columbia accused of the crime of growing marijuana. In defense, my attorney, John Carr, argued that any sane man who knew marijuana could help to retain his sight would break the law to obtain the marijuana he medically required. In November 1976, the court agreed and ruled that my use of marijuana was not criminal, but an act of "medical necessity." I was found not guilty. In the same month, federal drug control agencies began providing me with legal, medically supervised access to marijuana for use in the control of my glaucoma.

From November 1976 through January 1978 I received marijuana through Dr. John C. Merritt, an ophthalmologist at Howard University in Washington, D.C. Merritt ignored my previous medical records and started from scratch. First, I was tested on conventional glaucoma control drugs. These failed to adequately reduce my IOP. Next, Merritt tested my IOP-response to orally administered synthetic THC pills. These also failed to reduce my ocular pressure. Finally, Merritt tested my IOP-response to smoked marijuana. Marijuana significantly reduced my ocular tensions to below 20 mm Hg. After fine-tuning my dose, Merritt determined that I required daily between eight to ten 0.9 gram prerolled NIDA cigarettes of 2 percent THC potency or greater to control my elevated IOP.

Merritt acted as my treating physician for a period of 14 months. During this period I routinely visited his office for evaluation of my IOP-response to marijuana therapy. In addition, my IOP was monitored at home using a Schiotz tonometer. At times this monitoring was very extensive and involved IOP checks every half hour. After 14 months of therapy, Merritt concluded that marijuana effectively lowered my IOP and that the resulting decrease in ocular tension was preventing further damage to my optic nerve.

Despite Merritt's findings, federal agencies disrupted my medical access to legal supplies of marijuana in January 1978. In part this was in retaliation for my refusal to keep my medical access to marijuana a secret. It was also when Merritt left the Washington area. It should be noted that this disruption in access to marijuana occurred despite the fact that another board-certified ophthalmologist was ready and willing to monitor my medical use of marijuana.

In May 1978 my legal access to marijuana was restored as the result of an out-of-court settlement. On the basis of this out-of-court settlement I was guaranteed legal, medically supervised access to government supplies of marijuana of medicinal quality. Under this arrangement my private physician monitors my condition and writes prescriptions for marijuana that are honored by a designated pharmacy in the Washington, D.C., area.

The legal settlement specifically prohibits federal agencies from manipulating my medical care and from forcing me into unethical research programs. This legal settlement has provided me with FDA-approved medically supervised access to marijuana as a glaucoma control drug for nearly two decades. Employing marijuana as a mainstay drug, I have been able to eliminate several far more dangerous glaucoma control agents, including timolol and oral diuretics while still retaining stable control over my ocular pressure.

The resulting therapy has afforded me continuous control over elevated IOP for nearly two decades. My IOP now usually falls in a range from 12–18 mm Hg. Computerized visual field analysis consistently demonstrates that there has been no significant progression of sight loss since I began legally receiving marijuana. By any standard of glaucoma assessment marijuana has successfully stopped the rampant progression of sight loss.

I would be the first to admit surprise at this outcome. In 1976 when I was fighting for the legal right to smoke marijuana, I anticipated that like other glaucoma control drugs, marijuana would work for a brief period of time and then fail. But that has not been the case. As I finish this chapter in the spring of 1996, marijuana is providing the same degree of IOP-reduction as it did in 1976. Moreover, this therapeutic benefit has been achieved without any obvious mental or physical side effects.

Official Denial

While a marijuana-based therapy has been highly successful in helping to retain my vision, the FDA and other federal agencies, including the National Eye Institute (NEI), have virtually ignored marijuana's important role in glaucoma therapy. In the late 1970s the NEI poured nearly $2 million into efforts to develop synthetic THC-based topical eyedrops (Colasanti et al. 1984a, b). The resulting product was an abysmal failure. Not only did the NEI's THC-based eyedrops fail to reduce IOP, but the oil-based eyedrops caused severe ocular irritation. The NEI dropped additional research in this area in the early 1980s. Significantly, the NEI and FDA have refused to aggressively pursue marijuana's IOP-reducing properties.

The failure of the THC-based eyedrops could have easily been predicted. As early as 1974, Dr. Mario Perez-Reyes at Research Triangle Park in North Carolina reported that at least five chemicals in marijuana are responsible for the plant's IOP-reducing actions. Significantly, delta-9-THC is not the most impressive IOP-lowering agent in marijuana.

Other researchers, including Keith Greene, report chemicals not soluble in marijuana may also significantly contribute to reduced ocular tensions. Quite obviously, marijuana smoke contains numerous ingredients that are responsible for the plant's IOP-lowering effect.

Current Situation

At the present time only three Americans afflicted by glaucoma have legal, medically supervised access to marijuana. Significantly, the other two patients, Elvy Musikka and Corrine Millet, also report that marijuana has effectively lowered their ocular pressures and successfully prevented further erosion of their vision.

Despite these promising facts, United States law still prohibits marijuana's prescriptive medical use. Over the past decade, while United States researchers have ignored marijuana's important role in glaucoma therapy, investigators in the West Indies and elsewhere have been less reluctant to explore the plant's therapeutic usefulness. In particular, the work of Dr. Manley West in Jamaica has resulted in the creation of topical, cannabis-based eyedrops (Canasol) that appear to have some value as an IOP-reducing agent.

Over the years I have spoken with several individuals who have explored Canasol as a therapeutic agent. They consistently report the topical marijuana eyedrops can successfully reduce IOP. However, they also report concern over the eyedrops' long-term use. In one case the patient reported Canasol worked well for several months, then abruptly failed.

While I find West's work exciting I am not prepared to risk my vision on Canasol. Speaking personally, I already know that smoking marijuana successfully, consistently, and safely reduces my IOP. After more than 20 years of stable and reliable treatment, I would be foolish to abandon a therapy that I know works well and replace it with one that might or might not work. In short, I do not have enough remaining eyesight to risk the stability of my current care for a treatment that is uncertain and, therefore, risky.

Clearly, however, Canasol may have an important role to play in glaucoma therapy. And there may be very real advantages to a topical, marijuana-based agent. Some people, for example, do not wish to smoke. Others may find eyedrops less troublesome to use. In a rational world the decision to use marijuana or Canasol or some future cannabinoid-based synthetic to lower IOP should be made by treating physicians and their patients, not by vice cops and bureaucrats.

Finally, it is important to remember that the goal of successful glaucoma treatment is the preservation of sight. If this medical objective can be successfully achieved through the use of smoked marijuana, then smoked marijuana should be legally available, by prescription, for use by those patients who choose to use it.

References

Colasanti, B.K., C.R. Craig, and R.D. Allara. 1984a. Intraocular pressure, ocular toxicity, and neurotoxicity after administration of cannabinol or cannabigerol. *Experimental Eye Research* 39: 251–259.

Colasanti, B.K., S.R. Powell, and C.R. Craig. 1984b. Intraocular pressure, ocular toxicity, and neurotoxicity after administration of delta-9-tetrahydrocannabinol or cannabichromene. *Experimental Eye Research* 38: 63–71.

Hepler, R.S. and I.M. Frank. 1971. Marijuana smoking and intraocular pressure. *Journal of the American Medical Association* 217 (10): 1392.

8

The Use of Certain
Cannabis Derivatives
(Canasol) in Glaucoma

MANLEY WEST

Introduction

Glaucoma may be defined as a group of ocular conditions characterized by raised intraocular pressure. Approximately 300 persons per 100,000 suffer from glaucoma. The prevalence increases with age and involves about 1 percent of the population over 40. Almost 80,000 Americans are blind from glaucoma, which makes the disease the leading cause of preventable blindness in the United States. More than 2 million Americans have glaucoma of one form or another. Primary open angle glaucoma is the most common form; it causes insidious, asymptomatic, bilateral visual loss. About 15 percent of Caucasians with glaucoma have closed angle glaucoma, and this percentage may even be higher in Asians. Glaucoma is more prevalent, begins earlier in life, and progresses faster among blacks than among other races. Jamaica, in particular, with a population of about 3 million has about 3 percent of this number suffering from glaucoma.

Normal intraocular pressure is from 10 to 20 mm Hg. Elevated intraocular pressure is usually associated with damage to the optic disk and visual field loss. In spite of a fundamental interest and research in this area, the precise mechanism by which ocular hypertension damages the optic disk is not clearly understood.

Aqueous humor is the fluid that circulates within the eyes to provide nourishment to the tissues. It is produced by the ciliary processes in the

Manley West, O.M., Ph.D., is a professor of pharmacology at the University of the West Indies in Kingston, Jamaica.

posterior chamber of the eyes and passes from the posterior chamber through the pupil to the anterior chamber of the eyes and exits through the outflow system at the peripheral angle of the anterior chamber. Two factors are really important in the dynamics of aqueous humor: (1) irregularities in the inflow mechanism or aqueous humor production, and (2) abnormalities in drainage or outflow of the aqueous humor. The inflow should balance outflow to maintain a steady state of intraocular pressure. Reducing aqueous production and hence inflow should be an accepted method of reducing intraocular pressure in all forms of glaucoma. The treatment involves a medical or surgical approach. The surgical approach should be used only after all medical attempts have failed.

At present we do not know how either endogenous or exogenous stimulators or inhibitors may alter aqueous humor formation and intraocular pressure. However, the adenylate cyclase complex in the ciliary process acts to reduce flow in a manner that is not known. It is known that the cholera toxin induces a watery diarrhea by stimulating an intestinal epithelia adenylate cyclase with the result of sodium and water being drawn into the lumen of the intestines (Gregory et al. 1981). This same toxin increases endolymph production in the inner ear. Stimulation of adenylate cyclase activity will accelerate production of cyclic AMP in epithelial cells and cause movement of fluid from the basal to the apical portion of the cells and hence into the lumen. It is known that cyclic AMP will increase the permeability of luminal membranes. It is also known that adrenaline enhances the intraocular accumulation of cyclic AMP by activating adenylate cyclase. The same line of reasoning holds for the ciliary epithelium, but the movement of fluid is reversed due to the invagination of the optical vesicles during the development of the eye. Therefore, it should not be difficult to accept that the receptor complex in the secretory tissues of eye, the ciliary processes, may be the area where research should be directed to find an acceptable medication for glaucoma.

Treatment

The management of glaucoma is best left to the ophthalmologist, but the size and importance of the problem calls for the cooperation of other health professionals. The medical treatment is divided into two major areas: (1) reduction of aqueous humor production and (2) facilitation of aqueous humor outflow. Canasol is a fairly new drug that reduces inflow and has significant advantages when compared to the synthetic drugs.

Current antiglaucoma medications are not always effective and have significant side effects. Pilocarpine and other miotic drugs (which constrict the pupil, thereby increasing the fluid outflow) may cause blurred vision during the day due to ciliary body spasm and impaired vision at night caused by miosis. Furthermore, the miotics may contribute to the development of cataracts and may predispose the patient to uveitis and retinal detachment. The carbonic anhydrase inhibitors, such as Diamox, can produce electrolyte imbalance, fatigue, decreased appetite and weight loss, and kidney stones. Epinephrine eyedrops may cause eye pain or headache because they dilate the pupils (to inhibit the inflow of fluid). Because they can be absorbed into the circulation, they may also cause heart palpitations and nervousness. The most popular glaucoma medication is Timoptic (generic name, timolol maleate), a beta-blocker, which is believed to decrease eye fluid production. Initial adverse reactions noted were mild ocular irritation and a slight reduction in the resting heart rate. Later reports identified problems associated with nerves, digestion, vision, skin, and respiration (Miller 1980; the Harvard Medical School Health Letter 1979).

Canasol

For many years it was observed in Israel and the United States that the *Cannabis* plant has ocular hypotensive effects, and vast sums of money were invested in these countries in research to develop therapeutically useful compounds. These ocular hypotensive compounds represent a new class of chemicals that are more potent in reducing intraocular pressure than most of the other accepted drugs used clinically and with none of their side effects.

Canasol is a sterile ophthalmic preparation developed from Cannabis sativa specifically for the management of glaucoma. It is the result of ten years of basic scientific and clinical research done at the University of the West Indies in the pharmacology and ophthalmology departments and in private ophthalmic clinics (West and Lockhart 1978, 1980). (See Table 1 and Figure 1.)

Whereas international researchers concentrated their efforts on some cannabinoids that are psychoactive, at the University of the West Indies our research efforts were directed at other compounds of this plant since we were looking at long-term therapy. Now that the effectiveness of Canasol in glaucoma has been established in the Caribbean region and, according to private communication, in Australia, New Zealand, Colombia, and England, research is being directed at its mode and mechanism of action (Gutierrez and Gutierrez 1995). There is evidence that we may be looking at adrenergic receptor control of aqueous humor dynamics. Here Canasol could make a significant contribution to ophthalmology.

Pupil Size (mmm)	Before Use		2 Weeks		4 Weeks		8 Weeks	
	R	L	R	L	R	L	R	L
6	30	30	22	22	16	16	16	16
6	26	34	22	26	20	24	18	18
6	22	26	18	18	20	20	16	16
5	32	32	26	26	20	20	18	18
6	38	28	22	22	16	16	18	18
6	26	26	20	20	14	14	16	16
6	34	34	26	26	20	20	18	18
Mean	28.29	30	28.28	22.86	18.00	18.57	17.14	17.14
S.E.	1.53	1.31	1.11	1.12	0.97	1.29	0.40	0.40
6	30	30	16	16	18	18		
4	30	32	24	24	18	18		
5	26	26	16	16	18	18		
6	28	28	24	24	20	20		
4	30	40	26	28	22	22		
5	32	34	24	24	18	18		
6	28	26	22	20	16	16		
4	30	30	24	24	16	16		
5	42	34	28	28	32	32		
6	40	32	38	30	38	30		
6	28	28	20	20	22	24		
4	30	30	22	24	18	18		
5	40	40	30	30	26	26		
6	44	46	38	38	24	24		
5	26	26	20	20	20	20		
5	32	32	22	18	22	18		
Mean	32.25	32.13	24.63	24.00	21.75	21.13		
S.E.	1.46	1.42	1.70	1.61	1.49	1.21		

Table 1. Canasol 0.1 Percent in Glaucoma

Reduction in intraocular pressure in patients with glaucoma after treatment with Canasol 0.1 percent w/v eyedrops over eight weeks. The lower portion of the table shows the changes over four weeks.

R = right eye   L = left eye

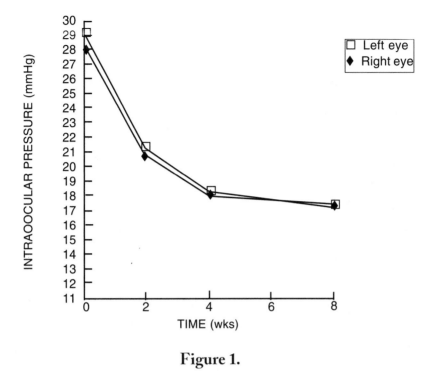

Figure 1.

Effect of Canasol ophthalmic solution 0.1 percent w/v applied topically to the human eye with glaucoma.

(Standard errors of mean are omitted on this and the following three figures.)

For Jamaica the introduction of this drug is timely considering the proportion of the population with glaucoma and the severe foreign exchange problems that now exist. For this reason the treatment of Jamaicans facilitates research in this area.

Pharmacology

Canasol is unique in that when applied to one eye it does not cross over to the contralateral eye. There is now evidence that no appreciable amount passes into the systemic circulation and thus it has a predominantly local effect. This action of Canasol may be a function of its chemical nature. As demonstrated in animals and humans, the onset of action is very rapid and can be detected within minutes after a single topical application into the eye. At 15 minutes there is a decrease of approximately 50 percent in the original

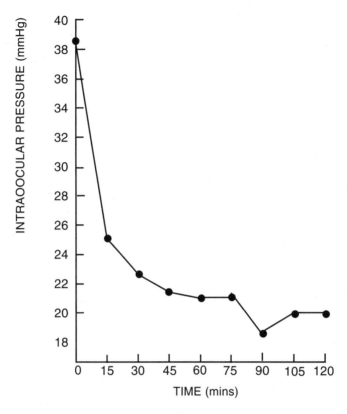

Figure 2.

Ocular hypotensive effect of Canasol 0.1 percent in dogs.

intraocular pressure, and this reaches a maximum at 90 minutes after application (see Figure 2).

Canasol has no effect on pupil size. Laboratory and clinical studies have
shown that Canasol is more effective on a weight basis in lowering intraocular
pressure when Canasol is combined with pilocarpine or timolol maleate (see
figures 3 and 4). Though there has been no scientific evaluation to verify this
claim, recent reports by ophthalmologists in Jamaica indicate that patients on
Canasol may have improved vision at night. Canasol lowers the pressure in
both the normal eye and the eye with glaucoma; however, the ocular hypotensive effect is most pronounced in the eye with glaucoma. The mode and mechanism of the action of Canasol is not clear at this time, but this is not unique
to Canasol; there are many drugs whose mechanisms of action were not worked
out until after they had been in clinical use, for example, digitalis.

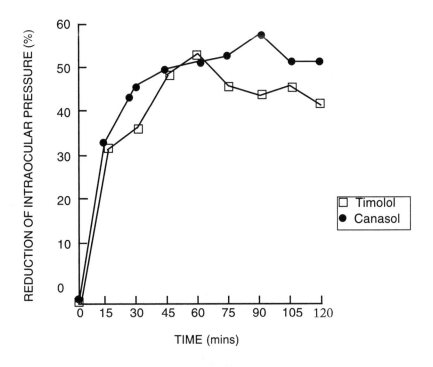

Figure 3.

Percentage change in ocular hypotension by Canasol 0.1 percent and Timolol 0.5 percent (in dogs).

However, the significant fall in intraocular pressure in animals is counteracted by several adrenolytic agents, whether they are applied topically to the eye or injected intravenously. Examples of these agents are tolazoline, azapetine, and phenoxybenzamine. Clinical experience has shown that when patients are already on antihypertensive medication, particularly alpha adrenergic blocking drugs, the frequency of dosing should be increased to produce the desired effect. The depletion of catecholamine stores in animals significantly reduces the effectiveness of Canasol. Extensive animal studies show that Canasol has no effect on the outflow mechanism. In animals, if the cervical (sympathetic) nerve is severed, the intraocular pressure is increased and Canasol may not reduce it. Present knowledge indicates that Canasol lowers intraocular pressure by adrenergic stimulations, and the site may be in the ciliary apparatus.

Canasol eyedrops may be used for (1) open or closed angle glaucoma or (2) raised intraocular pressure in patients who are at sufficient risk to require the lowering of their intraocular pressure. To date no adverse effects have

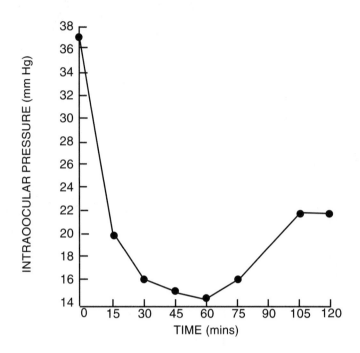

Figure 4.

Summation or potentiation of Timolol in the presence of Canasol. The potentiation is the same irrespective of which drug is instilled first (in dogs).

been reported following the use of over 90,000 phials (vials or small bottles) of sterile Canasol eyedrops.

Canasol is supplied in boxes of 25 phials. The solution is sterile and is contained in standard plastic eyedrop bottles (5 ml). Concentration is 0.1 percent weight/volume. It should be stored in a cool dark place. In Jamaica it is manufactured by Ampec Chemicals Limited and marketed by Medigrace Limited in Kingston.

References

Colasanti, B. 1986. Review of Ocular hypotensive effect of marihuana cannabioids: Correlate of central action or separate phenomenon? *Journal of Ocular Pharmacology* 2 (3): 295–304.

Crawford, W.J. and J.C. Merritt. 1979. Effects of tetrahydrocannabinol on arterial and intraocular hypertension. *International Journal of Clinical Pharmacology and Biopharmacology* 17: 191–196.

Green, K. 1979. The ocular effects of cannabinoids. In *Current Topics in Eye Research*, ed. J.A. Zadunaisky, 175–215. New York: Academic Press.

Gregory, D., M. Sears, L. Bausher, H. Mishima, and A. Mead. 1981. Intraocular pressure and aqueous flow are decreased by cholera toxin. *Investigative Ophthalmology and Visual Science* 20 (3): 371–381.

Gutierrez, A.M. and D.L. Gutierrez. 1995. Ocular hypertension treatment with Cannabis sativa. 1990 (Paper presented at the Annual Congress of Ophthamology, Cali, Columbia, August 1995).

The Harvard Medical School Health Letter Understanding glaucoma: preventing silent blindness. April 1979. 4 (6): 1–2.

Hepler, R.S. and I.M. Frank. 1971. Marihuana smoking and intraocular pressure. *Journal of the American Medical Association* 217 (10): 1392.

Merritt, J.C., W.J. Crawford, P.C. Alexander, A.L. Anduze, and S.S. Gelbart. 1980. Effect of marihuana on intraocular and blood pressure in glaucoma. *Ophthalmology* 87 (3): 222–228.

Merritt, J.C., J.L. Olsen, J.R. Armstrong, and S.M. McKinnon. 1980. Topical delta-9-tetrahydrocannabinol in hypertensive glaucomas. *Journal of Pharmacy and Pharmacology* 33: 40–41.

Miller, R.W. 1980. Keeping an eye on glaucoma. *FDA Consumer.* Rockville, MD: U.S. Department of Health and Human Services, HHS Publication No. (FDA) 80–3105.

West, M.E. and A.B. Lockhart. 1978. The treatment of glaucoma using a non-psychoactive preparation of Cannabis sativa. *West Indian Medical Journal* 27 (1): 16–25.

West, M.E. and A.B. Lockhart. 1980. The synergistic effect of Canasol and timolol maleate eye drops in glaucoma patients. World Conference on Clinical Pharmacology and Therapeutics (Paper No 0100). London.

9

Spasticity and Chronic Pain

Denis Petro

Historical Overview

As discussed in an earlier chapter, marijuana (Cannabis sativa) has been employed as a medication since ancient times. In Chinese and Hindu medicine marijuana found use as an analgesic, spasmolytic, and hypnotic. In the nineteenth century, cannabis extracts were used to treat muscle spasms associated with tetanus and rabies. Many other reports were published about the beneficial effects of marijuana in epilepsy, migraine headaches, and neuralgia.

Spasticity

One of the most difficult problems for a physician to manage is spasticity. When nerve pathways in the brain or spinal cord are damaged, spasticity of muscles controlled by that nerve pathway develops after the injury. Thus following spinal cord injury, spasticity is present in muscles below the site of injury. Patients with spasticity complain of impairment in control of the involved muscle with loss of fine movement, loss of muscle control with flexion of the associated limb, intermittent uncontrolled contractions, and pain. In addition, the severity of spasticity is usually dependent on the location and size of the damaged nerve pathway.

While many neurologic diseases can disrupt nerve pathways, the most common disorders causing spasticity include stroke, cerebral palsy, and multiple sclerosis. The prevalence of these disorders is well over 600 per 100,000

Denis Petro, M.D., is a practicing neurologist and clinical drug researcher in Arlington, Virginia.

individuals in the United States. To this group should be added the population of patients with traumatic brain and spinal injuries resulting from war, motor vehicle accidents, athletics, and violence. Well over 1 million persons in the United States have signs and symptoms of spasticity.

The goal of medical treatment is to normalize muscle activity in the affected area while minimizing side effects. The medical definition of spasticity is quite specific and distinguishes it from muscle spasm. Injuries to peripheral nerves such as in sciatica can cause localized irritation to muscles or muscle spasm. This finding is quite different from spasticity with important implications for treatment. Unfortunately, spasticity based on a fixed brain or spinal injury remains a challenge to the healthcare provider.

Marijuana in Spasticity

While the medical literature consists of the collected observations of physicians throughout the ages, nothing can surpass the impact of personal observation of a clinical response in an individual patient. For this author, the observations of patients in a neurology clinic in the 1970s proved to be a powerful stimulant of personal interest in the therapeutic potential of marijuana.

A 27-year-old man was referred to the neurology clinic for evaluation and treatment of his severe spasticity (Petro 1980). The patient had experienced several acute episodes of neurological impairment including vision loss and weakness of both legs. The weakness prevented him from climbing stairs without assistance, and his condition was made worse when he became overheated. These symptoms are typical for patients with multiple sclerosis, and his diagnosis was confirmed by the appropriate central nervous system (CNS) studies. In addition to the weakness and fatigability of the legs, he experienced frequent episodes of severe leg spasm in the evening and while in bed at night. The leg complaints were not relieved with the use of analgesics such as aspirin and Tylenol. He could not tolerate Valium or other antispasticity drugs due to their side effects.

At the suggestion of a friend, the patient tried marijuana. He smoked a marijuana cigarette in the evening when his symptoms of leg fatigue or spasms were intense. He stated that within a matter of minutes his symptoms were relieved. At the time of his initial clinic visit, he was asked to refrain from using marijuana and was scheduled for a follow-up visit in six weeks.

At the time of the second visit the patient described an increase in symptoms including leg pain, increased muscle spasm, and increased uncontrolled muscle contractions in the evening. He had experienced several episodes of urinary incontinence at night that were connected to the muscle spasms.

Bladder function can be affected by the loss of central motor control in spasticity. The patient's neurologic examination was consistent with the more prominent signs of spasticity, including extremely brisk reflexes and abnormal muscle tone. When the examiner moved the spastic limb, the increased muscle tone could be felt as an increased resistance.

At the patient's request, he left the clinic and returned one hour later. The neurologic examination was remarkable in that the findings of severe spasticity seen earlier were now absent. Deep tendon reflexes were now normal, and no abnormal reflexes were present. The classic neurologic sign of a CNS lesion is the Babinski reflex. When the outer portion of the sole of the foot is stroked with a blunt object such as a key, a pattern of toe response defines the reflex. An abnormal response indicates damage to motor centers in the brain or spinal cord. Dramatic changes in this reflex in a period of one hour are extremely unusual. The patient admitted to smoking a marijuana cigarette in the time between examinations. The case was presented to the attending neurology staff and discussed in conference. The consensus opinion was that conventional spasticity treatments offered little improvement over the patient's therapeutic use of marijuana. The patient has continued his pattern of marijuana use to control his symptoms of spasticity without adverse effects.

Marijuana appeared to offer this patient several advantages over conventional treatment. In normal practice the patient is given instructions to take the medication three or four times a day without exception. Unfortunately, many patients have good days and bad days with little to predict their symptoms. Since smoked marijuana is absorbed by the body rapidly, the effect is seen immediately, and one can titrate consumption to improve symptoms of spasticity without producing dysphoria or other CNS effects. On those days when spasticity is relatively quiescent, patients need not expose themselves to excessive medication. Needless to say, the cost of conventional drug treatment is much greater than the cost of homegrown marijuana.

This observation of the dramatic effect of marijuana on a spastic patient prompted review of the published literature supporting the muscle relaxant and analgesic properties of cannabis. Personal communication with surgeons involved in the care of veterans supported the beneficial effects of marijuana in those patients with traumatic spinal injuries and resultant spasticity. In these conversations, the use of marijuana was said to be very common in Veterans Administration patients with spinal injuries. The pattern of use was similar to the case seen in the clinic, with intermittent use to control increases in symptoms, especially in the evenings.

In a review of the medical literature, a single publication was found that reported a survey of ten males with spinal cord injuries who admitted to using marijuana. Five patients reported reduced spasticity, three patients noted no effect, and two patients did not suffer significant spasticity (Dunn and Davis 1974). Based on the observation of a dramatic effect in a single spastic patient and the indications in the literature that support marijuana in neurologic disorders, a rigorous study of marijuana in spasticity was undertaken.

Since marijuana is administered by smoking and can be difficult to administer in some patients not familiar with the technique, the oral formulation delta-9-THC was used in a double-blind, placebo-controlled, single-dose study (Petro and Ellenberger 1981). Considered the most "psychoactive" cannabinoid, THC might not be the best drug in patients with some neurologic conditions. At the time of the research, no other cannabinoids were available for use in patients. In this study, extreme care was taken to control conditions to insure scientific credibility.

Since spasticity includes a variety of signs and symptoms associated with the motor system, a precise clinical examination of the motor system was used to quantitate motor function. Motor reflexes were graded and strength measured. Nine patients with spasticity associated with multiple sclerosis were entered into the study. A trained observer examined each patient on three separate days, before and at 90-minute intervals after the oral administration of a capsule containing either 10 mg, 5 mg, or no THC. The observer rated muscle tone, motor reflexes, and muscle resistance to movement on a standard rating scale. In addition, the electromyographic activity of the quadriceps muscle in the leg was compared after each dose.

The results showed a beneficial effect of THC on muscle tone, reflexes, strength and electromyographic activity. The beneficial effects were seen at 90 minutes after the dose was administered and persisted for up to six hours. Side effects were recorded after each dose and were minimal. One patient reported feeling "high" after 10 mg THC and another reported feeling "high" after the placebo. No other side effects were noted. This study demonstrated that single doses of THC have an antispasticity effect with a favorable safety profile. The improvement in muscle tone and function was consistent with the observation of the first clinic patient who smoked marijuana to control symptoms of spasticity. This study was also reassuring in that no significant side effects were noted. If the most psychoactive component of marijuana is safe, one might expect that other cannabinoids may be even more effective on the motor system while sparing other CNS systems. While a single clinical study is of interest, the usual practice is to evaluate the body of evidence in support of a hypothesis. Fortunately, the observations described above have been supported by a series of reports by researchers throughout the world that confirm the efficacy of marijuana in treating the signs and symptoms of spasticity.

In a 20-day crossover study, oral THC (35 mg/day) was given to five patients with paraplegia associated with trauma (Truong and Hanigan 1986).

The patients had significant spasticity as a result of spinal injuries, and a series of neurologic tests including reflexes, muscle activity, and electrical measurements was recorded. All patients responded with a reduction in one or more measures of spastic activity during treatment with THC. The investigators documented an effect on the motor system at a site in the CNS but not at the peripheral nerve or muscle. This report is consistent with the initial clinical study and other animal studies that place the action of marijuana in the CNS affecting multisynaptic pathways. Since the location of the lesion causing spasticity in patients varies from one patient to another, one cannot generalize concerning the precise site of action nor can one predict the individual's response to marijuana.

In a publication from Germany, the effects of marijuana on the motor system in a 30-year-old male with spasticity associated with multiple sclerosis were presented (Meinck et al. 1989). This patient was confined to a wheelchair due to spasticity. He claimed that marijuana improved his motor system such that he could climb stairs and walk on even ground. In addition, he stated that his urinary system improved along with normalization of sexual function. He was asked to abstain from all drugs and was hospitalized for observation. On the fifth day in the hospital a range of motor function studies were conducted. The tests were conducted before and after the patient smoked a marijuana cigarette. Muscle force increased, tendon reflexes normalized, and other motor reflexes improved in a fashion similar to those responses seen in other studies. Also, recordings of hand tremor demonstrated a reduction in tremor after smoking the marijuana cigarette. The researchers concluded that this study confirmed the previous publications in demonstrating the beneficial effects of marijuana in spasticity. In addition to the antispasticity action, the researchers postulated an analgesic action as an additional benefit in patients with spasticity. This publication from Germany in essence repeated the observations presented in the initial case report from the United States.

In summary, a series of clinical studies have been conducted that confirm the observation that marijuana has beneficial effects in patients with spasticity. The observations were made in patients with spasticity associated with either traumatic spinal injury or multiple sclerosis. The effect has been seen with marijuana and with one of the constituent cannabinoids, delta-9-THC. No significant safety hazards were found in the published reports.

With the body of scientific evidence to support therapeutic effects and an obvious need on the part of spastic patients for more effective treatments of their condition, one might anticipate wide interest in the pharmaceutical industry for a research program to develop marijuana to treat spasticity. A potential sponsor need only complete "Phase 3" to submit a New Drug Application (NDA) to the FDA. In Phase 3, a drug in development is administered to a large group of patients such that dose-response activity and the risk-benefit ratio can be assessed in comparison to conventional approved treatments. Data from at least several hundred patients exposed to the drug for time periods of up to one year are usually presented to regulatory authorities prior to drug approval. This phase of drug development may take three years to complete and will cost up to $10 or $20 million. A corporate sponsor will make the appropriate projections of sales over the period of exclusive marketing of a drug and then proceed if the numbers are favorable. Since marijuana is a natural substance potentially found in one's backyard, no corporate sponsor is willing to expend the resources required for FDA approval only to be undersold by a local gardener.

With the publication of well-controlled studies that support the efficacy of marijuana in spasticity, one can ask: how widespread is the use of marijuana in the treatment of spasticity? Over the past decade personal communication with patients and physicians involved in the care of patients with spinal injuries has included hundreds of letters and telephone calls. Very few of these individuals have been willing to confront the daunting task of requesting marijuana from the government using the regulatory process. The practicing physician has neither the time nor the resources to face the regulatory bureaucracy.

An example from my own experience will illustrate the existing degree of regulatory arrogance. On one occasion the paperwork to provide marijuana to a patient with spinal injury in Long Island was prepared and submitted. Three months after the submission of all forms, I received a telephone call from a New York state regulatory bureaucrat concerning the case. All questions concerning the case were answered in the conversation. At the end of the call, the questioner stated that to evaluate the case adequately he would need to meet with me in his office in Albany. Since all questions concerning the case had been answered, I felt that no personal interview would be necessary or any remaining concerns could be addressed by correspondence. The bureaucrat stated that if I was not able to take the time to travel to Albany, he was not motivated to approve the request. The request for compassionate use of marijuana for this patient was denied. The patient continues to use marijuana provided by a friend without the supervision of governmental bureaucrats.

Since the number of patients with spasticity is quite large and amounts to well over 1 million people in the United States, it takes no leap of faith to assume that the number of patients using marijuana for spasticity is at least in the tens of thousands. In a survey of patients with spinal cord injuries seen at the University of Wisconsin, 24 of 43 responders reported marijuana use in the year prior to the survey (Malec et al. 1982). Of the 24 patients using marijuana, 21 indicated a reduction in spasticity due to marijuana use. Simply stated, 88 percent of those patients who use marijuana reported improvement in spasticity. If this simple survey is in any measure a reflection of the data in the United States, use of marijuana for spasticity may be even greater than the tens of thousands noted above. With this widespread use in mind, the need to characterize the therapeutic index for marijuana in spastic patients is obvious.

THERAPEUTIC INDEX OF MARIJUANA IN SPASTICITY

The therapeutic index is a quantitative comparison of the therapeutic and untoward effects of a drug. For example, aspirin is effective in the vast majority of patients in the management of pain with only rare cases of significant adverse effect or fatality. Yet even with aspirin one can expect occasional severe or even fatal reactions, such as anaphylaxis or bleeding disorder. In the treatment of spasticity, one might ask whether marijuana is a reasonable alternative to traditional medical management of spasticity. The two major treatments for spasticity are dantrolene and baclofen.

Dantrolene (trade name: Dantrium) acts directly on skeletal muscle to increase the weakness of the spastic muscle. Since the drug is distributed throughout the body, all skeletal muscles are weakened including those distant from the area of spasticity. The dosage of dantrolene is begun at 25 mg daily and gradually raised to a maximum of 400 mg/day. Unlike marijuana, this drug subjects the patient to weeks or months of treatment to evaluate the potential effectiveness of dantrolene. In addition, CNS side effects, such as dizziness and drowsiness, are very common. If dizziness and drowsiness were the only problems with dantrolene, it might be considered a potential therapeutic agent. Unfortunately for the patient, dantrolene can cause hepatotoxicity, which can be fatal. Symptomatic hepatitis occurs at higher doses, and this effect is of such severity as to warrant a "box warning" in the labeling of the drug. The liver impairment can occur at any time and is more common in females, in patients over 35 years of age, and in patients also taking other prescription drugs. Liver function studies must be monitored to watch for impending disaster. Even though the drug is administered for chronic use, the long-term safety of dantrolene has not been established. In animal studies, hepatic and breast tumors were increased at high doses. As one can see from this brief description, dantrolene is a drug with a low therapeutic index and of limited value to the clinician.

Baclofen (trade name: Lioresal) is considered the most useful drug in spasticity not related to stroke. Baclofen works at sites in the CNS to increase inhibition of the motor system. In use, the drug is started at a dose of 15 mg daily and increased slowly to a maximum of 80 mg/day after two weeks. The drug is associated with sedation and unsteadiness of movement although tolerance to these effects will occur over time. While generally considered safer than dantrolene, baclofen can cause side effects including hallucinations, anxiety, and tachycardia (rapid heart rate) after abrupt drug withdrawal. For this reason, baclofen should be decreased slowly over four weeks for withdrawal. Lower doses are recommended in patients with impaired renal function. Patients with a history of stroke do not respond well to baclofen and have a poor tolerance for the drug. Use of baclofen in pregnancy is not recommended because of animal studies showing an increase in fetal abnormalities. Additional questions of safety were raised in the finding of increased ovarian cysts in female patients treated with baclofen for up to one year.

Recently, a new method of administration of baclofen has been approved in the United States. In this technique, baclofen is delivered by direct infusion into spinal fluid using a programmable infusion pump. The infusion system is implanted beneath the skin and a catheter is used from the pump to the spinal canal. This technique is reserved for those patients with spasticity who are unresponsive to oral baclofen or experience intolerable CNS side effects at usual therapeutic doses. Spinal infusion is considered an alternative to direct neurosurgical procedures such as cutting the motor nerve to the spastic muscle. Placement of an infusion pump is not without risk. The infusion pump must be appropriately positioned beneath the skin and must be placed in a patient of sufficient bulk to accept the device. Complications include battery failure, infection, movement of the device, and catheter blockage or kinking. In addition, the possibility of a drug administration error cannot be ruled out. In the premarketing studies, 13 deaths occurred in the 438 patients reported to have used the system. The relationship between the device and a fatal outcome could not be determined, but at least some patients may be at risk of death in association with this therapy.

Other drugs used in spasticity include the benzodiazepines, such as Valium, phenothiazines, and anticonvulsants. Valium acts in a manner similar to baclofen and inhibits synaptic transmission in the CNS. All of these agents are considered less effective than baclofen or dantrolene. Since no single agent is satisfactory, the clinician usually proceeds by trying the drugs in sequence, beginning with baclofen, dantrolene, the secondary drugs, and then going on to invasive methods such as baclofen infusion and to neurosurgical procedures such as cutting the involved motor nerves. The approach begins with the safest and most efficacious methods and proceeds to the more invasive and dangerous ones. With this review as background, one may ask whether marijuana should be considered as a treatment for spasticity.

Based on the brief review herein, one can safely say that marijuana is certainly no worse than several generally recognized approaches that have been implicated in patient fatalities. In recorded history, no evidence has been published relating the oral or inhaled exposure to marijuana to a fatal outcome. Fatal hepatotoxicity secondary to dantrolene is a documented finding.

Baclofen is considered much less dangerous than dantrolene, but the safety of baclofen is not unquestioned. The development of baclofen infusion is an admission of the failure of the oral formulation in many cases.

Many spastic patients have developed symptoms as a result of multiple sclerosis. Recently, interest in the treatment of multiple sclerosis has focused on interferon beta (Betaseron). Betaseron has shown some positive effects on exacerbation rates, severity of exacerbations, and CNS lesions. Unfortunately, the effect on neurologic disability has been less dramatic. Since spasticity is one of the many symptoms associated with multiple sclerosis, only time and clinical experience will provide clear answers to the questions concerning Betaseron. Since Betaseron may slow the progression of the underlying disease, extra years of productive life may be added with therapy. The treatment does not reverse areas of previous injury that might be found in patients with spasticity.

In addition to the clinical considerations regarding therapy, an important aspect of treatment of spasticity is the cost associated with medical care. The financial cost of ongoing physician care and drug therapy for spasticity can range to the thousands of dollars per year. In a time when rationing of health services is a consideration, an incentive exists to use only "conventional" treatments covered by health insurance. Certainly, a physician has little incentive to recommend marijuana if such a recommendation will lead to governmental censure even in the face of the evidence supporting marijuana in spasticity. In personal conversations with many physicians who have inquired about marijuana as treatment for spasticity over the years, the overwhelming majority has agreed with the position that marijuana has potential as a therapeutic agent. Unfortunately, the governmental obstacles to marijuana prescription remain daunting for practicing physicians. Without a corporate sponsor with deep pockets, the current situation will not change. After nearly 20 years of experience and at least several pendulum swings in regulatory approach, the prospect for a rational policy concerning medicinal marijuana remains still very much in doubt.

From the scientific evidence substantiating the efficacy of marijuana in treating spasticity, several conclusions can be drawn. Over the years, patients have self-medicated with marijuana to treat signs and symptoms of spasticity. Relief of spasms, improved muscle tone, and relief of discomfort have been commonly seen. Support for this observation has been obtained in well-controlled clinical trials. The risk-benefit ratio or therapeutic index for marijuana can only be characterized by large, long-term studies comparing marijuana with conventional treatments. At present, conventional treatments for spasticity are unsatisfactory. Based on scientific evidence, cannabis is an effective and safe alternative when compared to conventional treatments. Where cannabis and cannabis derivatives will ultimately be placed in the practice of medicine, a more enlightened society will decide. Separation of the therapeutic uses from the concerns regarding abuse should be a goal of all parties in this issue. Perhaps by the dawn of the millennium, answers to the clinical issues may be forthcoming.

Marijuana in Movement Disorders

With the reports of the beneficial effects of marijuana in spasticity, a series of studies were published on patients with other disorders of the motor system. In one report, a patient with multiple sclerosis noted decreased postural tremor of the head and neck after smoking marijuana. Postural tremor is the involuntary regular and repetitive shaking of a body part associated with sustained posture. The investigator then studied eight multiple sclerosis patients with disabling tremors and ataxia (Clifford 1983). Ataxia is an abnormality of movement characterized by errors in rate, range, direction, timing, duration, and force of motor activity. A series of neurologic tests of the motor system was carried out and compared before and after test doses of THC. Two of the eight patients were judged to have both subjective and objective improvement in motor function after THC. In a separate report, five patients with Parkinson's disease and severe tremor were studied. Marijuana was compared to Valium and conventional anti–Parkinson treatment. None of the patients improved on marijuana or Valium while conventional drugs such as levodopa and apomorphine were effective.

The cannabis derivative, cannabidiol (CBD), has been studied in a few patients with dystonia (Consroe et al. 1986; Snider and Consroe 1985). Dystonia is the slow, purposeless, involuntary movements affecting muscle groups of the face, neck, limbs, and trunk. Cannabidiol has fewer CNS dysphoric effects than delta-9-THC. In several reports, patients with dystonia of the head and trunk have responded to CBD. Like the other cannabinoids, CBD is an extremely interesting potential therapeutic agent. As with the other compounds, without a sponsor to support the costs of research, CBD will not be the subject of widespread study.

Marijuana in Chronic Pain

Since analgesia is ultimately expressed at the level of the central nervous system, neurologists often are consulted in managing patients with difficult pain problems. During residency training in a pain clinic, a 30-year-old female was seen to evaluate her pain management. She had received multiple injuries in a motor vehicle accident including fractures of the pelvis, right kneecap, the fifth lumbar vertebra, and multiple ribs. Her recovery was complicated by persistent muscle contraction pain of the neck and lower back. Her treatment included medication such as meperidine, pentazocine, and Valium.

When first seen in the clinic her neurologic examination was normal except for tenderness of the neck muscle area and a sensory loss to touch in the left shoulder region. She complained that her medication caused excessive sedation and interfered with her ability to work. In addition, she expressed concern regarding the addiction potential of her medication. Since the analgesic and muscle relaxant drugs she was using have been associated with serious untoward effects, several alternative approaches were tried. Acupuncture was attempted over a three-week course without effect. Transcutaneous electrical stimulation was likewise unsuccessful. Upon the recommendation of a physical therapist, the patient began using marijuana for her neck pain and tenderness. The physical therapist had experience in the hospital system of the Veterans Administration and suggested that marijuana was one of the options tried in post–Vietnam era veterans with neuromuscular problems. The patient tried marijuana in periods when her symptoms increased and used simple aspirin on occasion. Over a period of three months, she eliminated the use of all prescription drugs. The patient reported both analgesic and muscle-relaxant effects without the sedation associated with her opiate and benzodiazepine cocktail previously required.

On a separate occasion, a 34-year-old female was seen after experiencing a side effect associated with the treatment of migraine headaches. The patient experienced three to four classic migraine episodes per month with visual symptoms followed by prolonged headache, nausea, and photophobia. She could not tolerate beta-blockers or opiate analgesics. Her use of ergot antimigraine therapy had resulted in disturbing sensory changes in her arms and legs. As a "last resort" she tried smoking marijuana at the first sign (aura) of an impending headache. To her surprise, the severity of her headaches decreased dramatically. The frequency of her episodes dropped to one per month over the next year. Throughout the year she carried a marijuana cigarette for use only in an "emergency."

As in the case of spasticity, interesting observations on the use of marijuana in cases of pain have been reported over the years. Reports in the nineteenth century included use against the pain of rheumatism, neuralgia, menstrual cramps, and childbirth. The use of marijuana for these indications decreased with the development of drugs such as aspirin and the opiates. Interest in the cannabinoids as analgesic agents was renewed with the synthesis of more than 40 cannabinoids isolated from the cannabis plant in the last 30 years.

Drug development in the analgesic field has been explosive since World War II. Potent analgesics are essential in time of war, and access to opiates has influenced the conduct of wars over the ages. The localization of specialized brain receptors involved in the perception of pain has been successful and the effects of analgesics at these sites is well known. The cannabinoids have been studied in many models of pain with effects as great as those of "standard" analgesics such as morphine and codeine.

The methods used to evaluate analgesics in clinical trials have been generally recognized and standardized. New drugs are compared with standard drugs such as aspirin or codeine in models of pain such as postoperative, dental, renal colic, and arthritic pain and in cancer cases. Since a wide variety of therapeutic agents are marketed, and the total analgesic market amount to billions of dollars, the regulatory requirements for new analgesics include many studies on large numbers of patients. The regulatory barrier to a new cannabinoid analgesic agent would be extremely difficult to overcome since the drug would most likely be considered to have a potential for abuse and would be restricted by the DEA. With the wide variety of competing analgesic agents that do not face DEA restrictions, a corporate sponsor would not be willing to venture into the regulatory waters with a new cannabinoid analgesic agent.

Several interesting clinical studies using cannabinoids as analgesics have been published. In healthy subjects THC was shown to produce analgesia to a heat source. In cancer patients with severe pain, oral THC (10 mg) was equal in effect to codeine (60 mg). Higher doses of THC induced CNS side effects. Researchers are directing their efforts to manipulate the basic cannabinoid structure to retain analgesic action and limit sedation and other CNS side effects.

The evidence in support of cannabis as a treatment for pain exists both in preclinical animal studies and in a small number of clinical trials. Since cannabis contains many active cannabinoids in varying amounts in differing plants, a coherent recommendation concerning use against pain symptoms is lacking. Some patients may prefer marijuana to a cocktail of prescription drugs or, as in the case of the migraine patient, they may choose it to obtain a dramatic effect. Others may benefit from effects associated with marijuana such as appetite stimulation in patients with cancer or AIDS. Considering the alternative of addicting drugs such as the opiate analgesics, patients may opt for the relative safety of cannabis. Fatal overdose continues to be a significant problem with the opiates. The absence of any fatalities associated with cannabis remains an astonishing fact. The safety profile of cannabis is such as to allow the clinician to consider this treatment option in selected cases, such as cancer and severe chronic pain with manifestations such as depression, weight loss, or intolerance of opiates.

References

Bhargava, H.N. 1978. General potential therapeutic applications of naturally occurring and synthetic cannabinoids. *Gen. Pharmacology* 9: 195–213.

Clifford, D.B. 1983. Tetrahydrocannabinol for tremor in multiple sclerosis. *Annals of Neurology* 13 (6): 669–671.

Consroe, P., R. Sandyk, and S.R. Snider. 1986. Open label evaluation of cannabidiol in dystonic movement disorders. *International Journal of Neuroscience* 30: 277–282.

Consroe, P. and S.R. Snider. 1986. Therapeutic potential of cannabinoids in neurological disorders. In *Cannabinoids as Therapeutic Agents*, ed. R. Mechoulam, 22–49. Boca Raton, FL: CRC Press.

Dunn, M. and R. Davis. (1974). The perceived effects of marijuana on spinal cord injured males. *Paraplegia* 12:175.

Hanigan, W.C., R. Destree, and X.T. Truong. 1985. The effect of delta-9-THC on human spasticity. *Clinical Pharmacology and Therapeutics* 35: 198.

Johnson, M.R., L.S. Melvin, T.H. Althuis, J.S. Bindra, C.A. Harbert, G.M. Milne, and A. Weissman. 1981. Selective and potent analgetics derived from cannabinoids. *Journal of Clinical Pharmacology* 21 (Supplement 8–9): 271S–282S.

Malec, J., R.F. Harvey, and J.J. Cayner. 1982. Cannabis effect on spasticity in spinal cord injury. *Archives of Physical Medicine and Rehabilitation* 63: 116–118.

Maurer, M., V. Henn, A. Dittrich, and A. Hofmann. 1990. Delta-9-tetrahydrocannabinol shows antispastic and analgesic effects in a single case, double-blind trial. *European Archives of Psychiatry and Clinical Neuroscience* 240 (1): 1–4.

Meinck, H., P.N. Schonle, and B. Conrad. 1989. Effect of cannabinoids on spasticity and ataxia in multiple sclerosis. *Journal of Neurology* 236 (2): 120–122.

Moss, D.E., P.Z. Manderscheid, S.P. Montgomery, A.B. Norman, and P.R. Sanberg. 1989. Nicotine and cannabinoids as adjuncts to neuroleptics in the treatment of Tourette's syndrome and other motor disorders. *Life Sciences* 44: 1521–1525.

Noyes, R., Jr., S.F. Brunk, D.H. Avery, and A. Canter. 1975. The analgesic properties of delta-9-tetrahydrocannabinol and codeine. *Clinical Pharmacology and Therapeutics* 18 (1): 84–89.

Noyes, R., Jr., S.F. Brunk, D.A. Baram, and A. Canter. 1975. Analgesic effect of delta-9-tetrahydrocannabinol. *The Journal of Clinical Pharmacology* 15: 139–143.

Petro, D. 1980. Marihuana as a therapeutic agent for muscle spasm or spasticity. *Psychosomatics* 21 (1): 81–5.

Petro, D., and C. Ellenberger. 1981. Treatment of human spasticity with Δ-9-tetrahydrocannabinol. *Journal of Clinical Pharmacology* 21: 413S–416S.

Sandyk, R., P. Consroe, L.Z. Stern, and R. Snider. 1986. Effects of cannabidiol in Huntington's disease. *Neurology* 36 (Suppl 1): 342.

Segal, M. 1986. Cannabinoids and analgesia. In *Cannabinoids as Therapeutic Agents*, ed. R. Mechoulam, 105–120. Boca Raton, FL: CRC Press.

Snider, S. and P. Consroe. 1985. Beneficial and adverse effects of cannabidiol in a Parkinson patient with Sinemet-induced dystonic dyskinesia. *Neurology* 35: 201.

Truong, X.T, and W.C. Hanigan. 1986. Effect of delta-9-THC on EMG measurements in human spasticity. *Clinical Pharmacology and Therapeutics* 39 (2): 232.

Ungerleider, J.T., T. Andyrsiak, L. Fairbanks, G.W. Ellison, and L.W. Myers. 1988. Delta-9-THC in the treatment of spasticity associated with multiple sclerosis. *Pharmacological Issues in Alcohol and Substance Abuse* 7 (1): 39–50.

10

Seizure Disorders

Denis Petro

Background

A seizure is a transient disturbance of cerebral function due to excessive neuronal production of an excitatory neurotransmitter. The term *epilepsy* is used to refer to a condition characterized by recurrent seizures. In the United States the more than 1 million patients who suffer from seizures without obvious intercurrent causative illness represent a continuing challenge to the physician. While medical management of epilepsy has improved over the years, at least 20 percent of patients remain under unsatisfactory control.

Our understanding of the etiology of seizure disorders has advanced significantly over the past hundred years beginning with the work of Hughlings Jackson in the nineteenth century. Seizures can be due to many factors including congenital abnormalities and perinatal injuries, metabolic disorders, trauma, tumors, vascular diseases, degenerative disorders or infection. Regarding patients with seizures that have no specific cause, the term idiopathic epilepsy is used.

While seizures can be described in different ways, the International League Against Epilepsy has classified seizures based on clinical and electroencephalographic features. The classification begins by dividing seizures into those that are generalized without focal features and those that are partial by beginning in one hemisphere. Generalized seizures include tonic-clonic (grand mal) seizures, absence (petit mal), and myoclonic attacks. Partial seizures include simple partial seizures manifested in focal motor or somatosensory symptoms. Complex partial seizures may begin as simple partial seizures but include cognitive, affective, and psychomotor symptoms and involve impaired consciousness.

Denis Petro, M.D., is a practicing neurologist and clinical drug researcher in Arlington, Virginia.

While the manifestations of seizures can vary, the fundamental cause of seizures is thought to involve abnormalities of cerebral neurotransmitters. Excessive excitatory neurotransmission or impaired neuronal inhibition can be implicated in causing seizure disorders. The goal of therapy is to decrease excitation or to prevent the spread of the localized abnormality. Significant advances in the treatment of seizure disorders have been made in the past 50 years. The choice of anticonvulsant drug is based on the classification of the seizure type and the clinical experience with individual drugs. The most commonly used anticonvulsants are phenytoin, carbamazepine, phenobarbital, and valproic acid. The patient is usually treated with one of these drugs, and the dosage is increased slowly until seizures are controlled or side effects limit further increases. Plasma drug levels are monitored to check patient compliance and to assure that blood concentrations of the drug are within the generally accepted therapeutic range. In uncomplicated cases, control of seizures can be achieved with a single drug. In uncontrolled cases, a second drug can be added to reduce the severity and frequency of seizures. Unfortunately, many patients cannot tolerate multiple drugs without serious side effects.

An estimated 20 percent to 30 percent of patients with seizures do not achieve acceptable seizure control with conventional medical management. An option to consider in some patients with a focal seizure disorder is surgical excision of the excitatory lesion. Major neurologic centers have reported promising results with this technique, which includes careful EEG mapping to localize the lesion. At one center (Montreal), one-third of the patients became free of seizures, and another third noted a marked reduction in seizures after surgery. Several new anticonvulsants (gabapentin and felbamate) will become available in the near future pending final regulatory action, and these new drugs offer new hope to those patients whose seizures are not adequately managed with conventional treatment.

Marijuana in Seizure Disorders

Marijuana has been used as an anticonvulsant since ancient times in the Middle and Far East. In the nineteenth century cannabis extracts were widely used in India to treat seizures of varying causes. In modern times a few reports with mixed results have been published. Since marijuana contains many individual cannabinoids with differing psychoactive potentials, a clear picture of the role of marijuana in the treatment of epilepsy does not yet exist. Several case histories have been published that either suggest marijuana as a potential beneficial drug in epilepsy or implicate marijuana as a risk factor that increases seizures. In the mid–1970s a survey of illegal drug use at an outpatient epilepsy clinic was reported. Of the patients under 30 years of age 29 percent reported using marijuana. When asked what effect marijuana had on their symptoms, most reported no effect. One patient reported a decrease in seizures while using marijuana, and one patient reported that marijuana "caused" his seizures.

While little else has been published concerning the effect of marijuana on clinical seizures, studies of individual cannabinoids have been reported for delta-9-THC and cannabidiol (CBD). Seizures have been reported in patients after they used THC to control nausea in cancer chemotherapy. Since THC is psychoactive in many animal studies and is associated with other adverse effects, THC can be eliminated from consideration as a potential candidate for the treatment of epilepsy. In animal seizure models CBD has been shown to have anticonvulsant properties with potential in grand mal, cortical focal, and complex partial seizures. In a clinical study of patients with secondary generalized epilepsy with temporal focus, CBD was administered for up to four and a half months in eight patients (Cunha et al. 1980). Four of the eight subjects were considered to be improved, three were partially improved, and one did not improve while receiving CBD. No serious side effects were reported.

In summary, a review of the literature documents some reports of the effects of marijuana in seizure disorders. The data concerning marijuana is mixed with both positive and negative reports. The scientific evidence in support of CBD is stronger based on both preclinical and clinical studies (Carlini and Cunha 1981; Consroe et al. 1981; Consroe et al. 1975; Cunha et al. 1980; Karler and Turkanis 1981).

Clinical Experience

Over the past decade, individuals with seizure disorders who claimed to have benefited from marijuana have been contacted either to assist them in FDA regulatory filings or in association with legal proceedings after arrest. So far, 11 cases have been reviewed via personal telephone communication, medical record review and discussion with attending physicians. While no serious medical conclusions can be drawn, several observations are of interest. All cases are males ranging in age from 19 to 43 years. In cases in which a diagnostic classification is available, five of seven were reported to have complex partial seizures with secondary generalization. While conventional anticonvulsants were used in all cases, drug levels were not available in most cases. In cases associated with litigation, the question of compliance with the attending physician's clinical recommendations has been a recurrent difficulty. Since the medical literature is somewhat ambiguous concerning marijuana and epilepsy, a convincing argument in support of individuals who make a therapeutic claim in this area is weakened. In addition, with the anticipated arrival of new anticonvulsants, which have their advocates, support for the use of marijuana in epilepsy is undermined. However, even with this background, in selected cases of complex partial seizures the evidence for a therapeutic benefit of marijuana is enticing and should not be disregarded. With the possibility for a change in governmental policy concerning the therapeutic use of marijuana, one should not be discouraged in pursuit of improved control of seizure disorders by this medication.

References

Carlini, E.A. and J.M. Cunha. 1981. Hypnotic and anti-epileptic effects of cannabidiol. *Journal of Clinical Pharmacology* 21 Supplement (8 and 9): 417S–421S.

Consroe, P., A. Martin, and V. Singh. 1981. Antiepileptic potential of cannabidiol analogs. *Journal of Clinical Pharmacology* 21 Supplement (8 and 9): 428S–436S.

Consroe, P., and S. Snider. 1986. Therapeutic potential of cannabinoids in neurological disorders. In *Cannabinoids as Therapeutic Agents*, ed. R. Mechoulam, 22–49. Boca Raton, FL: CRC Press.

Consroe, P.F., G.C. Wood, and H. Buchsbaum. 1975. Anticonvulsant nature of marihuana smoking. *Journal of the American Medical Association* 234 (3): 306–307.

Cunha, J.M., E.A. Carlini, A.E. Pereira, O.L. Ramos, C. Pimentel, R. Gagliardi, W.L. Sanvito, N. Lander, and R. Mechoulam. 1980. Chronic administration of cannabidiol to healthy volunteers and epileptic patients. *Pharmacology* 21: 175–185.

Feeney, D. 1976. Marihuana use among epileptics. *Journal of the American Medical Association* 235: 1105.

Karler, R., and S.A. Turkanis. 1981. The cannabinoids as potential antiepileptics. *Journal of Clinical Pharmacology* 21 Supplement (8 and 9): 437S–448S.

Savaki, H.E., J.M. Cunha, E.A. Carlini, and T.A. Kephalas. 1976. Pharmacological activity of 3 fractions obtained by smoking cannabis through a water pipe. *Bulletin on Narcotics* 28 (2): 49–56.

11

Use of Cannabis or THC in Psychiatry

MILTON EARL BURGLASS

Why Might Cannabis Be Considered as a Medication with a Potential Use in the Treatment of Psychiatric Disorders?

Three possible applications of cannabis products in psychiatry have been considered and studied: (a) as a *substitute* for existing pharmaceutical drugs having specific effects and properties for the treatment of the major psychiatric disorders, like depression, psychosis, anxiety, or schizophrenia; (b) as an *adjunct* to verbal psychotherapy, that is, as an agent that might enhance or facilitate some aspect(s) of verbal psychotherapy; or (c) as a *preventive* agent the use of which might decrease a person's likelihood of developing a psychiatric disease or disorder. In this chapter we will consider the rationale and evidence for each of these indications.

Cannabis as a Substitute Drug

In modern psychiatry, pharmacological treatments of the major mental disorders are chosen based on the biological or biochemical explanations of the disease, wherein abnormal biochemical states and processes in the brain are thought to express themselves in the signs and symptoms of a disorder. For example, the alterations in mood, cognition, and bodily function seen in major depression are today understood in terms of a chemical imbalance of specific brain hormones, or neurotransmitters, such as serotonin and norepinephrine.

Milton Earl Burglass, M.D., M.P.H., M.Div., F.A.A.F.P., F.A.S.A.M., is a neuropsychiatrist at the Zinberg Center for Addictions Studies of the Harvard School of Medicine in Cambridge, Massachusetts.

Schizophrenia and other psychoses are understood as expressions of abnormalities involving the neurotransmitter dopamine. Anxiety is thought to involve an abnormality in the GABA (gamma-aminobutyric acid) neurotransmitter system. Hence, drugs used in the treatment of depression have effects that by one of several mechanisms increase the amount of serotonin and or norepinephrine in the brain. Antipsychotic drugs act to decrease the amount of available brain dopamine. Antianxiety drugs either increase the amount of GABA in the CNS (brain and spinal cord) or, due to their chemical structures being similar to GABA, they are able to bind to sites in the central nervous system (CNS) that normally bind to GABA, thereby causing a chain of neurophysiological reactions that results in the suppression of the physical and mental symptoms of anxiety.

Despite their having very specific physiological effects, none of the drugs used in psychiatry are entirely satisfactory. Antipsychotic and antidepressant drugs have undesirable short- and long-term side effects; both require extra work by the liver to be metabolized and may also tax the heart; both can be sedating, and antidepressants are painfully slow to relieve the symptoms of depression (10 to 21 days). Each generation of antianxiety drugs has demonstrated more specific target effects and fewer and less serious side effects. However, their potential for abuse and subsequent dependence remains a substantial concern for both patients and physicians.

Is Cannabis a Better or Safer Drug?

Over the years, despite numerous clinical anecdotes and case reports suggesting that the use of marijuana might improve or reverse a psychiatric disorder, focused research has not supported such a conclusion. Some psychiatric outpatients (with depression, schizophrenia, anxiety) have reported using marijuana to self-medicate both their primary psychiatric symptoms and the unpleasant effects of their prescribed medications and that while doing so they felt they had been able to function better. A survey on substance use by psychotic patients showed that those who preferred marijuana use had a lower hospitalization rate than those who used other substances or no substance (Warner et al. 1994). These patients also scored significantly lower on activation of symptoms and reported beneficial effects on depression, anxiety, insomnia, and physical discomfort. Although intriguing and provocative, these studies were not designed in ways that would justify the conclusion that marijuana use had been responsible for the patients' self-reported improvements. Therefore, cannabis cannot be considered to be a proven alternative pharmacologic treatment for major psychiatric diseases and disorders. Moreover, cannabis does not demonstrate the specific effects on brain chemistry that current psychiatric disease theory would ascribe to an effective treatment agent. Certainly, further research in this area is warranted, but the neuropharmacology of cannabis and mental illness, as presently conceptualized, are not closely related.

Although the principal active ingredient in cannabis, delta-9-tetrahydrocannabinol (THC), has been identified, isolated, and formulated as an orally administered pharmaceutical, in popular culture marijuana is typically smoked. Limited research has suggested that the health consequences and risks (bronchitis, emphysema, cancer, and heart disease) of smoking marijuana are at least as serious as are those associated with smoking tobacco. However, comparable amounts of the two substances are rarely used in practice.

There has been some conflicting evidence to suggest a possible role for marijuana in the treatment of addiction to alcohol and certain opioid drugs (heroin, opium, pain pills, etc.). At least some drug-dependent patients have been found to decrease or stop their use of alcohol or opioids while smoking marijuana regularly. However, no controlled study to date has been conclusive or even persuasive. Moreover, in today's abstinence-oriented environment, a treatment strategy that would substitute one psychoactive, euphorigenic drug (albeit an arguably less harmful one) for another is unlikely to gain the popular, governmental, or professional acceptance necessary to support the required preliminary basic scientific and clinical research.

Cannabis as an Adjunctive Agent

The psychological effects of marijuana are highly variable and extremely subjective. Research has shown that the psychological mind-set of the user and the social setting in which it is used are at least as important as the pharmacology of the substance in determining an individual's experience of marijuana's effects. The frequent subjective reports of "mellowing" and "getting in touch with feelings" described by users of marijuana as one of the drug's major effects has suggested to some patients and psychotherapists its potential usefulness as an adjunct to verbal psychotherapy. On the other hand, some users also report an increase in anxiety, hypervigilance, and paranoia associated with the subjective loss of control induced by the drug. Such effects would clearly be countertherapeutic. Clinicians cannot reliably predict which patients will experience which set of effects from marijuana, nor can users always be certain how the drug will affect them. Although there are scattered case reports in the mental health literature of the facilitating effects of marijuana in verbal psychotherapy, none has been conclusive. Most recently, interest in pharmacological adjuncts to psychotherapy has shifted away from marijuana and focused on a very different, pharmacologically unrelated drug, methylene-dioxy-methamphetamine (MDMA), known as "Ecstasy." Nonetheless, there remains a small group of patient and therapist activists who continue working at various levels to generate interest and support for formal research to study this application of marijuana.

Cannabis as a Preventive Agent

In the 1960s a shifting voice in the counterculture advocated the use of marijuana as an antidote to the mental and emotional "pollution" caused by mainstream culture. The rationale for this was based on the beliefs and teachings of Eastern and mystic philosophy and emerging alternative religious movements. There is as yet no way to responsibly associate the regular use of cannabis products with either a decrease in mental illness or an increase in mental health (howsoever defined) in a population group. Although the smoking of marijuana is a central element in the cultural and religious life of the Rastafarian community in Jamaica, little formal research has been done into the mental health consequences of the practice. Illegality causes its own set of problems by forcing users to engage with drug dealers and maintain secrecy regarding their use because of the potential legal risks.

Conclusion: The Challenge to Researchers and Clinicians

Based upon available research data, clinical reports, and the currently prevailing biochemical understanding of the various forms of mental illness, there is *at present* no place for cannabis in clinical psychiatry. Moreover, although clarification of many clinical questions and basic issues awaits further research, there is little evidence to suggest that such research will reveal cannabis to be substantially useful in the treatment or prevention of mental illness. Its value as an adjunct to verbal psychotherapy remains to be conclusively demonstrated. Although the drug will likely continue to be used for this purpose by at least a few practitioners, its recognition and endorsement by the major academic and clinical disciplines working in the mental health field is highly problematic.

Suggested Reading

Gorman, J. 1990. *The Essential Guide to Psychiatric Drugs*. New York: St. Martin's Press.
Hales, D., and R.E. Hales. 1995. *Caring for the Mind*. New York: Bantam Books.
Nicholi, A.M., ed. 1988. *The New Harvard Guide to Psychiatry*. Cambridge, MA: Harvard University Press.
Restak, R.M. 1995. *Receptors*. New York: Bantam Books.
Warner, R., D. Taylor, J. Wright, A. Sloat, G. Sprigett, S. Arnold, and H. Weinberg. 1994. Substance use among the mentally ill: prevalence, reasons for use, and effects on illness. *American Journal of Orthopsychiatry* 64 (1): 30–39.
Yodofsky, S., R.E. Hales, and T. Ferguson. 1991. *What You Need to Know About Psychiatric Drugs*. New York: Grove Press.
Zinberg, N.E., and W.M. Harding, eds. 1982. *Control Over Intoxicant Use*. New York: Human Sciences Press.

12

Cannabidiol as an Anxiolytic and Antipsychotic

ANTONIO W. ZUARDI
and FRANCISCO S. GUIMARÃES

Introduction

Although delta-9-tetrahydrocannabinol (delta-9-THC) is commonly accepted as the major psychoactive constituent of Cannabis sativa, several reports have demonstrated that other components of the plant influence its pharmacological activity (Carlini et al. 1970; Kubena and Barry 1972). One of these components is cannabidiol (CBD), which may constitute up to 40 percent of marijuana extracts (Grlic 1976) and is devoid of the typical psychological effects of marijuana on humans (Zuardi et al. 1982).

Interactive studies between delta-9-THC and CBD have produced apparently contradictory results both in animals (Karniol and Carlini 1973; Borgen and Davis 1974; Fernandes et al. 1974) and humans (Karniol et al. 1974; Hollister and Gillespie 1975; Dalton et al. 1976; Zuardi et al. 1982). Different schemes of drug administration used in these studies may help to explain the contradictions. It seems that when CBD is administered before delta-9-THC, it potentiates the effects of the latter compound, probably by a pharmacokinetic interaction. A potent inhibitor of hepatic drug metabolism, CBD (Paton and Pertwee 1972; Bornhein et al. 1981), increases delta-9-THC concentrations in the brain (Jones and Pertwee 1972). Concomitant use of both compounds, however, suggests that CBD is able to antagonize delta-9-THC effects (Karniol and Carlini 1973; Davis and Borges 1974; Zuardi et al. 1981, 1984; Zuardi and Karniol 1983).

Antonio W. Zuardi, M.D., Ph.D., is affiliated with the Department of Neuropsychiatry and Clinical Psychology of the University of São Paulo in Brazil.

Francisco S. Guimarães, M.D., Ph.D., is affiliated with the Department of Pharmacology at the School of Medicine at the University of São Paulo in Brazil.

Since high doses of delta-9-THC can induce psychopathological symptoms, including anxiety, panic attacks, and psychotic symptoms (Melges et al. 1974; Tassinari et al. 1976), the evidence that CBD can block some of the psychoactive effects of THC is of interest.

To further investigate this point, we tested the simultaneous oral administration of CBD (1 mg/Kg) with a high delta-9-THC dose (0.5 mg/Kg) in healthy volunteers, using a double-blind procedure[1] (Zuardi et al. 1982). Previous studies had already shown that at this dosage CBD is not able to change delta-9-THC blood levels (Agurell et al. 1981). We observed that delta-9-THC induced significant subjective anxiety and psychotic-like symptoms. Both effects were significantly lessened by simultaneous administration of CBD. This counteraction does not appear to be caused by a general blocking of delta-9-THC effects, since no significant change was detected in other measurements, such as an increase in pulse rate. Moreover, CBD does not bind to the cannabinoid receptor, and hence it is not a competitive antagonist of these receptors (Howlett et al. 1992). In addition, when administered alone, CBD had its own effects, such as induced sleepiness (Zuardi et al. 1982).

Several other studies have also shown that CBD has its own effects both in animals and humans. These include sedative (Pickens 1981; Zuardi et al. 1981), hypnotic (Monti 1977; Colasanti et al. 1984; Carlini et al. 1979), anticonvulsant (Carlini et al. 1973; Izquierdo et al. 1973; Cunha et al. 1980) and hormonal effects (Zuardi et al. 1984, 1993). Our results, therefore, led us to suspect that CBD could have anxiolytic and or antipsychotic effects.

Possible Anxiolytic Effects of CBD

PRECLINICAL STUDIES

Early studies produced contradictory results concerning a possible anxiolytic effect of CBD. For example, Zuardi and Karniol (1983) reported that CBD (10 mg/kg) induced a change in the lever-pressing behavior of rats similar to that obtained by typical anxiolytic compounds. However, Silveira Filho and Tufik (1981) did not find any anxiolytic effect of CBD in doses above 100 mg/kg. CBD was ineffective as an anxiolytic in a conflict test and in increasing food intake suppressed by neophobia.

There were large differences between doses of CBD used in these two studies. So we decided to investigate the effects of CBD over a wider range of doses in a new animal model that is now largely used to detect anxiolytic effects, the elevated plus maze (a maze that is shaped like a plus sign). This model of anxiety is based on the natural avoidance of the open (not enclosed)

---

[1]Neither the drug administrators nor the volunteers knew what they were given.

and elevated arms of a plus-maze displayed by normal rats or mice (Pellow et al. 1985). We showed that CBD (2.5–10 mg/kg) increases exploration of the open arm, an effect typical of anxiolytic compounds (Guimarães et al. 1990). The curve of the drug effect, however, has an inverted U-shape, and higher doses are no longer effective. Musty et al. (1984), measuring water-licking behavior suppressed by concomitant electric shock in rats, and Onaivi et al. (1990), measuring mice's exploration of an elevated plus maze, reported similar anxiolytic results. More recently, we tested three derivatives of CBD, HU-219, HU-252 and HU-291, in the elevated plus maze. All compounds increased exploration of the open arm, although over a limited range of doses (Guimarães et al. 1994). Preclinical studies, therefore, seem to support the presence of anxiolytic properties of CBD.

CLINICAL STUDIES

Safety Studies. Cannabidiol was extensively tested in laboratory animals to detect possible side or toxic effects (Cunha et al. 1980). In humans, acute oral intake (15 to 160 mg/day), inhalation (0.15 mg/kg), or intravenous administration (30 mg) of CBD were devoid of any significant side effects (Hollister 1973; Karniol et al. 1974; Dalton et al. 1976). Chronic oral ingestion of doses ranging from 10 to 400 mg daily for two to 30 days did not induce significant changes in neurological, clinical, psychiatric, blood, and urine examinations (Mincis et al. 1973; Cunha et al. 1980), with exception of mild somnolence in a few volunteers at the beginning of the trial. These results have justified the use of CBD in clinical trials. For example, Cunha et al. (1980) treated 15 patients with refractory epilepsy with CBD (200–300 mg/day) for as long as four and one-half months with no signs of toxicity. More recently Consroe et al. (1991) also failed to find toxic effects of the drug (in doses of about 700 mg/day) administered over six weeks to patients with Huntington's disease. Therefore, in addition to animal findings, clinical studies also suggest that CBD is a safe compound when administered to humans over a wide range of doses.

EFFECTS OF CBD IN A CLINICAL MODEL OF ANXIETY

The preclinical and safety studies reported above prompted us to test CBD in a clinical model of anxiety, the simulated public speaking test. In this test healthy volunteers (university students, both sexes, N = 10/group) performed baseline measures, including self-rating scales to evaluate subjective feelings, before receiving, in a double-blind design, a placebo, CBD (300 mg), or two anxiolytics, diazepam (10 mg) or ipsapirone (5 mg). After one hour and 20 minutes, the subject sat in front of a videocamera and video screen and watched a videotape with instructions about the task he or she would have to perform. Subjects were told that they would have two minutes to prepare a four-minute speech about a topic he or she had learned in a course during the previous year. The speech would be recorded on videotape and analyzed later by a psychologist. The subject then started the speech in front of the videocamera while viewing his or her own image on the screen. Self-rating subjective anxiety measures were taken before, during, and after the speech. The test induced significant increases in subjective anxiety (Figure 1) and in its physiological concomitants. This effect was lessened by CBD and the two anxiolytic compounds. No side effects of CBD were found, suggesting that the drug's effect on anxiety levels cannot be attributed to general sedative effects (Zuardi et al. 1993). The results thus suggest that CBD has anxiolytic properties when administered to healthy volunteers.

Possible Antipsychotic Effects of Cannabidiol

PRECLINICAL STUDIES

Typical antipsychotic drugs, although effective in decreasing psychotic symptoms in schizophrenic patients, may induce significant extrapyramidal, Parkinson-like side effects. These side effects are not produced by drugs such as clozapine, often classified as "atypical antipsychotics." The clinical use of clozapine, however, is limited by potentially fatal hematological adverse effects. Intensive research efforts have been made to develop new compounds with an antipsychotic profile similar to that of clozapine but without adverse hematological effects. Recently, we studied the effects of CBD in animal models often used to investigate antipsychotic properties of new compounds, comparing them to those of haloperidol, a typical antipsychotic drug. Both compounds lessened stereotypy (that is, repetitive movements, such as sniffing or biting, made without a clear objective) induced by a dopaminergic agonist, apomorphine (Zuardi et al. 1991). In contrast to haloperidol, however, the potency of CBD in increasing prolactin levels was very low, and the drug did not induce catalepsy (that is, maintenance of abnormal postural positions) at any dose tested (15–480 mg/kg). The ability of typical antipsychotics to provoke catalepsy in rodents is highly correlated with the appearance of Parkinson-like symptoms in patients treated with these drugs. The profile of CBD effects in these tests, therefore, is similar to that seen with clozapine and suggests that CBD may act as an "atypical" antipsychotic.

CLINICAL STUDY

Based on the preclinical study reported above and on the antagonism of psychotomimetic effects induced by high doses of delta-9-THC (Zuardi et al. 1982), we decided to test CBD on a schizophrenic patient who had significant hormonal side effects during treatment with typical antipsychotics (Zuardi et al. 1995). The patient, a 19-year-old woman, was referred to the inpatient

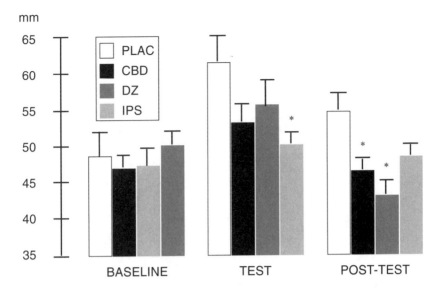

Figure 1.

Effects of cannabidiol (CBD, 300 mg), ipsapirone (IPS, 5 mg), diazepam (DZ, 10 mg) or placebo (PLAC) on anxiety induced by a simulated public speaking test. Bars are means of 10 healthy volunteers (+ SEM). Subjects were evaluated by the visual analogue mood scale (VAMS), anxiety factor, before drug administration (BASELINE), during speech performance (TEST), and 15 min. after speech (POST-TEST). See text for detailed explanation of phases. Asterisks indicate significant differences from placebo.

unit of the Clinical Hospital of Ribeirão Preto because of aggressiveness, self-injury, incoherent thoughts, and auditory hallucinations. After the study protocol was approved by the local Ethical Committee, informed consent was obtained from close relatives of the patient. The study began with four days of hospitalization during which the patient received placebo plus usual support measures. From days 4 to 30 she received CBD in progressively increased dosage, up to 1500 mg/day, in two divided doses. The CBD was then suspended and replaced by a placebo for four days. After that, haloperidol administration was started. Adjustment of the dosage was based on clinical evaluation. Diazepam was also administered in periods of great agitation. The mean daily dose of diazepam decreased after the beginning of CBD treatment from 16.3 to 5.7 mg/day. The patient was evaluated by two psychiatrists and two nurse auxiliaries, and the interviews were videotaped. At the end of the study the videotapes were analyzed blindly and in a random sequence by another psychiatrist. Symptoms decreased after CBD treatment (see Figure 2) and there was a trend for worsening of the symptoms after drug withdrawal.

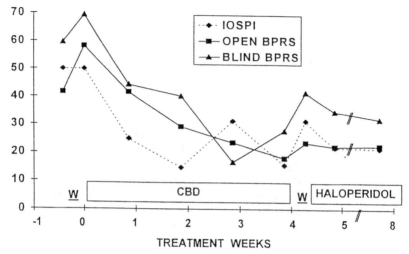

% of Maximum Possible Score

Figure 2.

Scores of the Brief Psychiatric Rating scale (BPRS) and the Interactive Observation Scale for Psychiatric Inpatients (IOSPI) from a patient treated with cannabidiol (CBD) or haloperidol. The BPRS was rated either by two independent psychiatrists (OPEN BPRS) or blindly by a psychiatrist based on videotaped interviews presented in a random order (BLIND BPRS). The IOSPI was evaluated independently by two nurse auxiliaries after daily observation periods of six hours. *W* indicates periods without medication.

The improvement obtained with CBD was not increased by haloperidol. This improvement was seen in all items of the rating scale employed, including those more closely related to psychotic symptoms, making it improbable that anxiolytic action was solely responsible for the antipsychotic effect. The drug was well tolerated during the study, and no Parkinson-like symptom was reported. The results, therefore, suggest that CBD may indeed possess antipsychotic properties devoid of Parkinson-like side effects. The presence of such properties may explain, as suggested by Rottanburg et al. (1982), the finding that patients admitted to a psychiatric hospital in South Africa show a much higher frequency of acute psychotic episodes associated with the use of Cannabis sativa than in other countries. Cannabidiol is virtually absent from the plant variety in that region. (Turner and Hadley 1973).

Concluding Remarks

The studies reviewed here suggest that CBD may possess anxiolytic and antipsychotic properties. More research efforts, however, are needed to ascertain a role for CBD in our therapeutic armamentarium. Larger, controlled, and double-blind clinical studies on patients suffering from anxiety and schizophrenia are clearly needed to confirm the anxiolytic and antipsychotic properties suggested by our initial findings. Preclinical studies, on the other hand, should concentrate on the elucidation of possible mechanisms of the actions of CBD. Such knowledge may help to develop new and more potent drugs with potential for clinical use.

References

Agurell, S., S. Carlsson, J.E. Lindgren, A. Ohlsson, H. Gillespie, and L. Hollister. 1981. Interactions of delta-9-tetrahydrocannabinol with cannabinol and cannabidiol following oral administration in man: Assay of cannabinol and cannabidiol by mass fragmentography. *Experientia* 37 (10): 1090–1092.

Borgen, L.A., and W.M. Davis. 1974. Cannabidiol interaction with delta-9-tetrahydrocannabinol. *Research Commununications in Chemical Patholology and Pharmacology* 7 (4): 663–670.

Bornhein, L.M., H.K. Borys, and R. Karler. 1981. Effect of cannabidiol on cytochrome P-450 and hexobarbital sleep time. *Biochemical Pharmacology* 30 (5): 503–507.

Carlini, E.A., J.R. Leite, M. Tannhauser, and A.C. Berardi (1973. Cannabidiol and Cannabis sativa extract protect mice and rats against convulsive agents. *Journal of Pharmacy and Pharmacology* 25 (8): 664–665.

Carlini, E.A., J. Masur, and C.C.P.B. Magalhães. 1979. Possível efeito hipnotico do canabidiol no ser humano: Estudo preliminar (Possible hypnotic effect of cannabidiol in man: Preliminary study). *Ciência e Cultura* 31: 315–322.

Carlini, E.A., M. Santos, V. Claussen, D. Bieniek, and F. Korte. 1970. Structure activity relationship of four tetrahydrocannabinols and the pharmacological activity of five semipurified extracts of Cannabis sativa. *Psychopharmacologia (Berl)* 18 (1): 82–93.

Colasanti, B.K., R.E. Brown, and C.R. Craig. 1984. Ocular hypotension, ocular toxicity, and neurotoxicity in response to marihuana extract and cannabidiol. *General Pharmacology* 15: 479–484.

Consroe, P., J. Laguna, J. Allender, S. Snider, L. Stern, R. Sandyk, K. Kennedy, and K. Schram. 1991. Controlled clinical trial of cannabidiol in Huntington's disease. *Pharmacology Biochemistry and Behavior* 40: 701–708.

Cunha, J., E.A. Carlini, A.E. Pereira, O.L. Ramos, C. Pimentel, R. Gagliardi, W.L. Sanvito, N. Lander, and R. Mechoulam. 1980. Chronic administration of cannabidiol to healthy volunteers and epileptic patients. *Pharmacology* 21 (3): 175–185.

Dalton, W.S., R. Martz, L. Lemberger, B.E. Rodda, and R.B. Forney. 1976. Influence of cannabidiol on delta-9-tetrahydrocannabinol effects. *Clinical Pharmacology and Therapeutics* 19 (3): 300–309.

Davis, W.M., and L.A. Borgen. 1974. Effects of cannabidiol and delta-9-tetrahydrocannabinol on operant behavior. *Research Communications in Chemical Pathology and Pharmacology* 9 (3): 453–462.

Dewey, W.L. 1986. Cannabidiol pharmacology. *Pharmacology Review* 38: 151–178.

Fernandes, M., A. Schabarek, H. Coper, and R. Hill. 1974. Modification of delta-9-THC actions by cannabinol and cannabidiol in the rat. *Psychopharmacologia (Berl.)* 38 (4): 329–338.

Grlie, L. 1976. A comparative study on some chemical and biological characteristics of various samples of cannabis resin. *Bulletin on Narcotics* 14: 37–46.

Guimarães, F.S., T.M. Chiaretti, F.G. Graeff, and A.W. Zuardi. 1990. Antianxiety effect of cannabidiol in the elevated plus-maze. *Psychopharmacology* 100 (4): 558–559.

Guimarães, F.S., J.C. de Aguiar, R. Mechoulam, and A. Breuer. 1994. Anxiolytic effect of cannabidiol derivatives in the elevated plus-maze. *General Pharmacology* 25: 161–164.

Hollister, L.E., and H. Gillespie. 1975. Interactions in man of delta-9-tetrahydrocannabinol: II. Cannabinol and cannabidiol. *Clinical Pharmacology and Therapeutics* 18 (1): 80–83.

Howlett, A.C., D. Evans, and D.B. Houston. 1992. The cannabinoid receptor. In *Marijuana/Cannabinoids: Neurobiology and Neurophysiology*, ed. L. Murphy and A. Bartke, 35–72. Boca Raton, FL: CRC Press.

Izquierdo, I., O.A. Orsingher, and A.C. Berardi. 1973. Effect of cannabidiol and other *Cannabis sativa* compounds on hippocampal seizure discharges. *Psychopharmacologia* 28 (1): 95–102.

Jones, G., and R.G. Pertwee. 1972. A metabolic interaction in vivo between cannabidiol and delta-1-tetrahydrocannabinol. *British Journal of Pharmacology* 45 (2): 375–377.

Karniol, I.G., and E.A. Carlini. 1973. Pharmacological interaction between cannabidiol and delta-9-tetrahydrocannabinol. *Psychopharmacologia (Berl.)* 33 (1): 53–70.

Karniol, I.G., I. Shirakawa, N. Kasinski, A. Pfeferman, and E.A. Carlini. 1974. Cannabidiol interferes with the effects of delta-9-tetrahydrocannabinol in man. *European Journal of Pharmacology* 28 (1): 172–177.

Kubena, R.K., and H. Barry, III. 1972. Stimulus characteristics of marihuana components. *Nature* 235 (5338): 397–398.

Melges, F.T., J.R. Tinklenberg, C.M. Deardorff, N.H. Davies, R.E. Anderson, and C.A. Owen. 1974. Temporal disorganization and delusional-like ideation. *Archives of General Psychiatry* 30 (6): 855–861.

Meyer, R.E. 1978. Behavioral pharmacology of marihuana. In *Psychopharmacology: A Generation of Progress*, ed. M.A. Lipton, A. Dimascio and K.F. Killam, 1634–1652. New York: Raven Press.

Mincis, M., A. Pfeferman, R.X. Guimarães, O.L. Ramos, E. Zukerman, I.G. Karniol, and E.A. Carlini. 1973. Administração cornica de cannabidiol em seres humanos (Chronic administration of cannabidiol in human beings). *Res. Assoc. Med. Brasil* 19: 185–190.

Monti, J.M. 1977. Hypnotic-like effects of cannabidiol in the rat. *Psychopharmacology* 55 (3): 263–265.

Musty, R.E., L.H. Conti, and R. Mechoulam. 1984. Anxiolytic properties of cannabidiol. In *Marihuana '84: Proceedings of the Oxford Symposium on Cannabis*, ed. D.J. Harvey. 713–719. Oxford: IRL Press.

Onaivi, E.S., M.R. Green, and B.R. Martin. 1990. Pharmacological characterization of cannabinoids in the elevated plus maze. *Journal of Pharmacology and Experimental Therapeutics* 253: 1002–1009.

Paton, W.D.M., and R.G. Pertwee. 1972. Effect of cannabis and certain of its constituents on pentobarbitone sleeping time and phenazone metabolism. *British Journal of Pharmacology* 44 (2): 250–261.

Pellow, S., P. Chopin, S.E. File, and M. Briley. 1985. Validation of open:closed arm entries in an elevated plus-maze as a measure of anxiety in the rat. *Journal of Neuroscience Methods.* 14: 149–167.

Pickens, J.T. 1981. Sedative activity of cannabis in relation to its delta-1-*trans*-tetrahydrocannabinol and cannabidiol content. *British Journal of Pharmacology* 72 (4): 649–656.

Rottanburg, D., A.H. Robins, O. Ben-Arie, A. Teggin, and R. Elk, 1982. Cannabis-associated psychosis with hypomanic features. *Lancet* 2 (8312): 1364–1366.

Silveira Filho, N.G., and S. Tufik. 1981. Comparative effects between cannabidiol and diazepam on neophobia, food intake, and conflict behavior. *Research Communications in Psychology, Psychiatry and Behavior* 6: 25–26.

Tassinari, C.A., G. Ambrosetto, M.R. Peraita-Adrados, and H. Gestaut. 1976. The neuropsychiatric syndrome of delta-9-tetrahydrocannabinol and cannabis intoxication in naive subjects: A clinical and polygraphic study during wakefulness and sleep. In *The Pharmacology of Marihuana*, ed. M.C. Braude and S. Szara, 357–375. New York: Raven Press.

Turner, C.E. and K. Hadley. 1973. Constituents of *Cannabis sativa* L. II. Absence of cannabidiol in an African variant. *Journal of Pharmaceutical Sciences* 62: 251–255.

Zuardi, A.W., R.A. Cosme, F.G. Graeff, and F.S. Guimarães. 1993. Effects of ipsapirone and cannabidiol on human experimental anxiety. *Journal of Psychopharmacology* 7: 82–88.

Zuardi, A.W., E. Finkelfarb, O.F.A. Bueno, R.E. Musty, and I.G. Karniol. 1981. Characteristics of the stimulus produced by the mixture of cannabidiol with delta-9-tetrahydrocannabinol. *Archives Internationales de Pharmacodynamie et de Therapie* 249 (1): 137–146.

Zuardi, A.W., F.S. Guimarães, and A.C. Moreira. 1993. Effect of cannabidiol on plasma prolactin, growth hormone, and cortisol in human volunteers. *Brazil Journal of Medical Biology Research* 26: 213–217.

Zuardi, A.W., and I.G. Karniol. 1983. Changes in the conditioned emotional response of rats induced by delta-9-THC, CBD and mixture of the two cannabinoids. *Arquivas de Biologia Tecnologia* 26: 391–397.

Zuardi, A.W., and I.G. Karniol. 1983. Effects of variable interval performance in rats of delta-9-tetrahydrocannabinol and cannabidiol, separately and in combination. *Brazilian Journal of Medical and Biological Research* 16: 141–146.

Zuardi, A.W., S.L. Morais, F.S. Guimarães, and R. Mechoulam. 1995. Antipsychotic effect of cannabidiol. *Journal of Clinical Psychiatry* 56 (10): 485–486.

Zuardi, A.W., J.A. Rodrigues, and J.M. Cunha. 1991. Effects of cannabidiol in animal models predictive of antipsychotic activity. *Psychopharmacology* 104: 260–264.

Zuardi, A.W., I. Shirakawa, E. Finkelfarb, and I. Karniol. 1982. Action of cannabidiol on the anxiety and other effects produced by delta-9-THC in normal subjects. *Psychopharmacology* 76 (3): 245–250.

Zuardi, A.W., N.A. Teixeira, and I.G. Karniol. 1984. Pharmacological interaction of the effects of delta-9-tetrahydrocannabinol and cannabidiol on serum corticosterone levels in rats. *Archives Internationales de Pharmacodynamie et de Therapie* 269 (1): 12–19.

13

Dosage and Administration of Cannabis

MADELYN Z. BRAZIS
and MARY LYNN MATHRE

As nurses, we are educated to administer and monitor the effects of medications and to educate patients about the safe and responsible use of their medications. Many medications can be quite toxic if used incorrectly or if inadvertently given to the wrong patient. With this understanding, nurses are aware of the importance of ensuring that patients receive the right medication, in the right dose, at the right time, and in the right form. To provide a framework for this chapter, we will simply ask some questions—the same basic questions patients should ask before using *any* medication. We will follow up with a description of cannabis administration to cancer patients.

What Is the Drug?

Cannabis is a natural plant with various cannabinoids and with varying amounts of these compounds found in its leaves, leaf buds and flowering tops. Its illegality can be a serious concern for the user because there is no assurance of quality control. It could be contaminated with pesticides, mold, bacteria, or other adulterants such as PCP. To avoid the danger of getting contaminated medicine, some people choose to grow their own cannabis. As noted in Krampf's chapter, cannabis buyers clubs have been organized by patients to assist in supplying other patients with clean, non-contaminated marijuana.

The THC pill is not synonymous with marijuana or cannabis. The THC pill is a synthetic form of just one of the 60 cannabinoids found in the cannabis

Madelyn (Katy) Z. Brazis, B.S.N., R.N., M.A., is a senior clinical research associate monitoring pharmaceutical clinical trials.
Mary Lynn Mathre, R.N., M.S.N., C.A.R.N., is an addictions consultant at the University of Virginia Medical Center in Charlottesville.

plant, the one believed to be the most psychoactive. It is a Schedule II drug and is available only by prescription.

What Are the Therapeutic Effects, Side Effects and Adverse Consequences of Cannabis?

Every medication available for prescription in the United States undergoes rigorous and often exhausting research evaluation before it is released to the general public in order to demonstrate that the medication has therapeutic benefit and that it is safe. Each medication is tested for therapeutic effects, side effects and adverse effects, and the appropriate dosing level is determined. Like any other medicine, cannabis or THC has many effects. And as with any other medicine, the patient should understand the potential risks and benefits of cannabis before using it so that the decision to use cannabis can be made by a careful evaluation of the risks and benefits.

THERAPEUTIC EFFECTS

An effect is therapeutic if it treats the problem or helps reach a goal. For example, cannabis may have the effect of appetite stimulation along with decreasing nausea, and therefore it may enhance weight gain. For cancer and AIDS patients who cannot maintain weight or suffer from the debilitating nausea and vomiting side effects of chemotherapy this is a major victory and would be considered a therapeutic effect of cannabis. For a glaucoma patient using cannabis, its ability to lower intraocular pressure would be considered the therapeutic effect, and appetite stimulation may be considered a side effect. In general, patients will experience the therapeutic effect with their first trial use. This is of great benefit, because the patient can soon determine whether or not to continue to use it and need not waste time trying to determine the most effective dose if the medication is not helpful. The preceding chapters discussed many of the therapeutic effects of cannabis.

SIDE EFFECTS

Side effects are effects accompanying the indicated therapeutic effect and are more of a nuisance and not usually a cause for concern. As with many medications, side effects from marijuana may or may not occur depending on such variables as dose, absorption factors, the environment, and attitudinal mindset of the patient. Potential side effects of THC/cannabis include:

Euphoria: A feeling of well-being or elation that may be accompanied by talkativeness, spontaneous laughter, or quiet introspection. It is usually at its most intense about 20 minutes after inhaling marijuana. This "high" is not necessary in order to obtain other therapeutic benefits, and patients may often develop a tolerance to the "high" but not to the therapeutic effects. For many patients trying to cope with the stress of a life threatening illness such as AIDS or cancer, this side effect may be therapeutic as well.

Drowsiness: Persons frequently complain of feeling sleepy after using marijuana. For this reason it is important for patients to avoid driving a car or operating dangerous equipment when using cannabis. Patients are easily aroused and this side effect is often dose related. As patients adjust to this medicine a dose can usually be achieved without causing drowsiness.

Conjunctival reddening of the eye: This "red eye" is due to a temporary dilation of the blood vessels of the lining of the eyeball. It is caused by systemic effects of THC, not cannabis smoke irritation.

Tachycardia or rapid heart rate: This is often dose related and due to the response of the sympathetic nervous system to the chemical constituents of THC. The "heart pounding" usually starts within 20 minutes and stops within 45 minutes after the THC dose (Kanakis et al. 1979). This may be a risk to persons with angina or other cardiac problems, and consequently should be used with caution under medical supervision.

Increased appetite: Commonly called "the munchies," an increased appetite often occurs within 10 to 60 minutes of taking marijuana. This can be a worrisome side effect for persons struggling to keep extra pounds off.

Dry Mouth: Patients are encouraged to have a beverage available to decrease this mild discomfort.

In addition to the above side effects, less common effects include an alteration in the perception of the passage of time in that it seems slower, sensory or perceptual distortions, mood changes ranging from a very relaxed state to anxiety or panic, a raising or lowering of the blood pressure, and dizziness. Research by Perez-Reyes et al. indicates that smoking high potency cannabis or taking more than 35mg of oral THC may cause dizziness when standing up quickly and a slow heart beat (vasovagal syndrome) (1990).

ADVERSE EFFECTS

Cannabis in doses exceeding the therapeutic levels or in individuals who are specifically vulnerable to its effects may lead to the experience of an adverse effect. Adverse effects are those that may be detrimental to the patient. Depression, hallucinations, paranoia, depersonalization, and confusion have been reported by a small percentage of people during or after cannabis use. These effects generally only last as long as the effects of the cannabis and are best treated by reassuring the patient and by providing a supportive and calm environment. No medication is required to counteract the adverse effects, although administration of aspirin, ibuprofen, or other non-steroidal anti-inflammatory drugs may help (Perez-Reyes et al. 1991). However, in cases where these symptoms are exhibited, the patient should probably discontinue the use of cannabis or THC.

What Is the Correct Dose?

Dosage is the most complex and important factor in using a medication and is the most frequent cause of serious injury or death from medications. Correct dosage includes the correct *amount* of the drug as well as the *route* and *frequency* of administration. As stated previously, cannabis has a very wide margin of safety and it is virtually impossible to overdose on it. However, other risks can be reduced by determining the lowest effective dose.

INHALED CANNABIS

When medicine is inhaled, it is immediately absorbed into the blood stream through the enormous network of capillaries in the lungs, and in less than a minute it reaches the target area in the brain where it can produce the therapeutic effect. Studies on the psychoactive effects of inhaled cannabis indicate that they begin within five to ten minutes, peak in about an hour, and last for approximately three hours. The amount of delta-9-THC in cannabis determines the strength and potential for mind-altering effects.

When smoking cannabis the dose received can be altered within limits by changing how much smoke is inhaled, the time between inhalations, and the number of inhalations taken. Other factors that affect the actual amount of THC and other cannabinoids being inhaled include the strength of the cannabis smoked, the amount of unchanged THC present in the smoke inhaled (the amount not burned up by fire), the amount lost in sidestream smoke, the method of use (cigarette or pipe), and the amount of THC trapped in the mucosal lining of the mouth and airway on the way to the lungs (Huestis et al. 1992; Perez-Reyes 1990). It is believed that a person receives less than 50 percent of the THC content of cannabis cigarettes since part is destroyed in the burning process (pyrolysis) and part is lost in the smoke (Lemberger et al. 1972). One study showed 20 to 30 percent of the THC was lost during pyrolysis and 40 to 50 percent was lost in sidestream smoke, allowing less than 40 percent of the THC to reach the lungs (Perez-Reyes 1990).

Breath-holding during cannabis inhalation has been a habitual practice of many cannabis smokers. Research indicates that breath-holding for ten seconds can increase the plasma THC level over no breath-holding, but there is no significant increase in the plasma level for breath-holding longer than ten seconds (Azorlosa et al. 1995). Another study suggests that cannabis smokers could still achieve adequate plasma levels while lowering their exposure to carbon monoxide and other possibly toxic smoke constituents by limiting breath-holding (Zacny and Chait 1990).

The potency of THC can range from less than 0.1 percent in non-psychoactive hemp-type cannabis (grown for its stalk), to over 10 percent in extremely potent cannabis (sinsemilla). The higher the percentage of THC, the higher the likelihood of increased psychoactive effects (euphoria or dysphoria). There are reports of higher potency cannabis having been developed and a more dangerous drug thus being on the market. These reports are not true. The reality is that persons growing cannabis have developed their knowledge and growing skills and have learned to grow sinsemilla (seedless female plants) that develop flowers rather than seeds. These flowering tops or buds have a higher THC content than the leaves (Mikuriya and Aldrich 1988). Smoking these flowers can provide the same amount of THC with much less consumption of smoke required. Robert Randall smokes ten marijuana cigarettes a day to control his intraocular pressure. If he could get more potent cannabis, he might only need to smoke a fraction of that amount and could thus decrease the potentially harmful side effects from smoking.

For some patients the higher THC content may not mean more therapeutic value. The various combinations of cannabinoids seem to be a significant factor in the therapeutic effectiveness. One study examined the effects of the three main cannabinoids: THC, cannabidiol or CBD (a reputed biochemical precursor of THC), and cannabinol or CBN (the immediate degradation product of THC). Pure forms of these cannabinoids were injected into human subjects. For THC, the researchers found that 20 mcg per kilogram of body weight was the average minimum amount to induce a "high," and 50 mcg per kilogram was the average maximum amount. For CBN, the amounts were 200 and 270 mcg per kilogram respectively. No high was reported with CBD. However, other studies indicate that CBD can have a significant interaction with THC (Karniol et al. 1974; Perez-Reyes 1973). It appears that the CBN and CBD can increase the sedative effects of THC and block the excitant effects (the "high"). As the CBD content approaches that of THC, the "high" will be diminished in its intensity, but the effects are prolonged. These findings indicate various plant hybrids may assist in identifying particular strains for specific therapeutic effects. Further research is needed to determine the most effective combinations for desired effects.

Autotitration is the key advantage to smoking cannabis. Because the effects are so rapid in onset, the patient can easily determine how much to inhale to achieve an effective dose. The few patients legally prescribed medicinal marijuana receive their cannabis in prescription form and are aware of the THC content. Patients who rely on illegal access to marijuana have no way of determining the potency but can easily determine if a new supply is stronger or weaker and can adjust their intake accordingly. Patients who choose to grow their own can have the reassurance that all cannabis from the same plant will be similar in potency. In any case, a patient should wait several minutes between inhalations of smoke in order to prevent taking more than necessary.

Cannabis is commonly smoked in cigarette form or "joints" (the self-rolled cigarettes) and with this method the user also inhales the chemicals contained in the burning paper. Patients may prefer to smoke cannabis in a pipe because it avoids inhalation of the chemicals in the papers.

The water pipe (hookah) or bong offer other methods to inhale cannabis. With the water pipe, cannabis smoke is cooled by water and the larger particles are filtered out before the smoke is inhaled. Water pipes facilitate the use of small amounts of higher potency cannabis. Bongs operate similarly, but are designed to deliver single inhalations of smoke per pipe bowl followed by a wash of fresh air to the lungs. There are numerous designs for water pipes and bongs, but the basic principle is the same. Both are classified as drug paraphernalia in many states and are illegal to purchase or possess. Only four states (Alaska, Iowa, North Dakota and South Carolina) are without some form of paraphernalia law (Burris et al. 1996).

Decreasing the amount of smoke inhaled is necessary because of the pulmonary risks associated with smoking. Despite the potential negative health consequences related to smoking cannabis, the patient and the healthcare provider should also realize that the cannabis-smoking patient inhales only a fraction of the smoke that a cigarette smoker does. Additional research directed toward limiting any health risks of smoking cannabis should be undertaken.

Hopefully, an aerosol or nebulizer method can be developed that would allow for the quick onset of action and the patient's ability to autotitrate but would also keep the burning smoke and other chemicals from being inhaled. In the meantime, if patients use a pipe or water pipe, it should be cleaned regularly to decrease the tarry buildup and other contaminants that adhere to

Top: *Various types of pipes used to smoke small amounts of cannabis.* Bottom: *"Bongs" used to smoke cannabis. The stem of the pipe is below the water line and the top serves as the mouthpiece from which the patient inhales. On the left is a commercial glass bong. The bong on the right is homemade using a graduated cylinder. Both photos supplied by I-CARE.*

the mouthpiece and accumulate in the water. Rubbing alcohol (pure grain alcohol) is a good solvent to use in cleaning any smoking device.

ORAL CANNABIS

Most medicines ingested by mouth take at least 20 to 30 minutes to become absorbed. The effects are experienced more slowly, are more variable, are of longer duration, and the response cannot be altered minute by minute. With the THC pills, the psychological effects begin within 30 to 60 minutes, peak at approximately three hours, and usually last more than four hours (Lemberger et al. 1972).

Prior to the Marihuana Tax Act of 1937, various pharmaceutical companies marketed a tincture of cannabis — cannabis extract prepared in an alcohol base. Eli Lilly and Company's Tincture *Cannabis indica* contained: "Fl. ext. *Cannabis indica*, Lilly, 1⅜ fl. ozs.; alcohol, 14⅜ fl. ozs." Without great concern for overdose but with the intent to minimize side effects, the directions for use were: "Dose, 10 minims, increased til its effects are experienced" (10 minims equal 0.6 ml, usually taken by dropper).

Patients who do not want to smoke cannabis may take it orally in tea, brownies, or cookies. Jamaican women frequently make a ganja tea using fresh cannabis leaves. When baking cannabis, it has been found that sautéing the cannabis in butter before adding it to the batter decreases the haylike flavor and changes the consistency to make it more palatable as well as extracting it efficiently. Another method of ingestion may be the use of a cannabis butter.

The THC pill Marinol (dronabinol) comes in 2.5, 5, and 10 mg capsules. As with the oral cannabis, it is more difficult to titrate the dosage because of the delayed onset of action. Based on anecdotal comments from patients who have tried both inhaled cannabis and oral THC, there seem to be more complaints of dysphoria and or hallucinations with the pill.

OTHER ROUTES OF ADMINISTRATION

Dr. West discussed the ophthalmic preparation of cannabis, Canasol, that is being used in some countries for glaucoma. Because the desired effect is to decrease intraocular pressure, eyedrops delivering the medication directly to the area of intent can maximize this effect and minimize other effects.

Other routes of administration include rectal by suppositories and topical with salves and compresses. There is a salve preparation available that is recommended for minor burns and cuts.

FREQUENCY

Depending on the desired effect, a patient may need to use cannabis on a continual basis to maintain a therapeutic level as with glaucoma. For patients with a seizure disorder or frequent spasticity problems, a regular pattern of use (e.g., every four hours) may be preferred to prevent symptoms from occurring. Other patients may use cannabis on an "as needed" basis, such as before chemotherapy to control the nausea and vomiting. Cannabis may be used prior to meals if the desired effect is to increase the appetite.

Marinol has been approved for use as an antiemetic for chemotherapy-induced nausea and vomiting, and in March 1993 it was also approved as an appetite stimulant for AIDS patients with the wasting syndrome. *The Physicians Desk Reference*'s (PDR) recommendation for Marinol administration as an antiemetic is: "an initial dose of 5 mg given one to three hours before treatment, then every two to four hours after treatment for a total of 4–6 doses per day." The patient should start at the lowest dosage and adjust the dose in small increments until the therapeutic effect is obtained. The recommended daily dose of Marinol as an appetite stimulant is: "two 2.5 mg. capsules; one before lunch and one before dinner." Marinol is available by prescription in a one-month supply of sixty 2.5 mg capsules. The cost is $150 per month or greater; however, the manufacturer, Roxane Pharmaceuticals, offers an assistance program for indigent AIDS patients.[1]

What About Interactions with Other Drugs?

A drug interaction should always be considered when taking more than one medication or drug. A problem with patients using cannabis is that they may not report their use of it to their healthcare provider because of its illegality, and therefore their healthcare provider may not be aware of the possible interactions (Mathre 1985).

Cannabis and THC have been shown to alter the absorption and elimination of other drugs (Benowitz and Jones 1977, Paton and Pertwee 1972). Because of possible additive or synergistic action, cannabis should not be used in combination with alcohol, sedatives, or sleeping pills since that would increase sedation. For patients using theophylline, cannabis will increase the metabolic processing of that drug (Jusko et al. 1979).

Griffith's *Complete Guide to Prescription and Nonprescription Drugs* is a great reference for possible interactions of drugs. Under each medication listed, up-to-date information is provided about possible drug interactions, including mention of possible interactions with marijuana.

Am I Allergic to Cannabis?

This possibility should be considered with any drug. An allergic reaction may be as mild as an upset stomach, could manifest as a rash or it could be as serious as impaired breathing that requires emergency care. Despite its

---

[1]*Information about Roxane Pharmaceuticals' assistance program is available at 1-800-274-8651.*

widespread use throughout history, hypersensitivity or allergic reactions to cannabis have rarely been reported (Liskow et al. 1971, Kagen et al. 1983, Añibarro and Fontella 1996). Cannabis has been identified as the possible cause of some occupational respiratory diseases (Zuskin et al. 1990, Vidal et al. 1991).

If a person is aware of an allergy to cannabis, as with other medication allergies, this should be included in the patient's record and future use should be avoided. Without access to a known source of unadulterated cannabis a patient may suffer an allergic reaction to the additivies. If chemicals are utilized in the growing process of the cannabis plant, patients may also be at risk for an allergic reaction to the chemical; therefore, organically grown cannabis is recommended.

Will I Develop Tolerance to the Effects?

Drug tolerance means that if a drug is used frequently and regularly over time increasing doses will be required to produce the same effects. In regard to the medical use of marijuana patients have found that tolerance to the therapeutic effects develops more slowly, if at all, than tolerance to the "high" and other side effects. Robert Randall has been successfully using the same amount of marijuana for more than 20 years to control his intraocular pressure. (For more detailed information see Chapter 15.)

Will I Develop Physical Dependence to Cannabis?

Physical dependence means that if a drug is used over time in a sufficiently high dose on a regular basis, the person will experience withdrawal symptoms if the drug is abruptly withheld. This will be covered in greater detail in the chapter on dependence and addiction. For patients using marijuana as a medicine, abrupt cessation of cannabis use will not cause any severe withdrawal symptoms, and they do not need to be concerned about this issue.

How Should Cannabis Be Stored

Once cannabis is harvested, the potency will deteriorate if the plant is not stored properly. Tetrahydrocannabinol oxidizes to cannabinol rapidly in samples stored at room temperature, and the concentration of THC may decrease at a rate of 10 percent per year (Starks 1977). It is best to leave the plants uncleaned (with small stems and seeds) in storage rather than manicuring it or crushing it, which would increase exposure to air and thus accelerate the deterioration process.

Dampness is another factor that should be avoided because of the possibility of the cannabis getting moldy, especially with Aspergillus, specifically *A. flavus* or *A. fumigatis*. To prevent mold, the cannabis must be dried properly and should not be stored in plastic bags. For most persons with a healthy immune system, the body can resist infection and is not in danger from exposure to aspergillus. However, in AIDS patients and other patients with a compromised immune system, moldy cannabis might cause serious and possibly fatal lung infections if the spores are inhaled (Sutton et al. 1986). At the Boston University School of Medicine, it was determined that baking cannabis at 300°F (150°C) for 15 minutes would destroy the aspergillus fungi (Levitz and Diamond 1991). This procedure is recommended for immuno-compromised patients to avoid accidental inhalation of undetected mold.

Temperature and light are additional factors that can affect the potency. Cooler temperatures slow the deterioration process. Exposure to light should be limited. Cannabis stored over a one-year period had a decrease in THC of 36 percent in the light compared to a 13 percent decrease when stored in the dark. Dark glass bottles or metal tins are preferred containers. In summary, recommended storage is in an airtight, opaque container kept in a cool location. For long-term storage, the freezer may be preferred.

Administration of Marijuana During the Lynn Pierson Study

On the morning of the first marijuana treatment, the chemotherapy nurse notified Brazis (the research nurse,) of the patient's presence in the treatment room. The pharmacy was presented with a prescription for either marijuana cigarettes or THC capsules, depending on the previously discussed choice made by the patient. The marijuana for the study was provided by the National Institute on Drug Abuse. The cannabis was (and still is) grown at the University of Mississippi by the Research Institute of Pharmaceutical Sciences. The marijuana cigarettes were manufactured on a modified tobacco cigarette machine and were stored partially dehydrated and frozen at the Research Triangle Institute, North Carolina. The marijuana cigarettes came in 10-inch round tin cans each containing 50 or 100 cigarettes, each weighing 800 to 900 mg. Because of the storage method, NIDA recommended humidifying the cigarettes at room temperature prior to use. The cigarettes had been irradiated to assure that no fungus or other contaminant was present so as to avoid the respiratory consequences of inhaling moldy marijuana. A typical prescription for cigarettes read: "THC Cigarettes #12: Smoke one cigarette every 4 to 6 hours as needed for nausea and vomiting."

The oral THC came in capsules containing 5 milligrams (mg) of THC extract dissolved in sesame oil, packaged in amber bottles each containing 25 capsules. The prescription for capsules read: "THC Capsules #30: Take one to three capsules every 4 to 6 hours as needed for nausea and vomiting." In this way the patient could titrate the dosage in order to achieve the most therapeutic

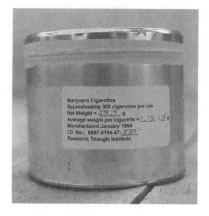

Marijuana cigarettes manufactured for the NIDA by the Research Triangle Institute. Photos supplied by I-CARE.

response while avoiding potential side effects. The amount prescribed was limited to the amount needed for one cycle of chemotherapy.

The NIDA research marijuana used in this study contained 2 percent THC. If the patient selected THC capsules rather than cigarettes, the dosage was three 5 mg capsules given orally approximately 30 minutes before chemotherapy treatment. Additional lead time was required with the capsules in order to assure adequate gastrointestinal absorption and release of the medicine into the blood stream.

If the patient had selected marijuana cigarettes, he or she was taken to a quiet, well-ventilated room, or, in nice weather, outside to a patio near the hospital or doctor's office. This was done in order to assure privacy and confidentiality, and to prevent sidestream smoke from reaching nearby office air vents. In a study done several years later on passive smoke exposure, it was determined that the behavioral effects of passive exposure to smoke of 16 marijuana cigarettes in a small, unventilated room was equal to that observed after the active smoking of one marijuana cigarette (Cone 1990). Since patients on the program used only one cigarette every four to six hours at a rate of one to three inhalations at a time, sidestream smoke was kept to a minimum.

During the initial visit the patient was instructed to inhale as much of an entire marijuana cigarette as possible, holding each inhalation for the count of ten. The smoking of the cigarette would occur ten minutes before chemotherapy treatment. During the study, family members and friends of the patient were not permitted in the room during the actual smoking process to avoid unintentional respiratory exposure. The patient was reminded to avoid sidestream smoke exposure to family members at home and to use discretion when utilizing marijuana in public settings for relief of vomiting.

For hospitalized patients, smoking marijuana in a hospital room was a novel experience; however, with the advent of the program, most of the healthcare providers who came in contact with the patient became quickly aware and supportive of the program. For individuals who received treatment in clinics, marijuana between visits was usually taken at home or in a clinic room just before chemotherapy. Some patients expressed anxiety before their first marijuana treatment and asked many questions that were addressed before and during all phases of the treatment. Some patients asked whether they should tell their family, doctor, or boss about their participation in the program. It was essential that the treating physician be aware of the patient's treatment with marijuana as well as all other medications used by the patient in order to maximize the outcome of treatment and minimize the incidence of side effects related to drug interactions.

The common side effects were dealt with efficiently by supplying a thorough and complete explanation of why and how they occur, how long they would last and treatment options. Patients were comforted and satisfied if they knew exactly how, what, why, when, and where they would receive treatment. It is of great importance that the patient be allowed to maintain an element of control over his or her treatment and life. Doing so ensures treatment compliance and reduces the fear of the unknown.

If disturbing effects were experienced, the dosage was reduced or discontinued. Of over 200 patients in the Lynn Pierson Program, only three experienced adverse effects requiring medical intervention. Two had panic attacks and one had an episode of an extremely fast heartbeat.

First Chemotherapy-Marijuana Session

A patient was first evaluated by his or her oncologist to determine whether chemotherapy would be administered that day. If chemotherapy was prescribed, an intravenous line was inserted and the patient was then moved to the marijuana treatment room and given the marijuana as described above. After the marijuana was given, the patient was moved into the chemotherapy treatment room, at which time chemotherapy was infused through the IV line. Following the infusion, the patient was moved to a comfortable recliner or bed in the original private room where the initial dose of marijuana was taken. At specified intervals, the patient's blood pressure, pulse, and response to marijuana were closely monitored. Psychological questionnaires were used to assess the various effects of the marijuana treatment. The patient's THC blood levels were measured in samples of blood drawn from the IV line during the four-hour observation period. Because individual smoking patterns are different and the rate of absorption of THC capsules varies from inhaled marijuana, the best way to determine how much THC is actually absorbed is by measuring its level in the blood.

Brazis remained with the patient during the four-hour initial chemotherapy and marijuana session and discussed the normal and temporary nature of the particular responses as they were experienced by the patient. After using marijuana, some patients fell asleep; others became talkative or hungry. At the end of the four-hour observation period, the patient was given another dose of marijuana and a zip-lock bag containing the prescribed number of cigarettes or a bottle containing the prescribed number of THC capsules.

Since not all nausea and vomiting symptoms are equal, the amount and duration of the marijuana prescription was individualized based on the patient's report of the intensity and duration of the vomiting. Some patients received medicine for up to ten days, while other patients received only enough for four days. Additional prescriptions were dispensed if follow-up contact revealed a continuation of vomiting. If the patient declined further participation in the program, unused marijuana was returned to the pharmacy. If the patient remained on the program, frequent intermittent contact reassessed the response to the marijuana and the patient's well-being in general.

The dose of marijuana was adjusted by the patient to maintain the delicate balance between a therapeutic effect and minimal side effects. Once the patient became familiar with the effects of marijuana cigarettes, he or she had complete control over the dosing regimen. Some patients found that initially they needed to smoke an entire cigarette to obtain relief. They then supplemented the dose based on the perception of impending nausea. Some patients took one to two inhalations whenever they felt a tinge of nausea, without the initial dose of a complete cigarette. This provided enough relief until they experienced the next urge to vomit. The time intervals for marijuana or THC dosing were chosen to assure near-peak blood levels of the THC at the most likely time of onset of nausea and vomiting.

Patients who chose to smoke marijuana had the advantage of being able to titrate their drug effect and thus their marijuana exposure, whereas the effects of oral ingestion of marijuana take longer and do not allow enough reaction time for dosage adjustment. Some patients who began on the capsules but were unable to keep them in the stomach switched to cigarettes in order to attain initial relief. Capsules could then be reintroduced to maintain the relief.

The patients were cautioned not to operate machinery or drive during their use of marijuana. In most cases, family members were willing to transport them and provide support. During treatment some patients appreciated social interaction while others preferred to be alone.

Use of the THC capsules or marijuana before chemotherapy treatment was more helpful than use in response to imminent nausea. Once the vomiting had begun, some patients were unable to retain the capsules and did not feel well enough to smoke. The most difficult time for a patient undergoing chemotherapy seemed to be from three hours to five days after the treatment and one to two days before the next treatment. It became essential that patients used a preventive dosing regimen at least one day before receiving any treatments in order to develop an adequate blood level of the medicine and to avoid the development of anticipatory nausea and vomiting.

One 72-year-old female participating in the study, a retired teacher, decided that the marijuana grown by the government was much too dry and harsh. With her cane and her balding head wrapped in a turban, she went to a now illegal head shop. After questioning the entire store personnel, several of whom asked if she was an undercover narcotics agent, she purchased a water pipe. With this pipe she was able to cool the smoke, inhale less irritants, and increase the relief she experienced from smoking marijuana. In addition to the water pipe, this patient unrolled the cigarettes and used the marijuana to make brownies. According to Roger Roffman (1979), marijuana does not work if it is ingested in its raw form and some form of heating is necessary for the antinausea effect to occur. The THC in its natural form is a carboxylic acid, which is orally inactive. Heating it decarboxylates this compound to orally active THC.

There were no cases of overuse or requests for unjustified additional supplies. According to a later survey of patients who discontinued using either capsules or cigarettes, it appears that problems with capsules were more related to their inability to stop the vomiting while problems with cigarettes were associated with the mechanics of smoking and personal values.

The results of the study supported the use of marijuana cigarettes as well as capsules for the treatment of chemotherapy-induced nausea and vomiting. By the time the Lynn Pierson study came to an end in 1986, THC capsules, but not cigarettes, had become available to cancer patients by prescription as a result of a growing body of literature supporting the medicinal use of THC. Some of the study patients and their families expressed concern about the unavailability of marijuana cigarettes and stated that they would actively seek, purchase, or grow cannabis on their own.

References

Añibarro, B. and J.L. Fontela. 1996. Allergy to marihuana. *Allergy Net.* 200–201.

Azorlosa, J.L., M.K. Greenwald, and M.L. Stitzer. 1995. Marijuana smoking: Effects of varying puff volume and breathhold duration. *The Journal of Pharmacology and Experimental Therapeutics* 272 (20): 550–569.

Benowitz, N.L. and R.T. Jones. 1977. Effects of delta-9-tetrahydrocannabinol on drug distribution and metabolism: Antipyrine, pentobarbital, and ethanol. *Clinical Pharmacology and Therapeutics.* 22 (3): 259–268.

Burris, S., D. Finucane, H. Gallagher, and J. Grace. 1996. The legal strategies used in operating syringe exchange programs in the United States. *American Journal of Public Health.* 86 (8): 1161–1166.

Chait, L.D., and J. Pierri. 1989. Some physical characteristics of NIDA marijuana cigarettes. *Addictive Behaviors* 14: 61–67.

Cone, E.J. 1990. Marijuana effects and urinalysis after passive inhalation and oral ingestion. *NIDA Research Monograph* 99: 88–96.

Griffith, H.W. 1994. *Complete Guide to Prescription and Nonprescription Drugs*. New York: The Body Press/Perigee Books.

Huestis, M.A., A.H. Sampson, B.J. Holicky, J.E. Henningfield, and E.J. Cone. 1992. Characterization of the absorption phase of marijuana smoking. *Clinical Pharmacology and Therapeutics* 52 (1): 31–41.

Jusko, W.J., M.J. Gardner, A. Mangione, J.J. Schentag, J.R. Koup, and J.W. Vance. 1979. Factors affecting theophylline clearances: Age, tobacco, marijuana, cirrhosis, obesity, oral contraceptives, benzodiazepines, barbiturates, and ethanol. *Journal of Pharmaceutical Sciences*. 68 (11): 1358–1366.

Kagen, S.L., V.P. Kurup, P.G. Sohnle, and J.N. Fink. 1983. Marijuana smoking and fungal sensitization. *Journal of Allergy and Clinical Immunology* 71: 389–393.

Kanakis, C., J. Paijet, and K. Rosen. 1979. Lack of cardiovascular effects of delta-9-THC in chemically denervated men. *Annals of Internal Medicine* 91: 571–574.

Karniol, I.G., I. Shirakawa, N. Kasinski, A. Pfeferman, and E.A. Carlini. 1974. Cannabidiol interferes with the effects of delta-9-tetrahydrocannabinol in man. *European Journal of Pharmacology* 28 (1): 172–177.

Lemberger, L., J.L. Weiss, A.M. Watanabe, I.M. Galanter, R.J. Wyatt, and P.V. Cardon. 1972. Delta-9-tetrahdrocannabinol: Temporal correlation of the psychologic effects and blood levels after various routes of administration. *The New England Journal of Medicine* 286 (13): 685–688.

Levitz, S.M., and R.D. Diamond. 1991. Aspergillosis and marijuana. *Annals of Internal Medicine* 115 (7): 578–579.

Liskow, B., J.L. Liss, and C.W. Parker. 1971. Allergy to marihuana. *Annuls of Internal Medicine* 75: 571–573.

Mathre, M.L. 1985. Disclosure of Marijuana Use to Health Care Professionals. Unpublished master's thesis. Case Western Reserve University, Cleveland, OH.

Mattes, R.D., L.M. Shaw, J. Edling-Owens, K. Engelman, and M.A. Elsohly. 1993. Bypassing the first-pass effect for the therapeutic use of cannabinoids. *Pharmacology Biochemistry and Behavior* 44: 745–747.

Mikuriya, T.H., and M.R. Aldrich. 1988. Cannabis 1988: Old drug, new dangers—the potency question. *Journal of Psychoactive Drugs* 20 (1): 47–55.

Miller, M., and S. Burbank. 1995. *Teach Your Children Well: A Rational Guide to Family Drug Education*. Mosier, OR: Mothers Against Misuse and Abuse.

Paton, W.D.M., and R.G. Pertwee. 1972. Effect of cannabis and certain of its constituents on pentobarbitone sleeping time and phenazone metabolism. *British Journal of Pharmacology* 44 (2): 250–261.

Perez-Reyes, M. 1990. Marijuana smoking: Factors that influence the bioavailability of tetrahydrocannabinol. *NIDA Research Monograph* 99: 42–87.

Perez-Reyes, M., S.H. Burnstein, W.R. White, S.A. McDonald, and R.E. Hicks. 1991. Antagonism of marijuana effects by indomethacin. *Life Science* 48: 507–515.

Perez-Reyes, M., M.C. Timmons, K.H. Davis, and E.M. Wall. 1973. A comparison of the pharmacological activity in man of intravenously administered delta-9-tetrahydrocannabinol, cannabinol, and cannabidiol. *Experientia*. 29 (11): 1368–1369.

Roffman, R. 1982. *Marijuana as Medicine*. Seattle: Madrona Publishers.

Starks, M. (1977). *Marijuana Potency*. Berkeley, CA: And/Or Press.

Sutton, S., B.L. Lum, and F.M. Torti. 1986. Possible risk of invasive pulmonary aspergillosis with marijuana use during chemotherapy for small cell lung cancer. *Drug Intelligence and Clinical Pharmacy* 20: 289–290.

Vidal, C., R. Fuente, A. Iglesias, and A. Saez. 1991. Bronchial asthma due to *Cannabis sativa* seed. *Allergy* 46: 447–449.

Zacny, J.P., and L.D. Chait. 1990. Response to marijuana as a function of potency and breath-hold duration. *NIDA Research Monograph* 105: 308–309.

Zuskin, E., B. Kanceljak, D. Pokrajec, E.N. Schacter, and T.J. Witek. 1990. Respiratory symptoms and lung function in hemp workers. *British Journal of Indian Medicine* 47: 627–632.

Part IV
Special Considerations

14

Cannabis and Pregnancy

MELANIE C. DREHER

Background

Recently, a 1,600-year-old tomb explored by scientists from the Hebrew University in Jerusalem revealed a glimpse of the early obstetrical use of cannabis. These researchers recovered tiny amounts of delta-6-tetrahydro-cannabinol, a highly stable component of cannabis, in the abdominal area of a girl, about 14 years old, who apparently died in childbirth around A.D. 400 (Zias et al. 1993). Reports of the use of cannabis as a medicine appeared in an Egyptian papyrus from the sixteenth century B.C. In addition, medical texts from the nineteenth century held that cannabis increases the force of uterine contractions and reduces the pain of labor. Accounts from other cultures also have suggested the association of cannabis with pregnancy and perinatal health. Cambodian women who have just given birth, for example, are given a small glass of cannabis tea by the midwife before each meal in order to combat postpartum stiffness and to increase the milk supply of nursing mothers. Vietnamese women use cannabis tea for dysmenorrhea and to produce a feeling of well-being after childbirth.

In spite of this historical and cross-cultural evidence, medical research on cannabis has not focused on its potential therapeutic value in childbirth and pregnancy but rather on its possible damaging effects. Since the thalidomide tragedy, there has been widespread public concern about protecting pregnant women and their fetuses from the harmful effects of substances ingested during pregnancy. Today, the most commonly used illicit substance worldwide is cannabis. The United States Census Bureau estimates that 28 percent of Americans aged 18 to 25 use cannabis and that 10 percent of the

Melanie C. Dreher, R.N., Ph.D., F.A.A.N. is the dean of the College of Nursing of the University of Iowa in Iowa City.

women in that age group use it. Indeed, one of the questions pregnant women most frequently ask of obstetricians and nurse-midwives is whether or not they can continue to smoke cannabis. Yet it is one of the substances about which we know least.

As vulnerable populations, unborn fetuses have been legally protected from the experimental administration of drugs in research protocols. Therefore, much of the early research on the effects of prenatal cannabis exposure on pregnancy outcomes was conducted on primates and small mammals. Although there are several problems with drawing conclusions from animal studies and applying them to human populations, these very important studies have shown us that the psychoactive ingredient in cannabis, delta-9-THC, crosses the placenta. Since the blood supply of the placenta is rich, fairly large amounts of THC can be found there. Yet only relatively small amounts of the psychoactive ingredient actually cross the placental barrier to the fetus. The highest concentrations of THC that do cross the placental barrier are found in the fetal nervous system. Again, using non-human populations, researchers have also traced THC as it enters the milk of lactating animals and is transferred to the suckling offspring. There is, of course, reason to believe that the exposure of newborns to cannabis in breast milk may have effects. Since the period of greatest brain growth coincides with the nursing period, the potential for harmful substances to damage the brain suggests that the babies of mothers who smoke cannabis may be at risk.

More recently, medical research on cannabis has been conducted on human mothers and their offspring. Among these studies is research linking the use of cannabis to neurological abnormalities, poor maternal weight gain, duration and progress of labor, fetal distress, major malformations, length of gestation, and lower birth weight (Day et al. 1991; Fried 1982; Fried et al. 1984; Gibson et al. 1983; Greenland et al. 1982; Hingson et al. 1982; Linn et al. 1983; Zuckerman 1989). In 1980, Fried provided the first published data regarding the effects of perinatal cannabis use on the human neonate. The subjects of the study were 291 pregnant women of whom 57 were reported marijuana users before or during pregnancy. Eleven of the users were described as heavy users (an average of five or more cannabis cigarettes per week) and eight of those remained heavy users throughout the pregnancy. No relationship was found between cannabis use and the amount of weight a mother gained during pregnancy, the length of pregnancy, the duration of labor, birthweight, or the Apgar scores (a score assessing the physiological status of newborns). A significant increase of symptoms associated with nervous system abnormalities in the newborns was found, however, including the presence of a "*cri-de-chat*," a high-pitched cry indicating neurological abnormality or immaturity. Also, abnormal visual responses were found in two- or three-day-old newborns. Within one month, however, the infants of cannabis users could not be distinguished from the other infants except for the "*cri-de-chat*," and by the age of one year there were virtually no differences between exposed and nonexposed infants.

Since Fried's groundbreaking work, other studies have explored cannabis as a perinatal risk factor. The results of these studies, however, have been inconclusive and often contradictory mainly because it has been difficult to isolate the effects of cannabis from the many other variables that could influence the outcomes of pregnancy. The cannabis users in these studies generally had lower incomes and education, were more likely to represent a minority ethnic group, have less prenatal care, be multiple drug users, and have poorer health habits, nutrition, and social support than nonusers (Fried 1991; Richardson et al. 1989; Tennes et al. 1985). Greenland, for example, found cannabis users to have a greater incidence of abnormal progress of labor and a greater incidence of meconium staining—a sign of fetal distress (1982). When Greenland repeated his study, however, the results showed that when the mothers had better living standards, more education, and better prenatal care, there was no meconium staining (1983). Greenland's research demonstrates that clinical findings are extremely difficult to understand unless they are interpreted in relation to other lifestyle characteristics of the users. Even in Fried's research the dose-related effect was confounded by the association of heavy use with lower family income, lower education, and greater poly-drug use. In a subsequent study that included an additional 129 subjects, he identified characteristics of cannabis smokers that might have an adverse effect on newborn development. These included lower socioeconomic status, less formal education, less prenatal care, and a greater consumption of both alcohol and nicotine compared to the mothers not using cannabis.

Moreover, because of the legal and social sanctions against cannabis use, it has often been difficult to recruit subjects for these studies. Once recruited, it has been difficult to determine the validity of their reports about the amount and frequency of their use of cannabis and other illegal drugs. Hingson, for example, in a study of hundreds of women at Boston City Hospital, found a discrepancy between the verbal and biological reports of drug use (1986). The urine assays of THC revealed that more women smoked cannabis during pregnancy than were willing to admit it. The study also found that when women were told that their urine would be tested, they were more likely to increase the accuracy of their verbal reports.

Cross-Cultural Research—Why Jamaica?

Another important reason that studies of prenatal exposure have been so inconclusive is that virtually all of the research on prenatal cannabis exposure has been conducted in the United States and Canada, where cannabis is thought of almost exclusively in terms of its psychoactive properties—as a recreational drug. This perspective stands in marked contrast to societies in which cannabis has religious and medicinal functions. Research on cannabis conducted in other countries has shown us the importance of cultural factors in understanding the outcomes of cannabis use. We have learned, for example, from studies in Greece, Costa Rica, and Jamaica that concepts associated with cannabis use in this country such as the "amotivational syndrome" and the "stepping-stone hypothesis" simply do not hold up cross-culturally (Dreher 1982; Page et al. 1988; Comitas 1976).

One of the important contributions of anthropological research is to reexamine the assumptions and research findings of our own society by seeing whether they hold true in other societies. Jamaica was selected to study the use of cannabis during pregnancy because it is a society in which cannabis (or ganja, as it is called in Jamaica) has *not* been associated with the use of other illicit drugs and only minimally with the use of alcohol and tobacco. Furthermore, in Jamaica cannabis is not restricted to or thought of as just a recreational drug. Rather, it is considered an herb that has both religious and medicinal value. For members of the Rastafarian faith (a politico-religious movement in Jamaica), ganja is a sacred substance that is used in all religious and ceremonial activities. Even more pervasive in Jamaican society is the medicinal use of ganja. As part of an extensive repertoire of herbal remedies, ganja teas, tonics, and poultices have been used both prophylactically to maintain good health and prevent illness and therapeutically for a variety of complaints including upper respiratory infections, asthma, intestinal problems, glaucoma, gonorrhea, marasmus (wasting due to malnutrition) and infant diarrhea, endemic fevers, discomfort of teething, and skin burns and abrasions. Thus cannabis is integrated with many other dimensions of Jamaican culture, and even though it is officially illegal, it is governed by social rules that guide its use and inhibit abuse (Dreher 1982; Rubin and Comitas 1975).

WOMEN AND CANNABIS IN JAMAICA

In Jamaica, ganja smoking traditionally has been a working-class, male-dominated activity. Men have likely started smoking ganja at a younger age, more frequently, and in greater quantities than women. The female ganja smoker has been rare and even those women who cultivated and sold cannabis refrained from smoking the substance. On the other hand, ganja is not new to Jamaican women. As their male counterparts, they likely were exposed to ganja through the ingestion of teas and tonics as infants and small children. Subsequently, they may have experimented with smoking ganja in their teenage years. Finally, in their roles as homemakers and caregivers, women have had a long-standing involvement in the preparation of ganja teas and medicines for their families, a knowledge of which is shared through the generations. Typically, however, Jamaican females have been excluded from the adult male recreational and workgroup gatherings in which ganja is routinely exchanged and smoked. This exclusivity was rationalized by the ethnophysiological explanation that women "don't have the brains" for smoking and should restrict smoking to no more than occasional use and only in the company of their husbands or partners. Ganja tea, on the other hand, is acceptable because tea does not affect the brain but rather the blood, where it has health-promoting properties.

Men who were themselves ganja smokers and even those who claimed to appreciate women who would "take a draw" now and then nevertheless disapproved of the woman who attempted to smoke socially with her peers as men do with theirs. The few women who did smoke socially often were regarded as "brawling" and not respectable. The extent to which a young woman conforms to standards of respectability generally influences her success in acquiring and keeping a young man who is a cut above the rest—at least literate and steadily employed. Since the competition for such men is intense, the woman who ignored the injunctions on ganja smoking risked censure and gossip from both ganja smokers and nonsmokers. Moreover, she could be severely rebuked by her mate even though he might smoke regularly himself and require her to smoke with him in a presexual context.

Despite the social sanctions that limited ganja smoking by women, the number of women who smoke cannabis has increased dramatically. One reason for this increase has been the exponential growth of Rastafarianism, which endorses ganja as a sacred substance. As participating members of the religion, Rastafarian women not only are permitted to smoke ganja but are expected to do so in order to fulfill their religious obligations. A second reason for the increase in ganja smoking of females is the acknowledgment on the part of many women that in the fragile economy characterizing many rural Jamaican communities, the ability of men to provide routine support for a woman and her children is severely compromised. When there are no benefits for conforming to the social norms, those social rules tend to be observed less stringently.

Today it is no longer unusual to see Jamaican women smoking in a manner that is similar to the peer-oriented social smoking typical of their male counterparts. Furthermore, these women are not only grudgingly tolerated but have been given the commendatory title of "roots daughter." This term of praise and esteem is used to signify a woman who has "good brains," who can "smoke hard as a man," and with whom men can "reason" as they would with other men. The model "roots daughter" is not simply a ganja smoker, she is also a woman of dignity. She "must live up to a principle," "go about properly," and "keep a standard." If the "roots daughter" is involved in a stable union, her partner can expect her to be supportive and faithful. The "roots

"Roots daughter" smoking ganja. Photo supplied by Melanie Dreher.

daughter" typically describes herself as independent—a "worker," a "fighter," a "woman with a plan." They compare themselves favorably to "lazy" and "helpless" women who do not smoke ganja (Dreher 1987).

In summary, while the vast majority of women continue to abide by the gender-linked prohibitions on ganja smoking, increasing numbers of Jamaican women breach social norms and smoke ganja with sufficient frequency and quantity to be considered chronic users by United States' standards. These nonconformists smoke on a daily basis, in a manner not unlike that of men, and continue to smoke during pregnancy and the breast-feeding period.

GANJA, PREGNANCY AND CHILDBIRTH

In 1980 we began to explore the use of cannabis during pregnancy in an area of rural Jamaica known for its heavy use of ganja. The research began with simply talking to women of all ages to better understand their attitudes and behavior regarding the use of ganja during pregnancy. Through formal interviews and casual conversations with hundreds of women, we found a wide range of opinions about the effects of ganja before and after birth. Approximately half of the women reported that smoking ganja during pregnancy probably had no effect—good or bad—on either mother or baby but confirmed the health-promoting properties of ganja tea for both mother and baby. Among those who had an opinion, however, were women who claimed that ganja use during pregnancy was potentially harmful for both mother and baby. They cited babies being "slow" to develop and born "viled up" with "cracked skin," "black mouths," and "mashed up brains" as reasons not to smoke ganja. These comments were reinforced by nurses, midwives, school teachers, and other human service workers who counseled women that their babies might be "retarded" and weigh less.

At the other extreme there were many women, some of whom were Rastafarians, who claimed that smoking or drinking ganja was good for both the mother and the baby because it relieved the nausea of pregnancy, increased their appetites, gave them strength to work hard, helped them to relax and sleep at night, and in general, relieved the "bad feelings" associated with pregnancy. In addition to these reported physiological effects, women also reported the psychologically uplifting role of ganja during pregnancy, i.e., "it helps me forget problems; it keeps you lively; when feeling down-hearted, me use it fe cheer up me spirit; it mek I feel nice, or smoking mek me feel more comfortable." Thus, while all of the women who attended prenatal clinics were told that ganja may have harmful effects on their babies, of the 70 smokers who were interviewed, only 11 discontinued smoking during their pregnancies. Of these, eight shifted to using ganja tea instead. One woman claimed to smoke only when she was pregnant.

GANJA AND THE NEWBORN

In order to explore these various opinions and experiences regarding the effects of prenatal ganja use, we recruited, with the help of local midwives, 30 pregnant women who smoked ganja cigarettes and 30 pregnant women who did not smoke ganja. With the help of local midwives, the two groups were matched according to socioeconomic status, age, the number of children the women had prior to their current pregnancy. The study was fully explained to both the ganja users and the mothers in the comparison group. None refused to participate, and all signed an informed consent allowing us to have access to their clinic and hospital records. We then interviewed each mother-to-be in her home where we collected detailed health, obstetrical, and social histories. Field workers continued to have regular contact with the women throughout the pre- and postnatal periods.

Conducting the study in one rural area provided an opportunity to compare users and nonusers drawn from the same population in which there is little variation in such factors as nutrition and prenatal care. Field workers resided in the communities and developed long-term, trusting relationships with the participants. This enhanced the credibility of self-reports of consumption and permitted confirmation by direct observation. Data concerning labor and delivery and the status of the neonate, complications, birthweight, head circumference, and length of gestation, were retrieved from clinic and hospital records for each pregnancy and birth event.

The course of the pregnancies was similar in the two groups. All of the women had regular prenatal care beginning at least in the second trimester of their pregnancies. The use of alcohol and tobacco was minimal in both groups and did not exceed three beers or 10 to 15 tobacco cigarettes per week. The group of cannabis-using mothers were further classified as light, moderate, or heavy users depending on their frequency and amount of use. Light users were women who used cannabis tea only or smoked infrequently (less than ten cannabis cigarettes per week). Moderate users were women who smoked three or more days a week for a total of 11 to 20 cigarettes a week. Heavy users smoked daily, ranging from 21 to 70 cigarettes per week. Many moderate and heavy users also were regular cannabis tea drinkers. These classifications were based both on the mothers' reports and on direct observations by field-workers in homes and communities.

Each of the participants—whether smoker or nonsmoker—had been informed that ganja may be harmful to their babies, and each was warned by nurses and midwives in prenatal clinics and through government-sponsored prevention programs that their babies might be "slow" or "sickly" or "weigh less." Nevertheless, all of the smokers continued to use ganja during their pregnancies and into lactation. Supported by the folk belief that ganja has health-promoting properties and by the experience of relatives and neighbors, they used it as a vehicle for dealing with the difficult circumstances surrounding pregnancy and childbirth. Nineteen of the marijuana smokers in the sample reported that it increased their appetites throughout the prenatal period and or relieved the nausea of pregnancy. Fifteen reported using it to relieve fatigue and provide rest during pregnancy. All of the mothers considered the effects of ganja on nausea and fatigue to be good for both themselves and their babies, reporting that ganja "keeps you working," "gives you strength," makes you "feel relaxed," "sleep better," and "work harder." In addition to the physical effects of ganja, women frequently mentioned that smoking ganja made them feel less depressed about their "condition" of being pregnant again and having little or no support.

When it came time for them to deliver, the mothers carried a letter to the hospital indicating that they were participants in the study but did not say whether they were ganja smokers or nonsmokers. Each baby then was evaluated using the Brazelton Neonatal Assessment Scale (BNAS) (Als et al. 1977; Nugent 1981). In addition to the commonly used items on the scale that constitute "clusters" of neurobehavioral development, "supplementary" items were employed to assess aspects of the baby's behavior such as the quality of the infant's attention and how easy or difficult it is to get the infant's attention and facilitate his or her performance. We believed that these "supplementary" items would be particularly useful in differentiating infants who may be "at risk" through their cannabis exposure, and who may have difficulty in coping with the demands of the examination, from the less stressed, healthy infant.

The tests were administered by a Jamaican nurse who was trained in the use of the Brazelton exam and who did not know whether or not the baby had been exposed prenatally to ganja. The examinations were administered at one day, three days, and one month of life. Because of the rural setting and lack of transportation and communication, some of the women did not get to the hospital in time for delivery but took their babies to the hospital immediately afterward. Therefore, in order to keep the conditions of the evaluation as consistent as possible, only the three-day and one-month exams were considered in the analysis. The assessment of infant behavior at the end of the first month also can provide a functional assessment of the effects of the caregiving environment on newborn behavior. The Brazelton scores at the end of the first month, therefore, can be interpreted not only in terms of direct cannabis effects but also as a result of the effects of the environment on behavior.

The course of the pregnancies was similar in each group, and the two groups of infants were not significantly different according to physical exam data, including birth weight and length and gestational age. Since Apgar scores were not recorded by hospital nurses at standard time intervals, they were less reliable. Nevertheless, there were no significant differences in the Apgar scores between the two groups. At day three, there were no significant differences between the exposed and nonexposed babies on any of the items on the Brazelton exam. In order to examine the degree to which *heavy* marijuana use may have an effect on neurobehavioral outcomes, we then compared the performance of the heavily exposed and nonexposed infants on the BNAS on day three. Again, on day three there were no significant differences in performance on the items of the Brazelton scale.

At one month, however, when we compared the exposed and the nonexposed infants, the offspring of the ganja-using mothers were less irritable and had better motor responses than those of the nonusing mothers. The infants of heavy users also had higher scores on response to both sound and touch and visual stimuli. As a group, they were more alert, less irritable, and had a greater capacity to be consoled. They also had fewer startles and tremors. When we looked at the supplementary items, we found that the infants of the mothers who were heavy users had significantly better scores on all dimensions of the assessment including the quality of alertness, endurance, irritability, and the amount of persistence needed by the examiner to engage the babies.

In summary, although the comparison of exposed and unexposed newborns at three days of life revealed no positive or negative neurobehavioral effects of prenatal exposure, there were significant differences between the exposed and nonexposed infants at the end of the first month. In the general comparison between cannabis users and nonusers, the infants of using mothers showed better physiological stability at one month. In addition, these infants required less examiner facilitation to reach an organized state and become available for social stimulation. The results of the comparison of newborns of the mothers who were heavy users and those of the nonusing mothers were even more striking. The infants of the mothers who were heavy users were more socially responsive and were more autonomically stable at 30 days in comparison to their matched counterparts. The quality of their alertness was higher; their motor and autonomic systems were more robust; they were less irritable; they were less likely to demonstrate any imbalance of tone; they needed less examiner facilitation to become organized; they had better self-regulation; and were judged to be more rewarding for caregivers than the infants of nonusing mothers at one month of age. These findings are particularly remarkable considering that all of the heavily exposed infants were breast-fed and their mothers continued to smoke ganja routinely during the neonatal/breastfeeding period.

Conclusions

Given the consequences of exposure to substances and the public concern over protecting the unborn child, the medical establishment's conservative approach to the cannabis-smoking mother is understandable. Although cannabis is a very complex substance and has many identifiable components, it is THC, the psychoactive ingredient, that has dominated our attention in the United States and taken precedence over other functions of this plant. As such, it has generated considerable public censure, and ultimately laws were enacted to restrict or eliminate its use. It is therefore predictable that nurses, midwives, and public health officials claim that women who smoke cannabis during pregnancy selfishly place greater value on the immediate pleasures derived from recreational ganja smoking than on the health of their babies.

The findings from Jamaica, however, suggest that prenatal cannabis exposure is considerably more complex than we might first have thought. Loss of appetite, nausea, and fatigue compound the "bad feelings" that women in this study commonly reported. For many women, ganja was seen as an option that provided a solution to these problems, i.e., to increase their appetites, control and prevent the nausea of pregnancy, assist them to sleep, and give them the energy they needed to work. For women who are responsible for the full support of their households and who need to accomplish work while not feeling well, ganja smoking is an available and inexpensive solution to this problem. The women with several pregnancies, in particular, reported that the feelings of depression and desperation attending motherhood in their impoverished communities were alleviated by both social and private smoking. In this respect, the role of cannabis in providing both physical comfort and a more optimistic outlook may need to be reconceptualized, not as a recreational vehicle of escapism, but as a serious attempt to deal with difficult physical, emotional, and financial circumstances.

The use of cannabis by pregnant women and neonatal outcomes can be understood only with reference to the cultural context. Unlike the research participants in the United States and Fried's participants in Canada, who may be multiple drug users and who score higher on neuroticism and aggression and lower on agreeableness and conscientiousness, the Jamaican women who smoke ganja heavily are often regarded as "conscientious," "reasonable," and "dignified," and their administration of ganja to themselves and to their children (in the form of tea) actually is considered a sign of accountable, rather than derelict, parenting. Whether or not the effects of cannabis on Jamaican women in the prenatal period are real or only perceived, it is clear that for them it has at least symbolic value in assisting them through the difficulties of pregnancy, childbirth, and the postnatal experience. Thus, while it would be misguided to conclude from this study that smoking cannabis actually improves pregnancy outcomes, the Jamaican experience does suggest the importance of using the experience of other cultures to better understand human behavior and responses. Using the experience of another culture, however, makes it clear that the problem is considerably more complex than conventional pharmacological or medical research would suggest. It is obvious that ganja use during pregnancy is profoundly influenced by the social context in which it occurs and thus requires a carefully constructed risk analysis that allows us to examine not only the potential hazards but also the relative benefits of cannabis for both the mother and the baby.

References

Als, H., E. Tronick, B.M. Lester, and T.B. Brazelton. 1977. The Brazelton Neonatal Assessment Scale (BNAS). *Journal of Abnormal Child Psychology* 5 (3): 215–231.

Comitas, L. 1976. Cannabis and work in Jamaica: A refutation of the amotivational syndrome. *Annals of the New York Academy of Sciences* 282: 24–32.

Day, N., U. Sambamoorthi, P. Taylor, G. Richardson, N. Robles, Y. Jhon, M. Scher, D. Stoffer, M. Cornelius, and D. Jasperse. 1991. Prenatal marijuana use and neonatal outcomes. *Neurotoxicology and Teratology* 13: 329–334.

Dreher, M. 1982. *Working Men and Ganja*. Philadelphia: ISHI.

Dreher, M.C. 1987. The evolution of a roots daughter. *Journal of Psychoactive Drugs* 19 (2): 165–170.

Fried, P.A. 1980. Marihuana use by pregnant women: Neurobehavioral effects in neonates. *Drug and Alcohol Dependence* 6: 415–424.

Fried, P.A. 1982. Marihuana use by pregnant women and effects on offspring: An update. *Neurobehavioral Toxicology and Teratology* 4: 451–454.

Fried, P.A. 1991. Marijuana use during pregnancy: Consequences for the offspring. *Seminars in Perinatology* 15 (4): 280–287.

Fried, P.A., B. Watkinson, and A. Willan. 1984. Marijuana use during pregnancy and decreased length of gestation. *American Journal of Obstetrics and Gynecology* 150 (1): 23–27.

Gibson, G.T., P.A. Baghurst, and D.P. Colley. 1983. Maternal alcohol, tobacco, and cannabis consumption and the outcomes of pregnancy. *Australia and New Zealand Journal of Obstetrics and Gynaecology* 23 (1): 15–19.

Greenland, S., G.A. Richwald, and G.D. Honda. 1983. The effects of marijuana use during pregnancy: A study in a low-risk home-delivery population. *Drug and Alcohol Dependence* 11: 359–366.

Greenland, S., K.J. Staisch, N. Brown, and S.J. Gross. 1982. The effects of marijuana use during pregnancy: A preliminary epidemiologic study. *American Journal of Obstetrics and Gynecology* 143 (4): 408–413.

Hingson, R., J.J. Alpert, N. Day, E. Dooling, H. Kayne, S. Morelock, E. Oppenheimer, and B. Zuckerman. 1982. Effects of maternal drinking and marijuana use on fetal growth and development. *Pediatrics* 70 (4): 539–546.

Hingson, R., B. Zuckerman, H. Amaro, D.A. Frank, H. Kayne, J.R. Sorenson, J. Mitchell, S. Parker, S. Morelock, and R. Timperi. 1986. Maternal marijuana use and neonatal outcome: Uncertainty posed by self-reports. *American Journal of Public Health* 76 (6): 667–669.

Linn, S., S.C. Schoenbaum, R.R. Monson, R. Rosner, P.C. Stubblefield, and K.J. Ryan. 1983. The association of marijuana use with outcome of pregnancy. *The American Journal of Public Health* 73 (10): 1161–1164.

Nugent, J.K. 1981. The Brazelton neonatal behavioral assessment scale: Implications for interventions. *Pediatric Nursing* 7 (3): 18–21, 67.

Page, J.B., J. Fletcher, and W.R. True. 1988. Psychosociocultural perspectives in chronic cannabis use: The Costa Rican follow-up. *Journal of Psychoactive Drugs* 20 (1): 57–65.

Richardson, G.A., N.L. Day, and P.M. Taylor. 1989. The effect of prenatal alcohol, marijuana, and tobacco exposure on neonatal behavior. *Infant Behavior and Development* 12: 199–209.

Rubin, V., and L. Comitas. 1975. *Ganja in Jamaica.* The Hague: Mouton Press.

Tennes, K., N. Avitable, C. Blackard, C. Boyles, B. Hassoun, L. Holmes, and M. Kreye. 1985. Marijuana: Prenatal and postnatal exposure in the human. In *Current Research on the Consequences of Maternal Drug Abuse*, ed. T.M. Pinkert, 48–60. Washington, DC: U.S. Government Printing Office, NIDA Research Monograph 59.

Zias, J., H. Stark, J. Seligman, R. Levy, E. Werker, A. Breuer, and R. Mechoulam. 1993. Early medical use of cannabis. *Nature* 363 (20): 215.

Zuckerman, B. 1989. Effects of maternal marijuana and cocaine use on fetal growth. *The New England Journal of Medicine* 320 (12): 762–768.

15

Risk of Dependence and Addiction

MARY LYNN MATHRE

Prejudice Against "Medical" Marijuana

When the subject of marijuana is brought up, the context is almost always that of substance abuse. An examination of pharmacology text books would show that marijuana is listed only under the chapters addressing substance abuse. In textbooks designed for healthcare professionals, marijuana is discussed under the health or medical problem of substance abuse. It may be discussed in detail including information regarding the number of "abusers," its intoxicating effects, dangerous health risks, and its addiction potential. And finally, in books on the topic of substance abuse or chemical dependency, a chapter is usually devoted to marijuana.

On the other hand, in trying to learn more about the treatment for spasticity, increased intraocular pressure, severe nausea and vomiting, and other such disorders discussed in the preceding chapters, one would be hard pressed to find marijuana or cannabis mentioned as a therapeutic remedy. Because of the governmental and political marijuana prohibition, a discussion of its merits has become taboo. Generations of American citizens have been raised under this information censorship and consequently their thinking about the drug is biased.

A New Paradigm for Substance Abuse

The prevailing black-and-white thinking about substance abuse in general is misleading and dangerous. Drugs are labeled according to their "abuse [or addictive] potential" and specific drugs are believed to "cause" an addic-

---

Mary Lynn Mathre, R.N., M.S.N., C.A.R.N., is an addictions specialist at the University of Virginia Medical Center in Charlottesville.

tion. Illogical thinking such as the following develops: "I would not have been an addict if I never had the opportunity to use this drug. ... It's not my fault, it's the drug's fault ... therefore this drug is bad and should not be available for use." This perpetuates the war on drugs propaganda that certain drugs are inherently bad and therefore should be banned and drug users are criminals who should be punished. The awareness that not all drug users are addicts (e.g., the moderate and responsible alcohol consumer) and that only a minority of drug users (7 to 20 percent) develop an addiction problem is soon forgotten. This zero tolerance approach limits the responsible behavior of the majority because of problems that occur among the minority.

More importantly, this zero tolerance approach fosters the unsafe and irrational belief that there are in fact "good drugs" and "bad drugs." The public is wrongly encouraged to believe that if a drug is sold over the counter, "it must be safe," and if a physician prescribes a controlled drug, "it must be good for me." This lack of personal responsibility regarding drug consumption often results in medical complications, drug dependence, or overdose because of the unsafe manner in which a "good" drug was used. A zero tolerance policy on illegal drugs deters rational dialogue regarding the benefits and risks of these substances, and so creates a shortage of reliable information for responsible citizens who need accurate information to make informed decisions about using drugs.

Drug addiction does not simply mean that the use of certain drugs makes people addicted. The problem is more complex. Drug addiction is about an unhealthy relationship with a drug or drugs and continued use despite the subsequent health and life problems. This can apply to OTC or prescription drugs as well as to alcohol or caffeine. Substance abuse and addiction indicate problems associated with the pattern of use of a drug. Why is the person using the drug? Is there a feeling of loss of control regarding the use of the drug? Is the pattern of use of this drug dangerous to the user? When under the influence of the drug, does the user find himself or herself doing things he or she would not normally do (and does not want to do)? These are the important questions to pursue instead of simply assuming that because a specific drug is consumed, the user has a substance abuse or addiction problem.

Drug abuse may be a symptom of a larger problem. Barry Beyerstein, a psychopharmacologist from Canada, did not simply believe that certain drugs will cause addiction, as was scientifically believed according to numerous animal studies. He believed that there may be factors other than simply a drug's inherent addictive potential that determined whether or not an animal became addicted. Most animal studies involve a caged animal with the opportunity to ingest a psychoactive drug. The drug's addictive potential is rated according to how eager the animal is to obtain and consume the drug. Beyerstein designed a study involving rats and morphine. The control rats were typically alone and caged, were given a sufficient supply of food and water, and had access to the morphine. The rats preferred the morphine over the water.

For the experimental rats, his students built a large cage, filled it with wood shavings and objects, and allowed both sexes to cohabitate. They called it "Rat Park." These rats were also provided with adequate food, water, and a morphine solution. His students closely observed these rats and the morphine supply and soon noted that the rats avoided the morphine. A sweetener was added to the morphine to entice the rats but to no avail. As a last resort, the water was removed. As the rats became thirsty, they soon began to drink the morphine, and Beyerstein's students kept careful records of the amounts consumed by each rat. They continued with this protocol for 57 days and then reintroduced the water. All of the rats abandoned the morphine in preference to the water. All of the rats experienced withdrawal symptoms from their abrupt cessation of morphine intake.

This study may not have been large enough to justify any broad conclusions, but it seems to indicate that caged rats given no quality of life may choose to escape this abnormal existence through the use of a psychoactive drug such as morphine. On the other hand, rats in a more normal and healthy environment had no urge to alter their mental status. They did consume the morphine only out of necessity when their water supply was withdrawn, yet all rejected the morphine when their water supply was returned. Certainly humans are more complex, but as with the rats, it is not simply the drug that determines whether or not addiction will develop. When discussing the addictive potential of drugs it is also important to note that animals do not self-administer cannabis or THC as they do with amphetamines, cocaine, nicotine, depressants, and opioids.

Stages of Drug Use

It has long been understood that there are different patterns of drug use. One way of describing these behaviors was to divide these patterns into stages or levels of use. The government described five stages of drug use (experimental, social or recreational, situational or circumstantial, intensified, and compulsive) to differentiate drug using behavior (National Commission on Marihuana and Drug Abuse 1973). Definitions of these stages are as follows:

Experimental use is short term use, a non-patterned trial of one or more drugs either concurrently or consecutively with variable intensity but maximum frequency of ten times per drug. Experimental use is primarily motivated by curiosity and usually takes place with others.

Social or *recreational use* occurs in social settings among friends or acquaintances who desire to share an experience perceived by them as both acceptable and pleasurable. This use is a voluntary act that tends not to escalate either in frequency or intensity to patterns of uncontrolled or uncontrollable use.[1] Also under the social use stage is the use of psychoactive drugs by various cultures for religious or sacred purposes.

Circumstantial or *situational use* is generally task-specific and self-limited. The level of drug use is motivated by a perceived need or desire to achieve a known and anticipated effect deemed desirable to cope with a specific, sometimes recurrent, situation or condition of a personal or vocational nature.

Intensified use occurs at least daily and is motivated by the user's perceived need to achieve relief from a persistent problem or stressful situation, or his or her desire to maintain a certain self-prescribed level of performance. Drug use becomes a normal and customary activity of daily life. However, the individual generally remains both socially and economically integrated in community life.

Finally, *compulsive use* includes a pattern of both high frequency and high intensity of relatively long duration, producing physiological or psychological dependence. The drug use is motivated by a need to elicit a sense of security, comfort or relief. At this stage drug use dominates the individual's existence and preoccupation with procuring and taking the drug precludes other social functioning.

These stages offer a framework for understanding that a person's use of a drug (or medicine) may range from a low risk activity to a major health problem. Currently healthcare professionals discuss drug use in terms of use, abuse, dependence, and addiction. The similarities between these terms and the stages of drug use are fairly clear.

Defining the Terms and Their Relevance to Cannabis

Before specifically addressing the dependence and addiction potential of cannabis, the relevant terms should be defined. The terms drug *use, abuse, dependence,* and *addiction* are often used interchangeably, and this accounts for much of the confusion surrounding "drug abuse" problems.

A *drug* is any substance other than food that by its chemical nature affects the structure or functioning of the living organism. Drugs do not always act in the same way for everyone. Body chemistry is different in different people, and this will be a factor in how the drug acts on each individual. The body chemistry of an individual also varies from day to day, and this will be a factor in how the drug works.

---

[1]*More recently the federal government's Center for Substance Abuse Prevention in its 1982 and 1983 Prevention Pipeline publications has instructed all readers no longer to use the phrase "recreational use of drugs" and instead simply refer to drug "use" "since no drug use is recreational." This new-speak by the government does not alter the reality that most people do use drugs in a social or recreational manner.*

In the context of substance abuse, the primary group of drugs considered are the "psychoactive drugs." These are drugs that change the way a person feels (e.g., happy, relaxed, energized, etc.) or that alter the senses (e.g., cause hallucinations or change perceptions of time or sound). Two factors important to consider when a person uses a psychoactive drug are the set and setting. *Set* refers to the mood and expectations of the user, and *setting* refers to the environment in which the drug is used. The intoxicating or "high" mental experience of a psychoactive drug is often influenced by these two factors.

Drug abuse is a very ambiguous and value-laden term, and therefore its usefulness is questionable. Drug abuse has been defined as use of a drug without a prescription. This narrow definition is not helpful for those persons and cultures that do not automatically accept the paternalistic notion that only a physician can decide whether or not a person should use a drug, when to use it, and how often to use it. This definition is also too narrow because it does not address the use of OTC drugs or other substances such as caffeine, chocolate, or alcohol that people may use without a prescription though their patterns of use could be harmful.

Another definition of drug abuse has been the use of a drug that is not socially approved. This definition is also limited because what constitutes drug abuse in one culture may be appropriate use in another culture, and therefore to determine the presence of drug abuse implies acceptance of a specific culture's values. Drug abuse is more usefully defined as the use of a drug in a manner that negatively affects the user's health or his or her social or economical functioning. This definition assumes the understanding that any drug can be abused and that drugs have different effects on different people; thus a drug that may be pleasant and therapeutic for one person may be unpleasant and detrimental for another.

Abuse of marijuana may be identified when a person with heart problems such as angina, uses cannabis and the subsequent increase in the heart rate from the cannabis causes harm to that person (health problem). Abuse of marijuana may be identified when a person uses cannabis to relax but continually smokes too much and falls asleep when socializing with friends and never seems to have the energy for social activities (social problem). Abuse of a drug may occur because the user lacks information about how the drug works or how it should be administered. It may also occur because the user is experiencing other problems and wants to escape from them. Despite many subjective judgments of healthcare professionals regarding drug abuse, abuse should be determined with agreement from the user. Is the person experiencing health problems because of the cannabis use and is that person aware of the connection? Is the person experiencing severe stress and using cannabis to medicate the stress to avoid dealing with the stressor? Are the results of the drug use other than what the user intended?

Tolerance is defined as the need for increased amounts of a drug to produce the desired effect. It is important to understand that while tolerance to one effect of a drug may develop, there may not be a tolerance to other effects of the drug, and at the same time the user may become more sensitive to other effects (reverse tolerance). As tolerance to the desired effects develops and the dose must be increased, the side effects of a drug may become more severe because the dosage is increased.

To develop tolerance, the user usually must consume enough of the drug with sufficient frequency for a long enough period of time. Studies have found that users can develop a tolerance to the "high" from cannabis, but only when the user consumes large amounts of cannabis (Wikler 1976). Robert Randall, the first legal medical marijuana patient in the Investigational New Drug Program has been smoking ten low-grade marijuana cigarettes per day since 1976 to control his glaucoma. He does not report experiencing a high from the cannabis, but he has consistently maintained his intraocular pressure with this same dose, thus he has experienced tolerance to the "high" but has not experienced tolerance to the desired medical benefits.

"Less is more" was a phrase used to deter recreational cannabis users from overusing cannabis, and in effect, it exemplifies the concept of tolerance with cannabis. The less frequently a person uses cannabis, the less likely is that person to develop tolerance to the original dose, thus the less likely would that person require higher doses (develop tolerance) to achieve the same effect. Hollister summarized tolerance to cannabis in his conclusions that relatively little tolerance develops when the doses are small or infrequent and the drug exposure is of limited duration. Tolerance clearly develops when persons consume high doses for a sustained period of time (1986).

Dependence is a term often misused as it is considered a synonym for addiction, or the term is separated into physical dependence and psychological dependence. For the purposes of this book, we will simplify the concept of dependence to what others sometimes more specifically refer to as physical dependence. Dependence is the result of continued regular use of a drug that produces a physiological change in the central nervous system to the extent that abrupt cessation of the drug causes withdrawal symptoms. The seriousness of the withdrawal symptoms depends on the particular drug used and the extent of its use (i.e., the amount used, the frequency, and duration of use). In order for a person to experience withdrawal symptoms the dose must be relatively high. However, the high dose is not enough, the drug must also have been consumed for a sufficiently long time period (days to months depending on the drug) on a frequency schedule that provides for a "continual neuronal exposure" to the drug. The frequency of use required for dependence to develop depends on the drug and its duration of action. For those drugs that can produce physical dependence, there is an expected physiological response that would occur in *anyone* who used the drug on a regular basis, but this is not by itself indicative of addiction. For example, it is expected that if a person was put on morphine on a regular basis (at least every four hours) for several days because of severe pain, that person would experience withdrawal symptoms if the morphine was suddenly taken away—similar to what happened to the rats in "Rat Park." To avoid this, the morphine dose is usually decreased gradually as the pain decreases, and thus the person does not experience withdrawal symptoms.

Chronic, heavy cannabis use (smoked every four hours) may produce a mild dependence with relatively benign withdrawal symptoms. Cannabis withdrawal symptoms *may* include irritability, restlessness, difficulty sleeping, nausea, and decreased appetite, and less frequently sweating and tremors. (Adams and Martin 1996, Jones et al. 1981, Wiesbeck et al. 1996). These symptoms generally peak in a few days then subside. There is no life-threatening withdrawal syndrome associated with cannabis dependence as seen in withdrawal from alcohol, barbiturates or benzodiazepines.

Patients requiring long-term high doses of cannabis may become mildly dependent upon it, but that is not necessarily a problem. The therapeutic benefit of the drug may well be worth the small risk of physical dependence. As mentioned earlier in this book, Corinne Millet, a patient suffering from glaucoma and receiving marijuana legally as a medicine, had her government supply arbitrarily stopped and was unable to get her medicine for six weeks. She experienced minor withdrawal symptoms, but of greater significance was that she lost 80 percent of her peripheral vision while she was without her medicine.

Addiction (also called psychological dependence) is defined as a pattern of drug abuse characterized by an overwhelming preoccupation with the compulsive use of a drug, securing its supply, and a high tendency to relapse if the drug is taken away. When a drug is described in terms of its "addictive potential," the intensity of the "high" is considered as well as the possibility of withdrawal symptoms. Tolerance and dependence (physical) are common results of addiction, but are not necessary components of addiction.

For patients receiving cannabis for medical reasons, the "high" effect is one of the first effects they lose as they develop a tolerance to this. Studies have shown that patients smoking cannabis titrate to the dose required to relieve symptoms and that once the dose is determined, they can be maintained on that dose for long periods of time. Examples of this have already been discussed in reference to glaucoma patients using cannabis to control their intraocular pressure and cancer patients receiving cannabis to combat the nausea and vomiting induced by chemotherapy.

Addiction to cannabis rarely occurs because in general, persons who have problems with drug addiction usually prefer more potent psychoactive drugs. Nicotine, alcohol, tranquilizers, cocaine, and opioids (narcotics) have a stronger effect on how a person feels, and therefore these are the drugs more commonly associated with addiction. Since the synthetic THC pill (the primary psychoactive cannabinoid in cannabis), Marinol, has been available, there has been little evidence of illicit marketing of this drug to drug addicts.

Schedule I Status of Cannabis Is Unjustified

As previously explained, marijuana is classified as a Schedule I drug and synthetic THC as a Schedule II drug. The three criteria for Schedule I classification are: (1) high potential for abuse, (2) has no therapeutic value, and (3) is not safe for medical use. Preceding chapters have discussed the remarkably wide margin of safety and the therapeutic value of cannabis.

According to the Controlled Substances Act of 1970, "a key criterion for controlling a substance, and the one which will be used most often, is the substance's potential for abuse." In reading about the determination of the potential for abuse (dependence liability) for all drugs, it must be noted that the dependence liability criteria are similar to the defining characteristics of addiction.

The Committee on Problems of Drug Dependence (CPDD) is responsible for applying standardized tests to evaluate the abuse liability and dependence potential of drugs for the National Institute on Drug Abuse (NIDA) to determine the level of regulation for the drug under the provisions of the Controlled Substances Act. Thomas Cicero, chairman of the Drug Evaluation Committee of the CPDD, identified five criteria to evaluate the degree to which a drug has dependence liability: (1) harmful, compulsive drug self-administration, (2) a preoccupation with drug-seeking behavior to the exclusion of all other activities, (3) craving for the drug, (4) tolerance, and (5) withdrawal symptoms (Cicero 1992). Cicero further states:

> Thus, it is essential that one look at the full spectrum of the drug's effects and the degree to which it satisfies the foregoing criteria before any conclusions regarding its dependence potential are drawn. However, it should be clear that the first three criteria mentioned above (harmful self-administration, compulsive drug-seeking behavior, and craving) must be satisfied in all cases to classify a drug as having significant dependence liability [p. 4].

Cicero elaborates on the self-administration criterion by explaining that people self-administer many substances because of the perceived beneficial effects. However, it is when this behavior results in adverse consequences that self-administration becomes an indication of drug dependence: "To summarize, self-administration of a drug to the point where the behavior becomes obsessive and detrimental to the individual is the primary criterion which must be met to classify a drug with significant potential for dependence" (p. 6).

Initially, animal studies are used to evaluate the abuse potential with the understanding that these do not necessarily reflect similar outcomes in humans. It is important to note that numerous studies conclude that while cannabis may produce a feeling of euphoria in humans, in general, animals will not self-administer THC (Office of Technological Assessment 1993; Abood and Martin 1992; Herkenham 1992). Unfortunately, rather than relying on scientific evidence to evaluate abuse potential, the DEA uses its rigid view of drug abuse according to which use of *any* illicit drug, regardless of its consequences or frequency of use (Cicero 1992) constitutes abuse.

In 1994 Dr. Jack E. Henningfield of the National Institute on Drug Abuse (NIDA) and Dr. Neal L. Benowitz of the University of California at San Francisco (UCSF) ranked six commonly used drugs by five criteria: withdrawal symptoms, reinforcement (craving), tolerance, dependence (addiction potential), and intoxication (Table 1). They ranked these drugs from 1 as most serious to 6 as least serious. Marijuana was ranked lowest for withdrawal symptoms, tolerance, and dependence (addiction) potential; it ranked close to caffeine in the degree of reinforcement and higher than caffeine and nicotine only in the degree of intoxication.

Conclusions

When used as a medicine, cannabis has a wide margin of safety due to its low toxicity. If taken in large amounts on a regular basis, patients often develop a tolerance to its psychoactive effects but not to its therapeutic effects. A mild physical dependence on cannabis might possibly occur for patients using cannabis in high doses, on a regular basis, over a long period of time. However, acute withdrawal from cannabis produces only mild discomfort (less problematic than caffeine withdrawal) rather than life-threatening symptoms as seen with many other medicines. Addiction to cannabis is not common, but if a person becomes addicted to cannabis, treatment is available.

References

Abood, M.E., and B.R. Martin. 1992. Neurobiology of marijuana abuse. *Trends in Pharmacological Sciences* 13: 201–206.

Adams, I.B. and B.R. Martin, 1996. Cannabis: pharmacology and toxicology in animals and humans. *Addiction* 91 (11): 1585–1614.

Cicero, T. 1992. *Assessment of dependence liability of psychotropic substances: Nature of the problem and the role of the Committee on Problems on Drug Dependence.* Contractor document for the Office of Technology assessment. Springfield, VA: National Technical Information Service (NTIS doc. #PB94-175643).

	Withdrawal		Reinforcement		Tolerance		Dependence		Intoxication	
	NIDA	UCSF	NIDA	UCSF	NIDA	UCSF	NIDA	UCSF	NIDA	UCSF
Nicotine	3	3	4	4	2	4	1	1	5	6
Heroin	2	2	2	2	1	2	2	2	2	2
Cocaine	4	3	1	1	4	1	3	3	3	3
Alcohol	1	1	3	3	3	4	4	4	1	1
Caffeine	5	4	6	5	5	3	5	5	6	5
Marijuana	6	5	5	6	6	5	6	6	4	4

Ranking scale: 1 = Most serious   6 = Least serious

Explanation of terms

Withdrawal—Presence and severity of characteristic withdrawal symptoms.
Reinforcement—Substance's ability, in human and animal tests, to get users to take it repeatedly, and instead of other substances.
Tolerance—Amount of substance needed to satisfy increasing cravings, and level of plateau that is eventually reached.
Dependence (Addiction)—Difficulty in ending use of substance, relapse rate, percentage of people who become addicted, addicts self-reporting of degree of need for substance, and continued use in face of evidence that is causes harm.
Intoxication—Level of intoxication associated with addiction, personal, and social damage that substance causes.

Table 1. Ranking of Risks of 6 Commonly Used Drugs

By Dr. Jack E. Henningfield of the National Institute on Drug Abuse (NIDA) and Dr. Neal L. Benowitz of the University of California at San Francisco (UCSF), from an article in the *New York Times* (August 2, 1994, p. C3).

Compton, D.R., W.L. Dewey, and B.R. Martin. 1990. Cannabis dependence and tolerance production. *Advances in Alcohol and Substance Abuse* 9 (1–2): 129–147.
Herkenham, M. 1992. Cannabinoid receptor localization in the brain: Relationship to motor and reward systems. *Annals of the American Academy of Sciences* 654: 19–32.
Hollister, L.E. 1986. Health aspects of cannabis. *Pharmacological Reviews* 38 (1): 1–20.
Jones, R.T., N. Benowitz, and J. Bachman. 1976. Clinical studies of cannabis tolerance and dependence. *Annals of New York Academy of Sciences* 282: 221–239.
National Commission on Marihuana and Drug Abuse. 1973. *Drug Use in America: Problem in Perspective*. Washington D.C.: U.S. Government Printing Office.
Office of Technology Assessment, U.S. Congress. 1993. *Biological Components of Substance Abuse and Addiction*. Washington, D.C.: U.S. Government Printing Office (OTA-BP-BBS-117).
Wiesbeck, G.A., M.A. Schuckit, J.A. Kalmijn, J.E. Tipp, K.K. Bucholz, and T.L. Smith. 1996. An evaluation of the history of a marijuana withdrawal syndrome in a large population. *Addiction* 91 (10): 1469–1478.
Wikler, A. 1976. Aspects of tolerance and dependence on cannabis. *Annals of New York Academy of Sciences* 282: 126–147.

16

Nutritional Value of Hemp Seed and Hemp Seed Oil

DON WIRTSHAFTER

The cultivation of Cannabis sativa is as old as agriculture. In many parts of the world hemp was grown for its valuable fibers. In other places people concentrated on its psychoactive properties. In either case, wherever cannabis was cultivated, the nutritious and delicious seeds of the plant were prized as food and medicine. Cultures around the world had their local recipes. The most common way to use the seeds was to grind them into a porridge called gruel. The seeds were also pressed to obtain an edible oil. Many cultures also developed fancy treats for traditional celebrations.

The prohibition against cannabis just about wiped out the use of this ancient food. Still, in parts of China freshly toasted hemp seeds are sold like popcorn outside movie theaters. Street vendors fill their customers' hands for a small coin. In the Ukraine's hemp growing regions, ancient hemp seed recipes are still shared. The Japanese use ground hemp seeds as a condiment. Some Polish cooks continue to bake them into holiday sweets.

Today, there is a resurgence of interest in using hemp seeds for human nutrition in the United States and Western Europe. The *Hemp Seed Cookbook* was written in 1991 by Carol Miller and this author. It contains information on hemp seed nutrition and 22 recipes for using the seeds. The use of hemp seeds for cooking has created so much demand for the seeds that they are currently in short supply.

Don Wirtshafter, J.D., is an environmental attorney and founder of the Ohio Hempery in Guysville, Ohio.

Hemp Seed Nutrition

The author commissioned a nutritional analysis of one batch of sterilized hemp seeds and hemp seed oil. The work was performed by several laboratories and is summarized in this article. These results confirm that hemp seeds are an extremely valuable human food with unique properties that deserve attention.

Where possible, the results of this testing program are compared to the Recommended Daily Allowances (RDAs) set by the United States Department of Agriculture. A complete mineral assay was performed on the sterilized hemp seeds. It can be seen that hemp is especially high in the most needed minerals: calcium, magnesium, phosphorus, potassium, and sulfur. It is also low in heavy metals like strontium, thorium, arsenic, and chromium. Heavy metals must be avoided in a healthy diet.

The vitamin results seem disappointing until one notes that hemp seed's vitamin content compares favorably with that of other grains. Vitamins are mostly provided by fresh vegetables. One would have to eat over a pound of hemp seeds to meet the RDA for many vitamins. The heat from the sterilization process may also affect the vitamin content. This will be the subject of further research. The fresh green leaves of the hemp plant could not be tested for nutrition. They are used in the Indian beverage called bhang, a conscious-altering frothy concoction of cannabis leaves, spices, milk, and honey.

PROTEIN

Hemp seeds contain up to 24 percent protein. A handful of seeds provides the minimum daily requirement for adults. Our testing confirms that hemp contains high quality protein that provides all eight essential amino acids in the correct proportions humans need. The basic proteins in hemp are easy to digest. Soybeans contain a higher total percentage of protein, but these are complex proteins that many people find difficult to digest. Widespread use of hemp seed for protein could nourish many of the world's hungry. Because hemp seeds are so digestible, many scientists suggest their use for nutrition blocking diseases and for treating malnourishment.

In addition to all this these seeds taste great. Hemp seeds can be used as a protein and flavor enhancer in any recipe. Once the seeds are cleaned and roasted, they can be substituted for up to one-fourth of the flour in any recipe. Less oil should be used than is called for in the recipe because hemp seeds contain so much of their own oil.

Hemp seeds remain an important Chinese medicine. Known as huó má rén, they are said to affect the meridians of the spleen, stomach, and large intestines. The seeds are prized for treating constipation in aged or debilitated persons. This is easy to understand as the high oil and fiber content of the seeds acts to clean the intestinal system.

Hemp Seed Oil

The hemp seeds tested contained 30 percent oil by weight. Varieties of hemp bred for high oil content contain up to 40 percent oil. This is said to be the most unsaturated oil derived from the vegetable kingdom. Hemp oil consists of up to 81 percent of the polyunsaturated essential fatty acids (EFAs) that are needed, but not produced by the human body. Furthermore, the proportions of these oils in hemp seed match the ratios previously determined to be the most beneficial to human nutrition (Erasmus 1993). The addition of hemp seeds or oil to our diet can supplement deficiencies of these needed nutrients.

The natural oil consists of three fatty acids bound on a glycerine molecule in what is called a triglyceride. Of the dozens of fatty acids we normally consume, only two have proven to be essential in sustaining human life. Originally, these were called the vitamin Fs. Perhaps because scientists found it impossible to put vitamin F in a vitamin pill, the name was changed to the essential fatty acids (EFAs) in the 1950s. They are a recognized part of the recommended daily requirement: 3 grams/day of the omega-6 linoleic acid (LA) and 2 grams/day of the omega-3 Linolenic Acid (LNA). No requirements for a third, important oil, the super omega-6, gamma linolenic acid (GLA) has been set.

Some scientists blame the increased prevalence of degenerative diseases in our society on the lack of essential fatty acids in the modern diet (Finnegan 1992; Rudin and Felix 1987). The present craze for "fat free" diets misses the need for EFAs. Some oils do plug up the system, but other oils are essential for sustaining life. Further, without oils in the diet, one does not get the fat-soluble vitamins, A, D, E, and K. Unless one is consistently eating the correct, extremely fresh foods, the "no fat" diet will eventually leave one devoid of these needed nutrients (Erasmus 1993).

The EFAs are used in a variety of body functions. They act as the lipids in the membranes of all body cells. They prevent buildup of arterial plaque. They are the precursors of the prostaglandins needed by our immune system. At least 200 articles a year studying the EFAs are published in scientific journals.

Because of the increased public awareness of EFA deficiencies, consumption of therapeutic oils that provide the EFAs has markedly increased. Flax oil has become a $6 million per year industry. It is popular because it is rich in LNA. Deficiency of LNA is much more common than LA deficiency. Flax oil is primarily used to treat cancer and arteriosclerosis.

Dr. Andrew Weil, author of *Natural Health, Natural Medicine,* and *Spontaneous Healing,* contrasted flax oil to the edible grade of hemp oil in the April/May 1993 issue of *Natural Health* magazine:

Most flax oil is not delicious. There is a great variation in taste among the brands currently sold in natural food stores, but the best of them still leaves much to be desired. I have been recommending flax oil as a dietary supplement to patients with autoimmune disorders, arthritis and other inflammatory conditions, but about half of them cannot tolerate it. Some say that it makes them gag, even when concealed in salad dressing or mashed into a baked potato. These people have to resort to taking flax oil capsules, which are large and expensive. Udo Erasmus, author of the classic book, *Fats and Oils* [Alive 1986], says that the problem is freshness. Unless you get flax oil right from the processor and freeze it until you start using it, it will already have deteriorated by the time you buy it.

Unlike flax oil, hemp oil also provides 1.7 percent gamma-linolenic acid (GLA). There is controversy about the value of adding this fatty acid to the diet, but many people take supplements of it in the form of capsules of evening primrose oil, black currant oil, and borage oil. My experience is that it stimulates growth of hair and nails, improves the health of the skin, and can reduce inflammation. I like the idea of having one food oil that supplies omega-3s and GLA without the need to take more capsules.

If you have a chance to try hemp oil, a long-forgotten, newly discovered food, I think you will see why I am enthusiastic about it.

Therapeutic use of evening primrose oil, borage oil and black currant seed oil has been accepted by naturopathic physicians and the general public. All are sources of super omega-6, gamma linolenic acid (GLA). The problem with these oils is that they are generally available in a solvent extracted form, not the much preferred cold pressing. Healthy bodies can process LA into GLA. This is why GLA is not officially considered an essential fatty acid. Systems under stress from autoimmune diseases, alcohol abuse, or other imbalances cannot make this transition, so supplementation with GLA can prove beneficial.

None of the previously available nutritional oils combine the needed EFAs in anything close to the proportions scientists have determined as ideal. One would have to carefully use a combination of these oils to get the optimal combination. Hemp oil is unique. It has a perfect 3:1 ratio of LA to LNA and a healthy GLA component (1.7 percent) as well. It's no wonder that Udo Erasmus in his new book, *Fats That Heal, Fats That Kill,* pronounced hemp "the most perfectly balanced, natural EFA-rich oil available" and "nature's most perfectly balanced oil" (Erasmus 1993, 287 and 400).

These therapeutic oils all share one difficulty; they are so reactive that they have a short shelf life. The better an oil is for us, the more quickly it will degrade. Unless properly protected, the good oils will go rancid in a matter of days. This is why our modern junk food diets are so devoid of EFAs. Food engineers design "convenience foods" to be low in EFAs so that their products can sit for years without going rancid. Manufacturers start with saturated fats (coconut and palm oils), or they artificially saturate the oils through the hydrogenation process. Hydrogenation produces the harmful trans-fatty acids that should be avoided in a healthy diet.

The shelf life problem is why one should be careful of many of the toasted hemp seed treats that are now sold in this country. Once the seeds are ground or toasted, the rancidity reactions begin. Cooked hemp seeds are safe in bakery goods that will be consumed within a few days but not for any product that must sit longer. The Food and Drug Administration issued a cease and desist order against one company that tried to wrap hemp granola bars in cellophane. Better technology could end this problem.

For years, no one was able to figure out how to put EFAs in a bottle or a pill and make them last. In 1986 advanced seed oil companies began using technology that could extract oils in the absence of heat, light, and air. This proprietary technology uses inert gases and vacuums to cold press an oil without contaminating it with oxygen. By keeping the oxygen away from the oil, the process does not start the chain reactions that create rancidity. Finally, the reactive oils, like hemp, can be pressed into a product that can be kept in opaque bottles for up to two years without going rancid.

The hemp oil available now is rather expensive, about twice the cost of flax oil. This is because the seeds have to be imported into the United States and the pressing technology is so expensive. Still, when one compares the grams of GLA per dollar, it turns out that hemp is already a better deal than many of its competitors such as evening primrose oil. The price will continue to go down with increased production and competition. When the U.S. government finally allows the growing of hemp seeds domestically, we will be able to produce a high quality hemp oil that may compete in price with corn oil.

Other Uses of Hemp Seed Oil

Skin cells readily absorb EFAs but not saturated oils. A coconut oil based skin cream will only coat the skin surface, offering some moisture protection simply by blocking the loss of additional moisture. A lotion rich in EFAs can be absorbed into the skin cells, replenishing the lipids damaged by sun rays and dry air. Hemp oil is especially effective in saving sunburned skin and preventing it from peeling.

Hemp oil was known in ancient times as *linum*, the root word for liniment. (True, flax is generally and taxonomically known by this name. It is wonderful to untangle the ways the oil and fibers of these plants have become intertwined through history.) There are many ancient recipes for making soothing rubs from the oil or even from the roots of the hemp plant. It makes a wonderful massage oil, except for its irritating ability to permanently stain bed sheets a light green color.

Why Sterilized Seeds?

The only hemp seeds legally available for purchase in America have been precooked under governmental supervision. This makes them legal to possess but compromises their value considerably. The problem is that this cooking destroys much of the nutritional potential of the seeds and leaves them prone to rancidity.

Allowing the sterilized seeds into commerce was a compromise worked out during congressional hearings for the 1937 Marihuana Tax Act. Representatives of the American bird food industry testified before the House Ways and Means Committee that parakeets would not sing unless they were fed hemp seeds. Pigeon growers had been unable to find a substitute for hemp seeds in their feed. Bowing to pressure from Harry Anslinger, the infamous commissioner of narcotics, the producers agreed to precook their seeds past the point of germination.

Legal hemp seeds are either heat sterilized or steam sterilized. Contrary to popular conception, none of the companies currently supplying legal seeds use gamma irradiation to treat their products. The only purpose for the sterilization is to keep the seeds from growing into new plants. The cooking does not affect the level of THC, which is already almost nonexistent in the live seeds, especially if the dust is rinsed off the seeds before use.

The word *sterilized* creates misconceptions. The seeds are not cooked to the point of killing bacteria, i.e., boiled for 15 minutes. Instead, the seeds are brought to a temperature of 160 degrees Fahrenheit for five minutes and then cooled. This is hot enough to alter some of the enzymes necessary for photosynthesis. If the seeds were cooked further, the seed coats would break, allowing the reactive oils in the seeds to go rancid quickly. As it is, the shelf life of the cooked seeds is considerably compromised. The heat opens microfissures in the hull that allow oxygen to penetrate into the delicate kernels. Live seeds can still sprout after being kept in a drawer for five years. The cooked seeds can go rancid in a few months, especially if not refrigerated.

Robert Stroud, known as the "Birdman of Alcatraz," became an expert on birds during the long years he avoided execution on California's death row. His 1939 book, *Diseases of Birds*, still stands as an authority in its field. Stroud explained how nutritious hemp seeds were but expressed frustration with the "sterilized" seeds that were coming on the market as a result of the 1937 Marihuana Tax Act.

> I want to make it perfectly clear right now that anything said in these pages about the virtues of hemp seed apply to fresh, unsterilized hemp seed—most assuredly not to the rancid trash now on the market. ...
> Because the seed is rich in the reproductive vitamin, an unlimited supply of

	Results	USRDA
Moisture	5.7%	
Fat	30.0%	
Protein (N x6.25)	22.5%	
Ash	5.9%	
Energy	503 calories/100 g	
Carbohydrates	35.8%	
Carotene (Vitamin A)	16,800 IU/lb	5000 IU/day
Thiamine (B_1)	0.9 mg/100 g	1.2 mg/day
Riboflavin (B_2)	1.1 mg/100 g	1.7 mg/day
Pyridoxine (B_6)	0.3 mg/100 g	2.0 mg/day
Niacin (B_3)	2.5 mg/100 g	20.0 mg/day
Vitamin C	1.4 mg/100 g	60.0 mg/day
Vitamin D	<10.0 IU/100 g	400.0 IU/day
Vitamin E	3.0 mg/100 g	30.0 IU/day
Insoluble dietary fiber	32.1%	
Soluble dietary fiber	3.0%	
Total dietary fiber	35.1%	

Table 1. Analysis of Hemp Seeds

it should be kept before the hens making eggs to insure a high percentage of hatchability…. The oil of hemp seed becomes rancid very quickly and what was once a valuable food becomes deadly poison. For this reason, hemp seed must always be used with care.

This is still important advice. Hemp seeds should be tasted before cooking. If the seeds are old enough to have lost their nutty flavor or taste rancid, they should be discarded. Many people are buying their seeds from animal feed stores that do not pay attention to the freshness of their product. Rancid oil seeds feel scratchy at the back of the throat. Tasting for rancidity is an acquired skill that one should learn to protect oneself from all sorts of spoiled foods.

The 1937 compromise agreed to by the bird food industry created many problems. Principally, the seeds could no longer be grown in this country. The seeds are now grown overseas, mainly in China. This greatly increases the price and lowers the quality of the currently available seeds. Organically certified seeds are very difficult to find at this time.

Element	Levels (ppm)	USRDA
Aluminum	54.00	
Antimony	1.75	
Arsenic	0.30	
Barium	6.48	
Beryllium	0.04	
Boron	9.50	
Cadmium	0.28	
Calcium	1680.00	800–1200 mg/day
Chromium	0.65	
Cobalt	0.53	
Copper	12.00	
Germanium	2.67	
Iodine	0.84	0.080–0.150 mg/day
Iron	179.00	18 mg/day
Lead	0.027	
Lithium	0.062	
Magnesium	6059.00	300–400 mg/day
Manganese	95.43	
Mercury	<0.02	
Molybdenum	0.51	
Nickel	5.0	
Phosphorus	8302.00	800–1200 mg/day
Platinum	9.23	
Potassium	170.00	
Selenium (< test limits)	<0.02	
Silicon	13.80	
Silver	0.40	
Sodium	22.0	
Strontium	7.33	
Sulfur	2394.00	
Thorium	8.12	
Tin	2.60	
Titanium	1.78	
Tungsten	1.84	
Vanadium	0.84	
Zinc	82.00	15 mg/day
Zirconium	1.23	

Table 2. Mineral Assay of Sterilized Hemp Seeds

Amino Acid	Mg/G
Phosphoserine	0.9
Aspartic acid + asparagine	19.8
Glutamic acid + glutamine	34.8
Threonine	3.7
Serine	8.6
Proline	7.3
Glycine	9.7
Alanine	9.6
Valine	3.0
Cystine + cysteine	1.2
Methionine	2.6
Cystathionine	0.9
Isoleucine	1.5
Leucine	7.1
Tyrosine	5.8
Phenylalamine	3.5
Tryptophan	0.6
Ethanolamine	0.4
Lysine	4.3
Histidine	2.5
Arginine	18.8

Table 3. Amino Acid Composition of Hemp Seeds

Component Name/Total Fatty Acids	Carbon Chain	% of Fatty Acids
Palmitic Acid	C16:0	6.1
Palmitoleic Acid	C16:1	0.3
Heptadecanoic Acid	C17:0	0.2
Stearic Acid	C18:0	2.1
Oleic Acid	C18:1	2.0
Linolenic Acid (LA)	C18:2	56.9
Gamma Linolenic Acid (GLA)	C18:3	1.7
Linolenic Acid (LNA)	C18:3	18.9
Arachidic Acid	C20:0	0.5
Eiscosenoic Acid	C20:1	0.3
Erucic Acid	C22:1	0.2
Lignoceric Acid	C24:0	0.3
Nervonic Acid	C24:1	0.2

Table 4. Fatty Acids in Hemp Seed Oil

Moisture	0.19%
Vitamin A	8,7000 IU/lb
Vitamin E	<1.0 mg/100g
Phosphatides	0.03%
Chlorophyll	6 ppm
Fat Stability AOM	5 hours
Fatty Free Acid	0.94%
Insoluble Matter	0.01%
Iodine Value	166.5
Saponification Value	192.8
Specific Gravity	0.9295 @ 20°C
Unsaponifiable matter	0.28%
Smoke point	165°C
Flash Point	141°C
Melting Point	(–8°C)

Table 5. Analysis of Hemp Seed Oil

Are These Seeds Really Legal?

Sterile hemp seeds are specifically excluded from the definition of marijuana and are not controlled substances under federal law according to Public Law 91-513, Section 102(15). The term *marijuana* is defined as:

> all parts of the plant *Cannabis sativa,* whether growing or not, the seeds thereof, the resin extracted from any part of such plant; and every compound, manufacture, salt, derivative, mixture or preparation of such plant, its seeds or resin; *but shall not include* the mature stalks of such plant, fiber provided from such stalks, oil or cake made from the seeds of such plant, any other compound, manufacture, salt, derivation, mixture or preparation of such mature stalks (except the resin extracted therefrom), fiber, oil or cake *or the sterilized seed of such plant, which is incapable of germination.* [Emphasis added.]

These exceptions to the definition of marijuana are what has allowed the resurgence of the American hemp industry.

The importation, sterilization, and commercial distribution of hemp seed is regulated by the DEA pursuant to the Controlled Substances Import and Export Act, U.S.C. 952 Et. Seq. and 21 C.F.R. 1311. In calendar year 1990 approximately 60 tons of seeds were imported into this country, mostly for use as birdseed. The seeds themselves contain almost no THC, the most psychoactive principal in marijuana. The THC is concentrated in the female flower top and leaves. Tiny quantities of THC are found in the dust of these crushed plant parts that inevitably end up being packaged with the seeds. The varieties of hemp grown for seed are genetically low in THC, so the residue that comes with commercial seeds is hardly worth smoking.

The DEA recognizes that legal, sterilized hemp seeds contain detectable quantities of THC. The DEA's official testing procedure requires laboratories to test for the viability of hemp seeds taken into evidence. Viability testing (rather than THC analysis) determines whether or not the material constitutes a controlled substance.

Conclusion

In the rush toward discovery of medical uses of the cannabinoids, we should not ignore the other important health and medical uses of the cannabis plant. Hemp seeds are clearly an important historical food with much to offer in our future. But the revival of their use must be accompanied by a close watch on their potential rancidity. What starts out as a health food can quickly turn into a health hazard unless proper steps are taken to preserve the freshness of hemp products. With this precaution in mind, the prolific hemp plant can be a strong ally in our common goals of achieving good health and solving malnutrition around the world.

References

Erasmus, U. 1986, repr. 1993. *Fats That Heal, Fats That Kill* (formerly, *Fats and Oils: The Complete Guide to Fats and Oils in Health and Nutrition*). Burnaby, BC, Canada: Alive Books.

Finnegan, J. 1992. *Fats and Oils: Promise or Poison, the Inside Story About Oils That Nourish Us and Those That Poison Us—and the New Breakthrough Methods of Producing Good Oils*. Malibu, CA: Elysian Arts.

Miller, C., and D. Wirtshafter. 1991. *The Hemp Seed Cookbook*. Athens, Ohio: Hempery.

Osborne, L., and J. Osborne. 1992. *Hemp Line Journal*. Maricopa, CA: Access Unlimited.

Robertson, L., C. Flinders, and B. Godfrey. 1976. *Laurel's Kitchen*. Bantam Press.

Rudin, D., and C. Felix. 1987. *The Omega-3 Phenomenon*. New York: Rawson Associates.

Weil, A. 1990. *Natural Health, Natural Medicine: A Comprehensive Manual for Wellness and Self-Care*. Boston: Houghton Mifflin.

Weil, A. 1993. Therapeutic hemp oil. *Natural Health*. March/April, 10–11.

Weil, A. 1995. *Spontaneous Healing: How to Discover and Enhance Your Body's Natural Ability to Maintain and Heal Itself*. New York: Knopf.

17

Economic and Environmental Potential of Cannabis

ROBERT C. CLARKE and DAVID W. PATE

Introduction

Cannabis has been cultivated throughout human agricultural history for its strong fiber and edible seed as well as for its drug properties. It has clothed our ancestors, sustained them in times of hunger, sailed them to the farthest reaches of the globe, provided books to record their history, soothed their ills, and strengthened communion with their deities. Today cannabis provides many valuable products that can supplement or potentially replace many of their marketplace equivalents. It possesses the unique ability to produce textiles, paper products, building materials, nutritious food (including a valuable oil), and effective natural medicines.

This extremely versatile plant also serves as a crop that fits into a healthy and balanced ecosystem model, slowing or even reversing the degradation of our environment through its potential for bioremediation and as a source of non-petrochemical raw materials (e.g., chemical feedstock) and biomass energy. Popularization of ecologically sound products and the establishment of appropriate global management strategies are important to our planet's future and cannabis can play a significant role.

Cannabis as a Plant

Almost all of the cannabis found worldwide is classified as Cannabis sativa. Many taxonomists argue that C. indica, C. afghanica, and C. ruderalis

Robert C. Clarke and *David W. Pate* are both cannabis biologists at the International Hemp Association in Amsterdam, The Netherlands.

are also valid species names for three different small subgroups of the genus *Cannabis*. However, even accounting for these additional putative species, 95 percent of the cultivated cannabis in the world would still be classified as Cannabis sativa.

A rapidly maturing annual crop like cannabis is well adapted for temperate climates. Ancient northern Asian and European cultures used cannabis mostly for its fiber and seed. Cannabis is also an aggressive weed at higher latitudes worldwide. South Asian and African cultures used cannabis mostly for its drug content as the more tropical climates allow maturation of the potent marijuana resin. More intense levels of ambient ultraviolet radiation and of insect predation in the tropics may also have contributed to a natural selection for these drug types (Pate 1994). In any case, cannabis has evolved into two basic races. Plants grown for their fiber, seed, and pulp are universally called hemp, while those grown for their drug content are commonly called drug cannabis or marijuana. This is really the only important taxonomic distinction most people need to make.

Most of the psychoactive properties of marijuana can be attributed to its content of a compound called delta-9-tetrahydrocannabinol (THC). In some literature, it is designated as delta-1-tetrahydrocannabinol due merely to a conflict between two methods of naming chemicals, but it is the very same molecule. Modern hemp varieties are nearly devoid of THC, and it is virtually impossible to divert hemp crops into the drug trade. Hemp has been heavily selected for high fiber content, high stalk yield, high seed yield, and low THC content (<0.3 percent). Drug-type cannabis varies widely in THC content from approximately 1 percent in unselected strains to over 10 percent in the most potent modern varieties. It is not feasible to "get high" on hemp (Karus et al. 1995), and marijuana produces very little low-quality fiber. Hemp should never be confused with marijuana as they are not interchangeable.

In temperate climates, cannabis is an annual crop sown in the spring or early summer and harvested in the summer or autumn. It is also sown during these seasons in more tropical climates to provide proper timing for seasonal rainfall for sufficient moisture to sustain the plants at least until flowering. A cannabis "seed" is actually a small hard-shelled nut (achene) with a single true seed inside. The seeds germinate within two or three days after they are moistened by rain and a pair of rounded green cotyledons (seed leaves) emerges from the soil. Cannabis grows quite rapidly when it receives plenty of water, nutrients, and sunlight. Alternating pairs of palmate leaves with an odd number of long leaflets form along the main stalk as it grows. The first pair of leaves has only a single leaflet, the second pair has three leaflets, the third five, and so on, up to a possible nine or eleven leaflets per leaf.

Hemp grown for fiber is sown densely, the plants only one or two inches

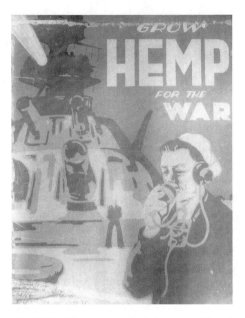

World War II poster emphasizing the military's need for hemp. Historic poster supplied by David Busch; photo I-CARE.

apart, so each plant must grow rapidly, tall, and straight to compete with the neighboring plants for sunlight. This results in single smooth stalks without any branches. Seed and marijuana crops are sown sparsely so that the plants have sufficient space and sunlight to grow long branches with many flowers. Widely spaced seed and marijuana crops begin to branch as soon as the primary leaves are fully formed. A small bud appears at the base of each leaf where it joins the main stalk and a branch begins to form. Seed and marijuana plants usually take on a conical or candelabra shape resulting from their extensive branching.

Short day-length triggers and promotes a usually dioecious flowering pattern (separate male and female plants) in cannabis. At this time, the number of leaflets on each leaf decreases from eleven or nine to seven, five, three, and then finally one as the flowers develop and ripen. Most types of cannabis in the Northern Hemisphere begin to flower in July and continue through August. Typical crops develop approximately half of each gender. Fiber hemp is usually harvested at the time when the male plants begin to shed pollen, and as a result few if any seeds are produced. This is done so that the stalks are uniform in fiber content and quality among both male and female plants. The male plants in seed crops are allowed to shed large amounts of pollen, and many seeds begin to form in the female plants a few days later. The male plants die soon after dispersing pollen, but the female plants continue to live up to two months longer as their seeds ripen. Seed crops are harvested when ripe, but before the seeds begin to fall from the flowers. If the crop is harvested too late, most of the seeds will be lost when the plants are handled during harvesting.

Male plants are often removed from marijuana crops before they shed any pollen so that no seeds will form in the female flowers, since female plants die when their seeds mature. This marijuana product is called sinsemilla, which is a slight corruption of the Spanish phrase *sin semilla* (without seed).

Sinsemilla is more potent than seeded marijuana because the female plants devote all of their energy to producing flowers and resin as they wait in vain for pollination. All drug cannabis crops are matured as long as climatic and other conditions allow in order to increase their potency.

Cannabis as a Resource

NATURAL MEDICINE

Most people in need of medicinal cannabis must obtain it illegally from friends. Improved varieties of cannabis are constantly being developed by amateur marijuana growers and used for personal small-scale cultivation of crude cannabis medicines. Criteria for medical use are imposed upon existing varieties in an effort to select promising candidates. The ultimate goal of breeders of medicinal cannabis is to create varieties that express specific reproducible cannabinoid chemotypes appropriate to the patient's individual medical requirements and personal preferences. Many of these amateur cannabis cultivators are in direct contact with patients who use the drug and are often provided with comments as to which varieties are more effective for various medical problems. Patients who are physically able will sometimes grow their own plants. This is especially true in regions of the United States where the movement for allowing the cultivation of cannabis for medical purposes is gaining popularity. Actively participating in such a nurturing hobby as gardening is good for a patient's attitude and helps foster a positive mental outlook for the fulfillment of life and expectations about death. Outdoor gardening is often included in recuperative therapy programs for ambulatory patients.

Cannabis is a very attractive and responsive plant that is well suited for indoor growth. Hospital wards for terminally ill cancer and AIDS patients could conceivably provide access to rooftop atriums or indoor grow rooms so that patients might enjoy participating in the growing and harvesting of their own herbal medicines without having to venture outdoors. However, there is some cause for concern as to whether these patients would have the ability to produce a consistent and contaminant-free cannabis product. In addition, there remains the unfortunate fact that many of these people do not have the time or strength to tend to such a project. Undoubtedly, these people would prefer to simply purchase this medicine at their local pharmacy. Until these scenarios are legally possible, however, patients will continue to patronize the various Cannabis Buyers' Clubs that have been established to provide access to this medicine.

Domestic cultivation of drug cannabis has increased steadily since the early 1970s and advanced glasshouse and grow room technologies have spread into American homes. It is now possible to set up nearly sterile grow rooms. This is a prophylactic measure designed to minimize contaminants (e.g., fungi) that might prove harmful to patients with suppressed immune systems (Randall 1991). The few extant persistent cannabis pests can be effectively controlled, if not eliminated, by using safe, nontoxic, biological controls. No chemical pesticides are required to grow high-quality, medicinal cannabis, and no chemical pesticides should be used because of the potential harm related to ingestion or inhalation of such chemicals. Many varieties are currently available that contain enough THC (5–10 percent) to be medically effective when only a small amount of the crude drug is smoked. Seeds and cuttings of improved strains are sold openly and legally in a number of seed shops in the Netherlands. In the near future, cannabis varieties with a high THC content and very low amounts of the other cannabinoids may be developed. This could serve as raw material for the extraction of natural THC useful in pharmaceutical preparations (Clarke and Pate 1994). When more of the naturally occurring cannabinoids are approved as therapeutic agents, additional single-cannabinoid varieties will likely be developed for this use.

Vaporizing purified cannabis resin is a much more efficient method for delivering concentrated doses of natural THC to the patient, simultaneously providing more immediate relief than orally ingested synthetic THC capsules and offering a healthier alternative to smoked whole marijuana or crude hashish. Resins from different varieties can be blended to provide differing effects.

The mechanical isolation of cannabis resin by filtration is a totally natural, solvent-free method of concentrating the medically active ingredients of cannabis and can be performed at home. First, the very dry female flowers and small leaflets are thoroughly crushed by hand or put through a coarse metal sieve, such as window mesh, above a tautly framed 135–150 micron pore silk-screen. This debris is then lightly brushed over the surface of the silk-screen, taking care not to press much of the green leafy material through the pores. The resin powder found underneath is then collected with a stiff card and can be further cleaned by rubbing it firmly over a 50 micron pore silk-screen, discarding any of the inert materials that have fallen through. The material remaining on top consists mostly of resin glands that are between approximately 50 and 130 microns in diameter and can contain more than 30 percent THC.

Nutritious Food

Hemp seed can be consumed whole, used to produce processed food, or employed as a feed for birds and fishes (Deferne and Pate 1996). Although nominally free of THC, it can contain traces of cannabinoids, probably as a residue of adherent resin originating from its flower bract (Matsunaga et al.

1990). Whole hemp seed contains approximately 20–25 percent protein, 20–30 percent carbohydrates, and 10–15 percent insoluble fiber, as well as a rich array of minerals, particularly phosphorous, potassium, magnesium, sulfur, and calcium along with modest amounts of iron and zinc. It is also a fair source of carotene, a vitamin A precursor. Most hemp seed also contains approximately 25–35 percent oil, although some strains have been claimed to exceed this range.

The crushed seed by-product of oil production is suitable for animal feed and as a human staple due to its spectrum of amino acids, including all eight of those essential to the human diet, as well as to its carbohydrates, fiber, and a small amount of residual oil. Its protein is primarily edestin, a highly assimilable globular protein of a type similar to the albumin found in egg whites and blood. This ease of digestibility is particularly important in the nutritional maintenance of patients with diseases such as tuberculosis and AIDS.

Analytical data reported for the fatty acid composition of hemp seed oil reveals that it is unusually high in polyunsaturated fatty acids (70–80 percent), while its content in saturated fatty acids (below 10 percent) compares favorably with the least saturated commonly consumed vegetable oils. This high degree of unsaturation explains its extreme sensitivity to oxidative rancidity, as the chemical double bonds that provide such unsaturation are vulnerable to attack by atmospheric oxygen. This degradation is accelerated by heat or light. For this reason, the oil is unsatisfactory for frying or baking, although moderate heat for short periods is probably tolerable. It is best consumed as a table oil in salads or as a butter or margarine substitute for dipping bread, similar in use to olive oil. Proper steam sterilization of the seed probably does not do significant damage to the oil, but it does destroy the integrity of the seed, allowing penetration by air and molds. By the same reasoning, one should avoid eating whole hemp seed that has been subjected to any cooking process, unless it is reasonably fresh.

The two polyunsaturated essential fatty acids, linoleic acid ($C_{18}H_{32}O_2$) or LA and linolenic acid ($C_{18}H_{30}O_2$) or LNA, account for approximately 50–70 percent and 15–25 percent respectively, of the total fatty acid content of the seed. Such a 3:1 balance has been claimed optimal for human nutrition and is apparently unique among the common plant oils, although black currant seed oil approaches this figure (Erasmus 1993). Preliminary studies indicate that cannabis seeds from tropical environments apparently lack significant quantities of LNA. Oils from temperate varieties are more unsaturated, perhaps due to a natural selection in northern latitudes for a seed energy storage medium that remains liquid at lower temperatures.

Hemp seed oil has also been reported (from sterilized seed in the United States) to contain 1.7 percent gamma-linoleic acid ($C_{18}H_{30}O_6$) or GLA

(Wirtschafter 1995), and considerably higher levels (3-6 percent) in other specimens have been measured by German investigators (Theimer and Mölleken, 1995, Theimer 1996), although it is apparently rare in most tropical varieties of cannabis. The metabolic conversion of LA to GLA is slow in mammals. Moreover, it has been suggested that due to stress, aging, or pathology (e.g., hypertension, diabetes, etc.), formation of a sufficient amount may be impaired. This problem may be relieved by direct GLA supplementation, although caution is warranted since overconsumption could be harmful. Its alleviating action on psoriasis, atopic eczema, and mastalgia are already well documented, and GLA preparations are now frequently prescribed for the treatment of the latter two maladies. The GLA has also been under investigation for its beneficial effects in cardiovascular, psychiatric, and immunological disorders.

TEXTILES

The stalks of some varieties of cannabis contain up to 35 percent usable textile fiber. These long, thin fibers can be extracted from the stalks by simple, albeit labor-intensive, methods. Thus hemp is an appropriate crop for rural peasant agriculture and the cottage industry manufacture of fiber products. The dried stalks are first retted (moistened and fermented) to free the fibers from the wood of the stalks by microbial decomposition, dried again, and then run through a brake that crushes their woody center. These broken pieces of pith or "hurds" are removed from the fibers by pulling them through the teeth of a hackle, an apparatus resembling an inverted turf rake. Afterward, the strands of fiber are combed to remove any remaining small debris and to lay the fibers parallel. They are then bundled and stored. Further processing and the spinning of yarn and weaving of cloth are traditionally performed within the hemp farmer's own home or village. In industrialized hemp agriculture, factories buy either dried stalks (Eastern Europe) or stripped fiber ribbons (China) from the farmers.

Although cannabis was traditionally seldom used for fine textile production, it has long served as the peasant's mainstay for cordage and cloth across Europe and Asia and was used extensively in the former colonies in the New World. A wide range of textile products can be made from hemp. New technology has made possible the manufacture of cloth with outstanding texture and versatility. Compared to cotton, hemp fibers are longer, more lustrous, more absorbent, have a higher tensile strength, and are more resistant to sunlight and mildew damage. These qualities of the basic fiber allow the manufacture of soft, warm (or cool), absorbent, and durable textile materials of all types and weights useful for clothing, mattresses, blankets, linens, carpets, draperies, wall coverings, upholstery, artist's canvas, sails, tarpaulins, sack cloth, etc. Rot-resistant maritime ropes and netting as well as cords, twine, thread, and carpet or linoleum-backing can also be manufactured from hemp.

Natural fiber textiles have steadily gained popularity since the early 1970s and the international textile market is eager for a new natural fiber. Pure hemp textiles possess a natural luster and resilient body that offers interesting and attractive opportunities for clothing designers. Hemp yarn can be woven along with yarns from other fibers to make blended textiles that incorporate much of the appearance and character of the other fiber and can be marketed at lower prices. Further, hemp fibers can be readily spun in combination with cotton, silk, wool, or other bast fibers to produce a wide variety of blended yarns.

If hemp is to replace or supplement other fibers, then the finished fibers must be made softer, and this effort can be initiated through genetic plant improvement. Chinese, Japanese, and Korean varieties produce a moderate content of long, thin, and supple primary fibers. Oriental hemp farmers have traditionally grown hemp that is harvested when it is very young, before flowering. Modern European varieties have traditionally been bred for high primary fiber content as well as higher coarse and stiff secondary fiber content. European hemp farmers usually allow their crop to mature longer, until flowering begins. The total fiber yields of the best Hungarian and Russian varieties are much higher than those of the East Asian varieties from China, Korea, and Japan, but the fiber quality is not as fine.

The advance of hemp fiber will also depend on the development and application of modern processing techniques. The Germans invented a hemp "cottonizing" process that was used from the 1930s through World War II, allowing the less expensive hemp fiber to be spun in combination with cotton and rayon. Later, the Hungarians also developed their own techniques. These processes rely on alkaline chemical digestion of the naturally occurring hardening and stiffening compounds (i.e., lignins) remaining on the fiber following the preliminary mechanical processes that isolate them from the plant. The Chinese have recently developed a patented hemp "degumming" process that softens the fibers so that they can be spun into supple, fine-count yarns. The feasibility of their techniques for the European hemp varieties possessing a higher secondary fiber content has not been established. It also remains to be seen if modern fiber processing steps can be performed on an increasing scale with a minimum of environmental stress. Forethought will be required to develop environmentally sound practices from the onset, since their implementation is more difficult in an already established industry.

Relatively coarse hemp textiles of a canvas grade and a somewhat lighter (but still heavy) clothing grade in several weights and weaves from China and Eastern Europe appeared in the United States around 1990. In the mid–1990s, hemp blends with cotton and silk became very popular. North America and northern Europe are realizing a hemp textile boom resulting from the resurgence of hemp in the news media. Many new hemp textile products are expected to be developed in the near future. Because of its resistance to wear and to the damaging effects of light and moisture, hemp textiles are well suited for upholstery, draperies, carpets, and other furnishings. Since hemp textiles are not restricted by the laws against cannabis drugs, this trade is expected to grow rapidly over the next few years. Currently, the problem is that hemp is in short supply. Hungary, Romania, and China are the only nations producing any commercial quantities of high quality hemp cloth, and they are not producing enough to satisfy current market demand in both the East and the West. As Western capitalization of the Hungarian and Chinese hemp industries continues, supplies of quality hemp products will rise to meet increasing consumer demand, and prices will become more competitive with cotton. However, this will require several years, and such developments must occur in many other regions before total world hemp textile production even approaches the current trade levels of the major natural fibers. Canada must import cotton and flax fiber and is eager to participate in this global expansion. During hemp's time of renewed industrialization, the demand for these textiles will exceed supply, so hemp will continue to command a high price in comparison with similar natural products. Traditional hand-made hemp cloth will always attract a premium price because of its beauty, rarity, and cultural significance. It remains to be seen to what degree hemp's presence in the marketplace will increase and whether it will eventually rival other sources of textile fiber.

PAPER PRODUCTS

Hemp provides a renewable resource for the production of the cellulose used in paper manufacture. This "tree-free paper" results in a low environmental cost because over a comparable period of time, the cellulose yield of hemp per hectare is many times greater than that of a forest. Further, if a forest burns down, it represents the loss of many years of biomass accumulation, but if a hemp field burns down or fails due to drought or other climatic conditions, only one year's growth is lost, and the crop can be replanted the following year. In addition, since hemp contains less than 25 percent of the natural lignin "glue" that binds wood fibers together, pulp processing can be milder and the environmentally safer peroxide bleaching process can be used. Hydrogen peroxide breaks down into oxygen and water, causing no environmental damage. The wood pulp industry almost universally uses a sulfite and chlorine process that produces large amounts of toxic waste (e.g., acids, chlorine, sulfur, and dioxin), which often enter the environment.

Hemp paper resists decomposition and does not exhibit the usual age-related sulfur-yellowing of wood-derived papers. Paper containing hemp cellulose is currently used for such high quality products as archival records, museum mounts, currency and other monetary instruments, artwork, fine books, and postage stamps. Paper produced from a mixture of the hurds and short fibers can be used for textbooks, computer paper, photocopy paper, bags, carton stock, and corrugated cardboard. Low-acid hemp fiber papers are also highly recyclable. In recent years, several hemp related books and journals have been printed on paper with hemp content.

Hemp fiber and hemp hurd pulp also blend well with pulp from other sources that may serve as a less expensive filler in specific paper formulations. One of the most economically viable uses for hemp fiber is to strengthen post-consumer pulp by adding a long, strong fiber to the short and weak fibers from recycled wood pulp paper, extending the number of recyclings possible with used paper pulp. Hemp crops have been grown for this purpose in the Netherlands.

Currently, 100 percent hemp paper is produced only in limited amounts for fine art use and limited printings. Pure hemp papers are not competitively priced with wood pulp papers unless purchased in very large amounts. However, several German, English and East European smooth-surfaced papers are currently available that incorporate 30–60 percent cannabis pulp blended with post-consumer waste. These papers are generally suited for office work and photocopying and many are of a sufficiently high quality to be suitable for printing paper or stationery. Many existing paper mills would be able to handle cannabis pulp, were sufficient amounts produced to make it practical. It is estimated that hemp stalks can be produced in Europe for ECU 50–70 (approximately U.S. $50–70) per ton (EC-AIR 1993). This is comparable to the price of softwood pulp. Cannabis-based cellulose pulp is also produced in France and Spain and is usually used in formulations for the high quality, low acid, blended-pulp specialty papers used in tea bags and cigarettes. Spanish pulp is used in the British and German hemp papers. Because hemp fiber is resistant to sun and moisture damage, it is also ideal for garden mulching paper, greenhouse weed mats, and the nonwoven geo-textiles used for landscaping and erosion control.

ADDITIONAL PRODUCTS

Hemp hurds make an excellent, naturally absorbent material for cat litter and for covering the floor of animal pens. The English, French, and Dutch produce a horse stable bedding by crushing dried cannabis stalks in a brake and packaging them in lightly compressed sacks. These hurds are readily composted, especially after they are saturated with nitrogenous animal wastes. This is a fine example of the direct use of a hemp product without complex processing.

Cannabis can also be used to make building materials. Suitably fireproofed hemp hurds are used as wall-fill insulation and are also being marketed by several companies in France as a constituent of construction blocks. Hemp hurd houses may be an answer to housing shortages in countries with few remaining forest resources, such as China and India. In Hungary, Poland, and the Netherlands particle board is manufactured from chipped hemp stalks. The dried hemp stalks are chopped into short pieces and pressed together with a binder to form the coarse interior matrix of a surfaced particle board. In 1991 Hungarian researchers were granted a patent for a more advanced and stronger laminated board made from crossed layers of whole hemp stalks also held together with a binder. So far, this type of product has not been marketed. An Austrian process that uses extreme pressure to compress hemp pulp into plasticlike molded products also shows great potential.

As a chemical feed stock, hurds can be treated in a manner similar to wood pulp and converted to the same wide range of products: plastics, propellants, explosives, etc. Cannabis seed oil makes a suitable ingredient in soap and other body care products, detergents, nontoxic paints, varnishes, and printer's ink. This oil can also be polymerized (the molecules linked) into plastics and other industrial materials that are currently derived from petrochemical sources, or it can serve as an alternative starting material for the production of these industrial chemicals (e.g., alcohols, ketones, aldehydes, etc.).

ENERGY APPLICATIONS

Cannabis is one of the plant kingdom's most efficient photosynthetic converters of atmospheric CO_2 into usable biomass and could serve as an inexpensive feed stock for fuel and energy production. Hemp seed oil is somewhat flammable and of limited use in lamps and diesel-type engines. The oil might also be "cracked" (a standard petroleum processing procedure) to break up its long chain molecules, providing a more easily combustible fuel. Perhaps microbial conversion of plant biomass to ethanol will also prove feasible. However, the real energy contribution of this plant might be best realized through the controlled pyrolytic conversion (i.e., at high temperatures in an oxygen-deprived atmosphere) of its whole biomass to methane, methanol, fuel oil, and charcoal. Unlike coal, these fuels contain little, if any, sulfur, a major contributor to the production of acid rain from industrial stack emissions. Certainly, the most direct energy utilization technique involves simply rolling the raw cannabis biomass into large bales and burning them in an electrical power generating facility. Growing a clean-burning, low-sulfur coal substitute at a rate of several tons per hectare (1 ha = 2.5 acres) could present an attractive alternative to fossil fuels. Much of the world's forest resources are burned for cooking and heating. Environmental pressure is particularly acute across much of Africa, Asia, and South America. Hemp and other renewable fuel sources can substitute for petrochemicals and save forests.

It will be necessary to perform a careful overall economic analysis of the potential of hemp for biomass production in comparison to other valuable crop candidates. Several sources of biomass are currently available and yet are not utilized for energy production. Many annual crops in the temperate zone have been shown to have a biomass limit of 20 tons of dry matter per hectare per crop cycle. Tropical sugarcane has been recorded as yielding up to 64 tons per hectare in a year, which is approximately comparable to temperate crops on a per month basis (Simmonds 1979). One would expect cannabis biomass production to approach the same approximate limits. In frost-free regions cannabis can be cultivated all year long. Late and slow-maturing varieties with indeterminate flowering could be adapted to tropical biomass production and be harvested without regard to floral maturity. In northern temperate regions, tropical cannabis varieties grow rapidly under the long photoperiod of summer, becoming very large but never maturing. Therefore, they do not produce either viable pollen and seed or much potent resin, but they do produce large amounts of biomass. In a single summer season, temperate hemp produces up to 12 tons of dry stalks per hectare per crop cycle, and foliage could add 50 percent to this total (EC-AIR 1993). Research must be carried out to determine just how efficient cannabis might be as a biomass producer under different cropping systems.

Multi-Use Strategies

Cannabis is the only plant that is used for fiber and pulp from its stalks, food and oil from its seed, and medicines from its resin. With the possible exception of certain members of the Cruciferae (i.e., turnip, kale, mustard, and canola are used for vegetables, fodder, and oil) no other crop plant is used for so many purposes (Simmonds 1976). Certainly no other single plant can be put to such a wide range of uses as cannabis.

As with other multiuse plants, specific cannabis varieties have been developed for differing purposes, selected from their widely diversified gene pool. Hemp fiber varieties have been selected for high yield of stalks, uniform maturation, low THC content, high fiber content, and, to some degree, high fiber quality. Seed varieties have been selected for factors contributing to high seed yield. Drug varieties have been selected for high THC content or high resin production and high flower/leaf ratios. The enforcement of these different sets of selection criteria has resulted in three groups of cannabis varieties suited for the manufacture of differing products. However, cannabis has never been intentionally bred for several other potentially valuable characteristics (e.g., bulk cellulose or seed protein or fatty acids). Varieties are also needed that are resistant to fungal pests encountered in the humid maritime climates of England, the Netherlands, and other parts of Northern Europe and Scandinavia. Tropical and semitropical hemp varieties low in THC are entirely lacking. It is expected that cannabis breeders will respond as do breeders of other crop plants: developing varieties that the agricultural industries find appropriate for making marketable products. It is unfortunate that hemp breeders must first overcome political obstacles, especially the lowering of plant THC content to very low limits, before they can begin to develop the other beneficial characteristics of cannabis.

It is unlikely that the primary use of cannabis will be for the production of industrial raw materials alone, since biomass is the low value by-product of all cannabis industries and is usually plowed back into the land. Hemp hurds and mill scraps are often wasted by the hemp textile industry because it is not cost-effective to transport them to a paper factory off-site. Production for these and other end uses may not prove economically feasible unless incorporated within the framework of an integrated plan to process hemp for multiple purposes simultaneously. The ultimate solution may be the development of a multiuse variety yielding an optimized combination of products from one plant. This would be especially advantageous in areas such as Western Europe, where arable land and manual labor are at a premium. Separate machinery would still be required for each of the differing product processing steps (as with single-use varieties), but total utilization of a uniform feed stock strain and decentralized processing on-site would make more efficient use of fuel and raw materials.

Plant breeders must overcome the effects of "resource partitioning" in order to develop a valuable multiuse variety with sufficient economic yield in each trait superior to that of existing single-use varieties. These partitioning effects tend to increase one economically valuable trait at the expense of another. Fortunately, because of the ancient cultural and geographical isolation of the early unimproved cannabis "land-races" (naturally established varietal types) and the selective breeding of these separate varieties for fiber, seed, and drug use, the gene pool is diverse, and overcoming partitioning effects may not be as much of a problem in cannabis as it has been with other crop plants.

Although the cultivation and processing of cannabis are perfectly adapted to manual peasant labor, the trend in modern agriculture toward automation continues. All modern industrial varieties must be selected for uniformity and acceptability for machine harvesting and processing. This could lead to a compromise between the quality of fiber, seed, or resin and the preferences of engineers who develop agricultural machinery. The modern tomato provides us with a typical example of a machine-harvestable and processable fruit that suffers from a lack of flavor and lowered vitamin content.

Conservation of the genetic diversity of cannabis is of the greatest importance to the future of breeding improved cannabis varieties. Many of the original, relatively unmodified land-races that formed the basic building blocks of modern drug and fiber hemp cannabis varieties have been lost. The remaining variability expressed in cannabis is crucial to the success of future breeding programs. Variability cannot be created in crop plants but can only be reshuffled into different combinations. Seed collections must be grown out in genetic isolation from other types periodically and on a large scale to keep each varietal line viable and genetically diverse. Every effort must be made to preserve all available varieties of cannabis before many more become extinct. We may already have lost unique varieties containing compounds of medical value or exhibiting other beneficial traits. Once a variety is lost, it is very difficult to recreate it through the recombination of other varieties and once its genes become extinct, it is essentially lost forever.

The successful industrialization of all newly introduced crops requires a period of "protected" introduction (often supported by government research grants and production subsidies to the farmer) before sufficient demand for the products of the new crop builds in the marketplace. This is being provided in the European Community, and similar incentives will be required if hemp is to enter quickly into mainstream agriculture in the United States. Eventually, demand alone will drive the market, where hemp proves to be superior as well as competitively priced. Unfortunately, it is likely that due to a lingering confusion between the value of cannabis as a crop plant and its misperceived threat as a drug problem, the United States will miss its opportunity to become a leading hemp-producing nation. Despite American agricultural prowess in other endeavors, the foreseeable future promises that this crop will come primarily from the new producers in Canada and Western Europe and from traditional producers in the semi-industrialized nations of Asia and Eastern Europe.

Environmentally Friendly Crop

Cannabis crops grow rapidly and tend to overgrow and shade out competing weeds. Herbicide use is usually not necessary in densely planted hemp fields provided with sufficient autumn and spring plowing. In the rare cases where herbicides may be required, they are usually applied only once as a pre-emergent before the seed is sown. Few insect pests attack field crops of cannabis, and pesticide applications are also rarely necessary. Hemp presents a stark contrast to cotton cultivation, which disastrously depletes the soil and consumes far more agricultural chemicals than any other crop. In glasshouses and grow rooms, insect pests and fungal diseases are a much more serious problem, but they can be controlled preventively through environmental manipulation and correctively through the use of natural biocontrols. The few chemical pesticides that may be required can be of low toxicity and can be incorporated into an "Integrated Pest Management" (IPM) approach to control.

Contrary to the often quoted report of Dewey (1913) stating that hemp requires little fertilizer and does not lower soil fertility, cannabis is actually a quite heavy feeder. It withdraws two to three times as much nitrogen, phosphorous, and potassium from the soil as cereals (Dempsey 1975), although farmers consider this crop beneficial to the soil structure. While high application rates of chemical fertilizers are not required for adequate yields, good harvests require sufficient soil fertility. Cannabis is particularly responsive to manuring (as marijuana growers are well aware). Hemp does not deplete the soil as much if the harvested plants are dried and processed (and their stalks retted) in the field, where they are repeatedly moistened by dew and acted upon by fungi. A significant amount of the nutrients contained in the foliage, plant debris, and roots is thereby returned to the soil when plowed under each autumn. This "dew-retting" is simple, easily automated, and causes little, if any, environmental damage. Unfortunately, it also produces an inferior grade of hemp suitable only for the coarsest applications such as the production of ropes and sacking.

Dutch researchers have developed an ensilaging system whereby hemp stalks can be stored in a partially anaerobic fermenting state without field drying and can be used later for pulp and fiber extraction as the need arises. This technique will allow hemp to be profitably cultivated in regions with humid summer and autumn climates where the field drying of hemp stalks is not possible (EC-AIR 1993).

"Water-retting" is used to produce hemp fiber of fine quality. It has traditionally been the preferred retting technique in China, Japan, and Eastern Europe and is often done in ponds, waterways, and ditches. The stems are submerged for up to a week and while they decompose, butyric acid, pectins, and other by-products are released into the water. Water-retting requires large amounts of fresh water, and this retting water must be changed often. Dumping this nutrient-rich retting water into streams and lakes can cause eutrophication. This is a process initiated by a rapid algal bloom caused by these added nutrients. However, when this sudden growth exhausts the nutrients, the abrupt death of these organisms results in deoxygenation of the aquatic environment due to the consequent decomposition process. This soon suffocates the other species living in that water. If the retting compounds are sufficiently diluted before release into the environment, they do not cause such an effect or may even prove useful if utilized as an organically enriched irrigation water for crops. Research is also being carried on to determine which microbial organisms are most appropriate for environmentally friendly water-retting.

OXYGEN PRODUCTION AND CARBON FIXATION

Burning several million years of stored fossil fuels in just a few decades has increased atmospheric carbon dioxide (CO_2) levels, causing the greenhouse effect (a trapping of planetary heat normally lost to outer space), resulting in global warming (the gradual increase of average temperatures worldwide). This, in turn, can result in climatic changes (i.e., extremes of temperature and moisture) and affect sea levels, potentially threatening established coastlines. Green plants are the primary organisms capable of using the energy of sunlight to "fix" (convert to a usable form) the carbon atoms contained in carbon dioxide, and the hydrogen and oxygen atoms contained in water into simple sugars (the building blocks of more complex molecules) through the biochemical process of photosynthesis. As plants perform this process, they also release vital life-supporting oxygen into the atmosphere. The increased cultivation of cannabis, like that of any other plant, would increase this oxygen production and carbon fixation, helping to replace at least this one function of our rapidly vanishing forests and other habitats not in plants, thus playing a critical role in the maintenance of planetary balance.

However, until comprehensive programs are in place to maintain and eventually increase our *total* photosynthetic capacity (rather than just tree-farming a limited percentage of the natural forests cut annually), cannabis or any other fast-growing and efficient plant will not be needed. What is really lacking is a coordinated international policy and a concerted, government-initiated effort to "green" our depleted planet. If cannabis merely replaces other crops because of the superior products that can be made from it, then there would be little or no *net* increase in global plant biomass and consequent photosynthesis and therefore, no increased direct benefit to the environment. One carbon-fixing and oxygen-producing crop would simply be replaced by another. Hemp, as a substitute for fossil fuels and forest resources, could utilize marginal or presently unused agricultural land to meet the growing demand for this new crop. Farmers would not need to cut down forests to grow hemp, so there could be a net increase in carbon fixation and oxygen production. Unlike fossil fuels, burning hemp would add no more CO_2 to the atmosphere than it had extracted during its growth. Certainly, forests could be better used for their unique wood products and appreciated for their intrinsic value rather than exploited as a source of pulp products better made from cannabis.

EROSION CONTROL

Cannabis is cultivated in a wide range of environments on every temperate continent and naturalizes readily as a weed throughout Eurasia and North America, especially in regions with a warm, moist summer growing season. One of the greatest adaptive tools of weeds is their heterozygosity (variation of genetic characteristics), allowing a broad range of inherited traits to be harbored within the population. This trait allows increased adaptation of a species to a wider variety of environmental conditions. Dioecious wind-pollinated plants, such as cannabis, are characteristically highly heterozygous, and this accounts in large part for their great adaptability. This heterozygosity is also the genetic basis for rapid progress in cannabis varietal improvement. Special varieties adapted for erosion control, possessing enhanced weed characteristics, such as rapid maturation and tolerance to environmental extremes, could be bred for their improved ability to colonize an area and establish reproductive populations. These varieties could incorporate traits such as increased root growth, low nutrient requirements, drought tolerance, and frost hardiness. However, caution should balance this initiative, lest an enhanced potential "pest plant" escape into the general environment.

LAND RECLAMATION

One method for absorbing and concentrating toxic compounds contained in contaminated soil is to cultivate plants that will selectively bioaccumulate them and then to properly dispose of the resulting crop. Cannabis is an active feeder and takes up large amounts of soil solutes. Its rapid biomass accumulation, weedy colonizing tendencies, and suitability for mechanized harvesting may make cannabis suitable for use in the reclamation of polluted land fills and dump sites. Preliminary experiments in Poland indicate that it may be useful for absorbing the heavy metal contamination of such soils (Kozlowski et al. 1995).

Future of Cannabis

Cannabis has largely been neglected by the formal agricultural community and has not received many of the benefits of modern research that have been applied to other more developed crops, although considering the legal and economic restrictions extant, it has progressed quite far. One can imagine that cannabis will become an even more productive crop plant as modern genetic techniques are brought to bear on its improvement.

Many members of the Fabaceae (bean family) contain the genes to provide a proper host environment in their roots for specially adapted *Rhizobium* bacteria. These nitrogen-fixing organisms fix atmospheric nitrogen gas (N_2) into the water-soluble ions of nitrate (NO_3) used by the host plant as a primary nutrient and ensure that the ecosystem as a whole receives a steady supply of usable nitrogen. This symbiotic (mutually beneficial) relationship with nitrogen-fixers reduces the amount of nitrogen fertilizer a crop requires and can potentially provide net gains of nitrogen to the soil through decomposition of the harvest remains. Through gene transfer techniques, cannabis could be genetically engineered to serve as a host to nitrogen-fixing organisms. This idea has been approached with limited success in other crops, such as corn. Lowered soil nitrogen requirements would enhance the potential for cannabis to be grown in marginal areas.

Cannabis can be readily manipulated to be reproduced asexually, yielding many identical individuals (clones). Vegetative cuttings are made from a mother plant, transplanted and grown to desired size, then induced to flower by photoperiod (day-length) reduction. This has become the normal method of drug-cannabis production in the modern glasshouse or grow room. Tiny sterile meristem (shoot tip) cuttings that are easily rooted and stored in sterile glass vessels represent the current state of the art. Cultures of undifferentiated cannabis cells have also been maintained for many years. This callus tissue is potentially useful for cleaning up varieties infected with viral or fungal pathogens, screening for stress resistance, and early selection or creation of mutants. Probably the most exciting potential use for callus is as a genetic archive for thousands of individually cloned potential plants stored in a frozen state. However, though lumps of cannabis callus grow well and develop roots in response to growth hormone applications, it has proven very difficult to initiate shoot formation. Unless these undifferentiated cells can be thawed and regenerated (without mutations) into whole plantlets and then grown to form healthy mature plants suitable for seed production, they will be useless (e.g., undifferentiated cannabis cells have never been shown to produce THC in vitro).

In the distant future, other organisms might be genetically engineered to produce THC or other cannabinoids. Perhaps a plant family that already produces terpenoid essential oils, such as the Labiatae (mints), could be genetically engineered to produce cannabinoids. Plants of this family also produce appropriate glandular trichomes (hairlike resin-producing structures) on the surface of their leaves. It does not seem economically feasible to attempt the genetic engineering of bacteria or other simple life forms to produce THC, since the natural plant source of cannabinoids is so inexpensive to grow.

Despite these present technical challenges, further "biotech" discoveries will undoubtedly create exciting new cannabis-based products. We must then take care to avoid narrowing the cannabis gene base through narrow breeding selection for specific applications or even abandoning the cannabis plant altogether in favor of artificially bioengineered substitutes. With care, one might expect that our 12,000-year-old relationship with this useful plant will last well through the *next* several millennia!

Conclusion

There is no need to overglamorize the potentials of cannabis, as its value as a beneficial crop plant is self-evident. Cannabis alone will not "save our planet," as hemp activists have often claimed, but it can certainly provide a variety of effective medicines and environmentally friendly products in the near future. Cannabis may also prove itself as a valuable land management tool and provider of biomass for raw materials and energy production. Until restrictions on the cultivation and use of cannabis are lifted and new policies enacted to actively pursue a better understanding of this plant's potential for improving our quality of life, it will remain a crop of secondary importance, clouded in misunderstanding. Progress in cannabis research is accelerating despite the legal obstacles associated with this plant, and once the legal flood-gates are opened, significant discoveries can be expected. That a single plant can produce so many different valuable commodities is a natural wonder. It is a great oversight on the part of many governments that we are not now receiving more benefits from a strong alliance with such a venerable ally.

References

Clarke, R.C., and D.W. Pate. 1994. Medical marijuana. *Journal of the International Hemp Association* 1 (1): 9–12.

Deferne, J.L., and D.W. Pate. 1996. Hemp seed oil: A source of valuable essential fatty acids. *Journal of the International Hemp Association* 3 (1): 1, 4–7.

Dempsey, J. M. 1975. Fiber crops. In *Hemp*, 46–87. Gainesville, FL: University of Florida Press.

Dewey, L.H. 1913. Hemp. *USDA Yearbook*, 283–246.

EC-AIR Meeting. (August 24, 1993). Wageningen, Netherlands.

Erasmus, U. 1993. *Fats That Heal, Fats That Kill*. Burnaby, B.C., Canada: Alive Books.

Karus, M., F. Grotenhermen, and H. Schaaf. 1995. Mißbrauchpotential THC-armer Faserhanfsorten als Rauschdroge. *Bioresource Hemp Symposium Proceedings*, 589–605. (2d ed.). Cologne, Germany: Nova-Institute.

Kozlowski, R., P. Baraniecki, L. Grabowska, and J. Mankowski. 1995. Recultivation of degraded areas through cultivation of hemp. *Bioresource Hemp Symposium Proceedings*. (2d ed.) 259–267.

Matsunaga, T., H. Nagatomo, I. Yamamoto, and H. Yoshimura. 1990. Identification and determination of cannabinoids in commercially available cannabis seeds. *Eisei Kagaku* 36 (6): 545–547.

Pate, D.W. 1994. Chemical ecology of cannabis. *Journal of the International Hemp Association* 1 (2): 29, 32–37.

Randall, R.C. 1991. *Marijuana and AIDS: Pot, Politics, and PWAs in America*. Washington, DC: Galen Press.

Simmonds, N.W., ed. 1976. *Evolution of Crop Plants* (pp. 203–204). London and New York: Longman.

Simmonds, N.W. 1979. *Principles of Crop Improvement* (p. 42). London: Longman Scientific and Technical.

Theimer, R. 1996. Personal communication.

Theimer, R.R., and H. Mölleken. 1995. Analysis of the oils from different hemp (*Cannabis sativa* L.) cultivars: Perspectives for economic utilization. *Bioresource Hemp Symposium Proceedings*. (2d ed.) 536–545a.

Wirtshafter, D. 1995. Nutrition of hemp seeds and hemp seed oil? In *Bioresource Hemp Symposium Proceedings*. (2d ed.) 546–555.

APPENDIX A

Organizations for Therapeutic Cannabis

Alliance for Cannabis Therapeutics (ACT)
P.O. Box 21210
Kalorama Station
Washington, D.C. 20009
(202) 483-8595
alliance@webcom.com
http://www.marijuana-as-medicine.org

This organization was founded in 1981 by Robert Randall. The Alliance for Cannabis Therapeutics is a nonprofit organization seeking to end the federal prohibition of cannabis (marijuana) in medicine. ACT works for fundamental reform of current regulations which prohibit the use of cannabis in medicine and inhibit neutral study of the plant's therapeutic properties. ACT concentrates solely on the question of marijuana's medical utility and adopts no policy regarding the nonmedical use of cannabis.

Cannabis Cultivator's Club
1444 Market Street
San Francisco, CA 94102
(415) 621-3986
FAX: (415) 621-0604

Founded by Dennis Peron, it is the largest cannabis buyers club in the United States, serving more than 10,000 patients. It was closed by state and federal officials during the summer of 1996. On January 15, 1997, the club was reopened by a Superior Court ruling for states' rights under the passage of Proposition 215.

Green + Cross Patient Co-Op (GCPC)
P.O. Box 10416
Bainbridge, Island, WA 98110
(206) 762-0630

Co-founded by JoAnna McKee and Stich Miller. The not-for-profit GCPC is patterned after the nationwide network of buyers' clubs that exist to provide people with AIDS with unapproved anti–AIDS drugs and treatments. The GCPC provides medicinal cannabis to people with AIDS, but its scope is not limited to AIDS. The GCPC is open to all who present a bona fide need for medicinal cannabis on the advice of their physician or other healthcare professionals.

International Cannabis Alliance of Researchers and Educators, Inc.

(I-CARE)
Fish Pond Plantation
1472 Fish Pond Road
Howardsville, VA 24562
(804) 263-4484
FAX: (804) 263-6753
I-CARE@ MedicalCannabis.com

A corporation formed to educate the public and health care professionals about the therapeutic use of cannabis. It has produced a 17-minute award-winning video, *Marijuana as Medicine*, which features the first five patients legally receiving marijuana as medicine through the IND program, as well as its second project, this book. Provides expert witnesses for legal cases involving therapeutic cannabis use; consults to corporate, government, political and professional organizations concerning therapeutic cannabis.

Patients Out of Time

Fish Pond Plantation
1472 Fish Pond Road
Howardsville, VA 24562
(804) 263-4484
FAX: (804) 263-6753
Patients@MedicalCannabis.com

A nonprofit organization dedicated to educating the public and healthcare professionals about the therapeutic value of cannabis. It urges professional healthcare organizations to proactively urge the federal government to allow patient access to therapeutic cannabis through a formal and public resolution/position paper and is available for consultation to assist in this endeavor. Patients Out of Time will continue to exist until cannabis becomes legally available to patients in need.

APPENDIX B

Organizations Supporting Access to Therapeutic Cannabis

AIDS Action Council 1996
Alliance for Cannabis Therapeutics
American Academy of Family
  Physicians 1977
American Bar Association (ABA)
American Civil Liberties Union
  (ACLU)
American Medical Students Association 1993
*American Public Health Association (APHA) 1995
Burlington Board of Health,
  Burlington, VT 1994
California Medical Association
  1993
California Nurses Association
  1995
California-Pacific Annual Conference of the United Methodist
  Church 1996
*Colorado Nurses Association
  1995
Conference of Episcopal Bishops
Cure AIDS Now
Florida Governor's Red Ribbon
  Panel on AIDS
International Cannabis Alliance
  of Researchers and Educators
  (I-CARE) 1992
Iowa Civil Liberties Union
Iowa Democratic Party
Lymphoma Foundation of America

Marin County Council, CA 1993
Minnesota Democratic Farm-
  Labor Party
*Mississippi Nurses Association
  1995
Mothers Against Misuse and
  Abuse (MAMA)
National Association of Attorneys
  General 1993
National Association of Criminal
  Defense Lawyers (NACDL)
National Association of People
  with AIDS
*National Nurses Society on
  Addictions (NNSA) 1995
*North Carolina Nurses Association 1996
Northern New England Psychiatric
  Society
Oakland City Council, California
  1996
Patients Out of Time 1995
The People of the State of Arizona
  1996
The People of the State of California 1996
Physicians Association for AIDS
  Cure
Preventive Medical Center,
  Netherlands 1993
San Francisco City Council, CA
  1992

Santa Cruz County Council, CA 1993

Stichting Institute of Medical Marijuana, The Netherlands 1993

Virginia Nurses Association 1994

Virginia Nurses Society on Addictions 1993

Compiled by Patients Out of Time.

*Therapeutic cannabis consultation and information provided by:
  Patients Out of Time
  Fish Pond Plantation
  1472 Fish Pond Road
  Howardsville, VA 24562
  (804) 263-4484

APPENDIX C

Resolution of the Virginia Nurses Association

Legalizing Marijuana for Medical Purposes

Submitted by: Council of District Presidents, Ethics Committee, and Committee on Preserving the Rights of HIV Infected Persons

Whereas Marijuana is a Schedule I drug, which means that it cannot be legally used as a medicine by patients or prescribed by physicians; and

Whereas Schedule I drugs must meet all of the following criteria: 1) have no therapeutic value, 2) are not safe for medical use, and 3) have a high abuse potential; and

Whereas Virginia nurses have an understanding a) of the negative health consequences that substance abuse and/or addiction can cause, b) that substance abuse and addiction are not about "bad" drugs, but rather about the unhealthy use of drugs, and c) that persons can develop a substance abuse or addiction problem from any psychoactive drugs, legal or illegal; and

Whereas Marijuana has been found to be effective in a) reducing intraocular pressure in glaucoma, b) reducing nausea and vomiting associated with chemotherapy, c) stimulating the appetite for patients living with AIDS and suffering from the wasting syndrome, d) controlling spasticity associated with spinal cord injury and multiple sclerosis, and e) controlling seizures associated with seizure disorders; and

Whereas Marijuana has a wide margin of safety for use under medical supervision and cannot cause lethal reactions; and

Whereas Thirty-six states, including Virginia, have recognized marijuana's therapeutic potential and have passed legislation supporting its medical use; and

Whereas   The Drug Enforcement Agency's own Administrative Law Judge ruled in 1988 that marijuana must be removed from the Schedule I category and made available for physicians to prescribe; and

Whereas   Desperate patients and/or their families have chosen to break the law to obtain this medicine when conventional medicines have not been effective or are too toxic. This places them at risk for criminal charges and at risk for obtaining contaminated medicines because of lack of quality control; and

Whereas   Nurses have an ethical obligation to be advocates for health care for all individuals. Medicines which enhance the quality of life for persons suffering from life threatening or debilitating illness; therefore be it

Resolved   That the Virginia Nurses Association support all reasonable efforts to end federal policies which prohibit or unnecessarily restrict marijuana's legal availability for legitimate medical uses; and be it

Resolved   That the Virginia Nurses Association provide education to the nurses of Virginia on the therapeutic use of marijuana and the federal prohibition of its use; and be it

Resolved   That the Virginia Nurses Association encourage other healthcare provider organizations to support medical access to marijuana; and be it

Resolved   That the Virginia Nurses Association submit a resolution to the American Nurses Association House of Delegates in 1995 that ANA educate American nurses about the therapeutic use of marijuana and the federal prohibition of its use; and be it

Resolved   That the Virginia Nurses Association submit a resolution to the American Nurses Association House of Delegates in 1995 that the ANA support a change in federal policy to permit medical access to marijuana for therapeutic purposes.

This resolution was passed by the Virginia Nurses Association Delegate Assembly on October 7, 1994. The VNA followed this resolution with a position paper, "Therapeutic Use of Cannabis/Marijuana," in March of 1995.

Virginia Nurses Association
7113 Three Chopt Rd.
Suite 204
Richmond, VA   23226
(804) 282-1808

APPENDIX D

Excerpt from the National Nurses Society on Addictions' Position Paper "Access to Therapeutic Cannabis"

As addictions nurses, members of the National Nurses Society on Addictions (NNSA) have an understanding of the negative health consequences that substance abuse and/or addiction can cause. Substance abuse and addiction are not about "bad" drugs, but rather about "bad" or unhealthy relationships with drugs. Persons can develop a substance abuse or addiction problem from any psychoactive drug, legal or illegal. Accordingly, our focus is on prevention of substance abuse and addiction as well as treatment for persons with such problems.

Addictions nurses understand that no drug is completely safe and that any drug can be abused. Prior to using any medication or drug, the patient should have an understanding of the expected benefits and associated risks so that he or she can make a responsible decision regarding its use.

As nurses, we have an ethical obligation to advocate for optimal health care for all individuals. Medicine which enhances the quality of life for persons suffering from life- and sense-threatening illnesses should not be prohibited because some persons may develop a substance abuse and/or addiction problem to that medicine. Cannabis does have therapeutic value and has a wide margin of safety, and therefore, practitioners should have the right to prescribe cannabis to patients when the potential benefits surpass the health risks.

NNSA's Position on Access to Therapeutic Cannabis

The National Nurses Society on Addictions urges the federal government to remove marijuana from the Schedule I category immediately and make it available for physicians to prescribe.

NNSA urges the American Nurses' Association and other healthcare-professional organizations to support patient access to this medicine.

NNSA supports ongoing human research to determine alternative active methods of administration to minimize health risks.

NNSA supports research regarding the various cannabinoids and combinations thereof to determine the greatest therapeutic potential.

Prepared by Mary Lynn Mathre, R.N., M.S.N., C.A.R.N., on behalf of the National Nurses Society on Addictions, effective May 1, 1995.
Complete text of this position paper can be obtained from the National Nurses Society on Addictions
4101 Lake Boone Trail, Suite 201
Raleigh, NC   27607
(919) 783-5871
nnsa@mercury.interpath.com

APPENDIX E

Resolution of the American Public Health Association

Access to Therapeutic Marijuana/Cannabis

The American Public Health Association,

Being aware that cannabis/marijuana has been used medicinally for centuries and that cannabis products were widely prescribed by physicians in the United States until 1937[1,2]; and

Being aware that "marijuana" prohibition began with the Marihuana Tax Act of 1937 under false claims despite disagreeing testimony from the AMA's representative[3,4]; and

Being further aware that the Controlled Substances Act of 1970 completely prohibited all medicinal use of marijuana by placing it in the most restrictive category of Schedule I, whereby drugs must meet three criteria for placement in this category: 1) have no therapeutic value, 2) are not safe for medical use, and 3) have a high abuse potential[5]; and

Being cognizant that the Drug Enforcement Administration's own administrative law judge ruled in 1988 that marijuana must be removed from Schedule I and made available for physicians to prescribe[6,7,8]; and

Knowing that 36 states have passed legislation recognizing marijuana's therapeutic value[9,10]; and

Also knowing that the only available access to legal marijuana which was through the Food and Drug Administration's Investigational New Drug Program has been closed by the Secretary of Health and Human Resources since 1992[11]; and

Understanding that while synthetic tetrahydrocannabinol (THC) is available in pill form, it is only one of approximately 60 cannabinoids which may have medicinal value individually or in some combination; and

Understanding that marijuana has an extremely wide margin of safety for use under medical supervision and cannot cause lethal reactions[6,32,34]; and

Understanding that marijuana has been found to be effective in a) reducing intraocular pressure in glaucoma,[12,13] b) reducing nausea and vomiting associated with chemotherapy,[14,15,16] c) stimulating the appetite for patients living with AIDS and suffering from the wasting syndrome,[17, 18, 19] d) controlling spasticity associated with spinal cord injury and multiple sclerosis,[20, 21, 22, 23, 24, 25] e) decreasing the suffering from chronic pain,[26, 27, 28] and f) controlling seizures associated with seizures disorders[29, 30, 31]; and

Understanding that marijuana seems to work differently than many conventional medications for the above problems, making it a possible option for persons resistant to the conventional medications[32, 33]; and

Being concerned that desperate patients and their families are choosing to break the law to obtain this medicine when conventional medicines or treatments have not been effective for them or are too toxic[34, 35]; and

Realizing that this places ill persons at risk for criminal charges and at risk for obtaining contaminated medicine because of the lack of quality control; and

Realizing that thousands of patients not helped by conventional medications and treatments, may find relief from their suffering with the use of marijuana if their primary care providers were able to prescribe this medicine; and

Concluding that cannabis/marijuana was wrongfully placed in Schedule I of the Controlled Substances depriving patients of its therapeutic potential; and

Recognizing that APHA adopted a resolution (7014) on Marijuana and the Law which urged federal and state drug laws to exclude marijuana from classification as a narcotic drug,[36] and

Concluding that greater harm is caused by the legal consequences of its prohibition than possible risks of medicinal use; therefore

1. Encourages research of the therapeutic properties of various cannabinoids and combinations of cannabinoids; and

2. Encourages research on alternative methods of administration to decrease the harmful effects related to smoking; and

3. Urges the Administration and Congress to move expeditiously to make cannabis available as a legal medicine where shown to be safe and effective and to immediately allow access to therapeutic cannabis through the Investigational New Drug Program.

References

1. Abel EA: Marihuana: The First Twelve Thousand Years. New York: McGraw-Hill Book Company, 1982.
2. Mikuriya TH, Ed: Marijuana: Medical Papers 1839–1972. Oakland, CA: Medi-Comp Press, 1973.
3. Bonnie RJ and Whitebread II, CH: The Marihuana Conviction: A History of Marihuana Prohibition in the United States. Charlottesville, VA: University Press of Virginia, 1974.
4. National Commission on Marihuana and Drug Abuse (RP Shafer, Chairman): Marihuana: a Signal of Misunderstanding. New York: the New American Library, Inc., 1972.
5. Controlled Substances Act of 1970 (Pub.L. 91-513, October 27, 1970, 21USC801 et seq.)
6. In the Matter of Marihuana Rescheduling Petition, Docket 86-22, Opinion, Recommended Ruling, Findings of Fact, Conclusions of Law, and Decision of Administrative Law Judge, September 6, 1988. Washington, D.C.: Drug Enforcement Agency, 1988.

7. Randall RC: Marijuana, Medicine and the Law. Washington, D.C.: Galen Press, 1988.
8. Randall RC: Marijuana, Medicine and the Law. (Volume II) Washington, D.C.: Galen Press, 1989.
9. Alliance for Cannabis Therapeutics: No accepted medical value?? ACT News Spring, 1995; p. 4.
10. Grinspoon L and Bakalar JB: Marihuana as medicine: a plea for consideration. JAMA 1995; 273(23):1875–1876.
11. Government extinguishes marijuana access, advocates smell politics. JAMA May 20, 1992; 267(19):2673–2674.
12. Colasanti BK: Review: Ocular hypotensive effect of marihuana cannabinoids: correlate of central action or separate phenomenon. J Ocular Pharmacol 1986; 2(3):295–304.
13. Hepler RS and Frank IM: Marihuana smoking and intraocular pressure. J Am Med Ass 1971 217:1392.
14. Sallan SE, Zinberg NE and Frei, III E: Antiemetic effect of delta-9-tetrahydrocannabinol in patients receiving cancer chemotherapy. New Engl J Med 1975; 293(16):795–797.
15. Sallan SE, Cronin C, Zelen M, and Zinberg NE: Antiemetics in patients receiving chemotherapy for cancer. New Engl J Med 1980; 302:135–138.
16. Vinciguerra V, Moore T, and Brennan, E: Inhalation marijuana as an antiemetic for cancer chemotherapy. N Y State J Med 1988; 88:525–527.
17. Nelson K, Walsh D, Deeter P, et al: A phase II study of delta-9-tetrahydrocannabinol for appetite stimulation in cancer-associated anorexia. J Palliative Care 1994; 10(1):14–18.
18. Regelson W, Butler JR, Schultz J et al: Delta-9-THC as an effective antidepressant and appetite stimulating agent in advanced cancer patients. In Int Conf Pharmacol Cannabis, Ed S Szara, MC Bruade. Savannah: Raven, 1975.
19. Foltin RW, Fischman MW, and Byrne MF: Effects of smoked marijuana on food intake and body weight of humans living in a residential laboratory. Appetite 1988; 11:1–14.
20. Clifford DB: Tetrahydrocannabinol for tremor in multiple sclerosis. Ann Neurol, 1983; 13:669–671.
21. Malec J, Harvey RF, and Cayner JJ: Cannabis effect on spasticity in spinal cord injury. Arch Phys Med Rehab 1982; 35:198.
22. Meinck H, Schonle PW, and Conrad B: Effect of cannabinoids on spasticity and ataxis in multiple sclerosis. J Neurol 1989; 236:120–122.
23. Petro D: Marihuana as a therapeutic agent for muscle spasm or spasticity. Psychosomatics 1980; 21:81–85.
24. Petro D and Ellenberger C: Treatment of human spasticity with delta-9-tetrahydro-cannabinol. J Clin Pharmacol 1981:21:413S–416S.
25. Ungerleider JT, Andyrsiak T, Fairbanks L., et al: Delta-9-THC in the treatment of spasticity associated with multiple sclerosis. Pharmacological Issues in Alcohol and Substance Abuse 7(1):39–50.
26. Johnson MR, Melvin LS, Althius, TH et al: Selective and potent analgesics derived from cannabinoids. J Clin Pharmacol 1981; 21:271S–282S.
27. Maurer M, Henn V, Dittrich A, et al: Delta-9-tetrahydrocannabinol shows antispastic and analgesic effects in a single case double-blind trial. Eur Arch Psychiatry Clin Neurosci 1990; 240:1–4.
28. Noyes, R, Jr., Brunk SF, Avery DH, et al: The analgesic properties of delta-9-tetrahydro-cannabinol and codeine. Clin Pharmacol Ther 1975; 18(1):84–89.
29. Cunha JM, Carlini EA, Pereira AE, et al: Chronic administration of cannabidiol to healthy volunteers and epileptic patients. Pharmacology 1980; 21:175–185.
30. Feeney D: Marihuana use among epileptics. JAMA 1976; 235:1105.
31. Karler R and Turkanis SA: The cannabinoids as potential antiepileptics. J Clin Pharmacol 1981; 21:437S–448S.
32. Institute of Medicine: Marijuana and Health. Washington, D.C.: National Academy Press, 1982.
33. Mechoulam R, Ed: Cannabinoids as Therapeutic Agents. Boca Raton, FL: CRC Press, 1986.
34. Cannabis clubs open for medicinal business. USA Today October 1, 1993: B1 and B5.

Resolution of the American Public Health Association • 223

35. Berger J: Mother's homemade marijuana: a plan to aid her son leads to arrest and push for change. The New York Times October 11, 1993.
36. American Public Health Association Resolution No. 7014: Marijuana and the Law. APHA Public Policy Statements, 1948–present, cumulative. Washington, DC: APHA, current volume.

American Public Health Association
1015 Fifteenth St., NW, Suite 300
Washington, DC   20005-2605
(202) 789-5674

APPENDIX F

Editorial from *The New England Journal of Medicine*
(Jan. 30, 1997)

Federal Foolishness and Marijuana (reprint)

The advanced stages of many illnesses and their treatments are often accompanied by intractable nausea, vomiting, or pain. Thousands of patients with cancer, AIDS, and other diseases report they have obtained striking relief from these devastating symptoms by smoking marijuana.[1] The alleviation of distress can be so striking that some patients and their families have been willing to risk a jail term to obtain or grow the marijuana.

Despite the desperation of these patients, within weeks after voters in Arizona and California approved propositions allowing physicians in their states to prescribe marijuana for medical indications, federal officials, including the President, the secretary of Health and Human Services, and the attorney general sprang into action. At a news conference, Secretary Donna E. Shalala gave an organ recital of the parts of the body that she asserted could be harmed by marijuana and warned of the evils of its spreading use. Attorney General Janet Reno announced that physicians in any state who prescribed the drug could lose the privilege of writing prescriptions, be excluded from Medicare and Medicaid reimbursement, and even be prosecuted for a federal crime. General Barry R. McCaffrey, director of the Office of National Drug Control Policy, reiterated his agency's position that marijuana is a dangerous drug and implied that voters in Arizona and California had been duped into voting for these propositions. He indicated that it is always possible to study the effects of any drug, including marijuana, but that the use of marijuana by seriously ill patients would require, at the least, scientifically valid research.

I believe that a federal policy that prohibits physicians from alleviating suffering by prescribing marijuana for seriously ill patients is misguided, heavy-handed, and inhumane. Marijuana may have long-term adverse effects and its use may presage serious additions, but neither long-term side effects nor addiction is a relevant issue in such patients. It is also hypocritical to forbid physicians to prescribe marijuana while permitting them to use morphine and meperidine to relieve extreme dyspnea and pain. With both these drugs the difference between the dose that relieves symptoms and the dose that hastens death is very narrow; by contrast, there is no risk of death from smoking marijuana. To demand evidence of therapeutic efficacy is equally hypocritical. The noxious sensations that patients experience are extremely difficult to quantify in controlled experiments. What really counts for a therapy with this kind of safety margin is whether a seriously ill patient feels relief as a result of the intervention, not whether a controlled trial "proves" its efficacy.

Paradoxically, dronabinol, a drug that contains one of the active ingredients in marijuana (tetrahydrocannabinol), has been available by prescription for more than a decade. But it is difficult to titrate the therapeutic dose of this drug, and it is not widely prescribed. By contrast, smoking marijuana produces a rapid increase in the blood level of the active ingredients and is thus more likely to be therapeutic. Needless to say, new drugs such as those that inhibit the nausea associated with chemotherapy may well be more beneficial than smoking marijuana, but their comparative efficacy has never been studied.

Whatever their reasons, federal officials are out of step with the public. Dozens of states have passed laws that ease restrictions on the prescribing of marijuana by physicians, and polls consistently show that the public favors the use of marijuana for such purposes.[1] Federal authorities should rescind their prohibition of the medicinal use of marijuana for seriously ill patients and allow physicians to decide which patients to treat. The government should change marijuana's status from that of a Schedule 1 drug (considered to be potentially addictive and with no current medical use) to that of a Schedule 2 drug (potentially addictive but with some accepted medical use) and regulate it accordingly. To ensure its proper distribution and use, the government could declare itself the only agency sanctioned to provide the marijuana. I believe that such a change in policy would have no adverse effects. The argument that it would be a signal to the young that "marijuana is OK" is, I believe, specious.

This proposal is not new. In 1986, after years of legal wrangling, the Drug Enforcement Administration (DEA) held extensive hearings on the transfer of marijuana to Schedule 2. In 1988, the DEA's own administrative-law judge concluded, "It would be unreasonable, arbitrary, and capricious for DEA to continue to stand between those sufferers and the benefits of this substance in light of the evidence in this record."[1] Nonetheless, the DEA overruled the judge's order to transfer marijuana to Schedule 2, and in 1992 it issued a final rejection of all requests for reclassification.[2]

Some physicians will have the courage to challenge the continued proscription of marijuana for the sick. Eventually, their actions will force the courts to adjudicate between the rights of those at death's door and the absolute power of bureaucrats whose decisions are based more on reflexive ideology and political correctness than on compassion.

References

1. Young F.L. Opinion and recommended ruling, marijuana rescheduling petition. Department of Justice, Drug Enforcement Administration. Docket 86-22. Washington, D.C.: Drug Enforcement Administration, September 6, 1988.
2. Department of Justice, Drug Enforcement Administration. Marijuana scheduling petition: denial of petition: remand. (Docket No. 86-22.) Fed Regist 1992;57(59):10489-508.

APPENDIX G

Organizations for
the Overall Use
of Cannabis

1. **Business Alliance for Commerce in Hemp** (BACH)
   P.O. Box 71093
   Los Angeles, CA 90071-0093
   (310) 288-4152   FAX: (510) 215-TEAM

   An organization dedicated to the restoration of industrial hemp, the reinstitution of medical marijuana, and private use of cannabis by citizens 18 years or older.

2. **Cannabis Action Network** (CAN)
   2560 Bancroft Way #46
   Berkeley, CA 94704
   (510) 486-8083
   caninfo@ccnet.com

   National grassroots nonprofit organization working to reform marijuana laws in the medical, industrial, spiritual and personal use areas.

3. **Help End Marijuana Prohibition** (H.E.M.P.)
   5632 Van Nuys Blvd., #310
   Van Nuys, CA 91401
   (818) 988-6210   FAX: (818) 988-3319
   e-mail: JackHerer@webtv.net
   http://www.fishnet.net/hemp

   This organization works towards the total relegalization of cannabis for medicine, industry, nutrition, as well as personal use for persons over 21. H.E.M.P. also wants the release of all non-violent prisoners incarcerated for marijuana-related offenses.

4. **Hemp Environmental Activists**
   P.O. Box 724
   Battle Creek, MI 49016
   (616) 968-2550

   A nonprofit organization focusing on the food, fuel, and fiber value of hemp.

5. **Hemp Industries Association** (HIA)
   P.O. Box 1080
   Occidental, CA 95465
   (500) HIA-HEMP
   (707) 874-3648   FAX: (707) 874-1104
   info@thehia.org   http://www.thehia.org

6. **The International Hemp Association** (IHA)
   Postbus 75007
   1070 AA Amsterdam
   The Netherlands
   Phone/Fax: 31-20-618-8758
   iha@euronet.nl

   The IHA acts as a liaison between academia, industry, and government, providing scientifically validated information on cannabis through the publication of its biannual, peer-reviewed journal. It also provides primary financial support for maintenance of the irreplaceable cannabis germplasm collection at the Vavilov Research Institute in St. Petersburg, Russia. Membership is invited by inquiry to the above address.

APPENDIX H

Sources of
Hemp Products

Ecolution
P.O. Box 2279
Merrifield, VA 22116
(703) 207-9001
http://www.ecolution.com

Grassroots of Hawaii
66-079 Kam Hwy.
Haleiwa, HI 96712
(808) 947-4367

Hemp Times
111 East 14th St., Suite 278
New York, NY 10003
(212) 260-0200

Lost Harvest
P.O. Box 615
Rye, NH 03870
(603) 431-5966
FAX: (603) 431-1489

New Age Hemp Co.
1 Steele St.
Burlington, VT 05401
(802) 865-5003

The Ohio Hempery, Inc.
7002 State Route 329
Guysville, OH 45735
Orders: 1-800-BUY-HEMP

FAX: (614) 662-6446
Inquiries: (614) 662-4367
hempery@hempery.com
http://www.hempery.com

Plant Hemp
423 Broome St.
New York, NY 10013
(800) 681-HEMP

Real Goods
555 Leslie St.
Ukiah, CA 95482-5576
Orders: (800) 762-7325
FAX: (707) 468-9394
foreign orders: (707) 468-9214
realgood@realgoods.com
http://www.realgoods.com

Sharon's Finest
P.O. Box 5020
Santa Rosa, CA 95402
(800) 656-9669
FAX: (705) 545-7116

U.S. Hemp
461 West Apache Trail, Ste. 130
Apache Junction, AZ 85220
(602) 983-7065
ushemp@ix.netcom.com

APPENDIX I
Additional Resources

1. **Families Against Mandatory Minimums** (FAMM)
   1612 K St. NW, Suite 1400
   Washington, DC 20006
   (202) 822-6700   FAX: (202) 822-6704
   famm@famm.org
   http://www.famm.org

   Nonprofit grassroots organization dedicated to state and federal drug sentencing reform.

2. **Fully Informed Jury Association** (FIJA)
   P.O. Box 59
   Helmville, MT 59843
   (800) TEL-JURY

   An organization concentrating on the restoration of the right of jurors to know they may nullify charges against a defendant if they believe the charge to be based on a bad law or capricious law enforcement.

3. **LibertyTapes.com**
   medicalTHC@LibertyTapes.com

   This company has numerous audio and video tapes from national conferences on drug law related issues, including many on medicinal cannabis.

Index

linoleic acid (LA) 183–184, 189, 197–198

linolenic acid (LNA) 183–184, 189, 197–198

linum 185

Lioresal *see* baclofen

Liskow, B. 150

LNA *see* linolenic acid

Ludlow, Fitz Hugh 46

Ludlow Library *see* Fitz Hugh Ludlow Library

Lynn Pierson Therapeutic Research Program 70–82, 151–158

ma 35; ideogram 36

marihuana *see* marijuana

Marihuana Tax Act of 1937 7, 49, 186

marijuana 56; disclosure of use 150, 161; use and use patterns 2, 8, 159–160, 162–166; *see also* cannabis; hemp

Marijuana: Medical Papers 45

marijuana prohibition 2–3, 7, 171, 190; legal issues concerning medical use 15–19, 22–28; Schedule I category 4, 51–53; state research programs 27

Marinol 16, 50, 57, 59, 148; adverse effects, side effects, and toxicity of 61–65, 88; cost of 17, 75, 87, 150; use with AIDS patients 86–87, 149–150; withdrawal symptoms from 62

Mechoulam, Raphael 38, 41, 45

medical necessity defense: definition of 22–28, 99–100; expert witnesses 15–19, 23–26, 29

medicine, definition of 6

Medigrace Limited, Kingston 110

Megace 85–86

Merritt, John C. 99–100

Messer, James 15, 16

metabolites, of cannabis *see* cannabis, metabolite of

Middle East 42, 126; ancient 38–39; medieval 40–41

migraines, use of cannabis 15, 122

Mikuriya, Tod 45

Miller, Carol 181

Miller, Mark 6

Millet, Corinne 1, 101, 177

minerals *see* hemp seeds

miotics 104–105

Moreau, Jacques Joseph 44

movement disorders, and use of cannabis 121

multiple sclerosis 113–114; cannabis, therapeutic use of 15, 24; medical necessity defense 22, 24; *see also* spasticity

Musikka, Elvy 101; medical necessity defense 14–15, 17, 19, 24–25

Muslims: cannabis, therapeutic use of 40–41

Napoleon 44

National Cancer Institute 70

National Eye Institute 100–101

National Institute of Drug Abuse (NIDA) 3, 21, 70, 92, 98, 151–152, 178, 179

National Organization for the Reform of Marijuana Laws (NORML) 51

Natural Health, Natural Medicine 183

nausea and vomiting: cannabis, use of 16, 75–80, 151–155; rating of 73–74, 79; *see also* chemotherapy

Netherlands: cannabis production 91, 196; hemp production 201, 202, 206

neurotransmitters 129–130

New Drug Application 116

newborn development *see* infant development

NIDA *see* National Institute of Drug Abuse

Nixon, Richard M. 4

NORML *see* National Organization for the Reform of Marijuana Laws

odanstron (Zofran) 75

Ohio State Medical Society 46

oncologists, recommend use of therapeutic cannabis 20

O'Shaughnessy, William B. 44–45, 46

over-the-counter drugs (OTC) 4, 5

Palmberg, Paul 25

Palmer, J.W. 46

Pantagruelion 42

paraphernalia laws 148

Parke-Davis 46